The Supreme Court
and American Capitalism

THE SUPREME COURT IN AMERICAN LIFE
Samuel Krislov, General Editor

Samuel Krislov, *The Supreme Court and Political Freedom*

Arthur Selwyn Miller, *The Supreme Court and American Capitalism*

Martin M. Shapiro, *The Supreme Court and Administrative Agencies*

The Supreme Court
and American Capitalism

ARTHUR SELWYN MILLER

Professor of Law, The George Washington University

THE FREE PRESS, *New York*

Collier-Macmillan Limited, *London*

347.7
m 61 s
65934
may 1969

First Printing

To Dagmar

Preface

The importance of the government-business relationship to the American people cannot be overestimated. Government and business are *the* key institutions of the nation; how they interact is of profound significance to all Americans. In this volume, certain aspects of that interrelation are developed as the Supreme Court of the United States has viewed them. The treatment is historical and contemporaneous; it is also predictive of possible future developments. Throughout, the exposition is written on the assumption that it is better to pose questions so as to stimulate thought than to give dogmatic answers. There are no final answers in constitutional law; it is always in a state of becoming, open-ended and fluid.

Constitutional law (and theory) is also controversial. Anyone who writes about it unavoidably brings certain predispositions and value premises to his task. Although I have tried to make the volume as factual as possible, certain passages are judgmental in nature. For that matter, even facts are inevitably colored by the manner in which they are selected and stated. Accordingly, it is desirable in such studies as this not only to attempt to be as objective as possible, but openly to face up to the question of valuation. The problem of personal valuations can be minimized, although not eliminated, by stating them.* This is seldom done at the present time, and much writing in constitutional matters tends to become the mutual exchange of unsupported assertions clothed in ostensibly objective language. At times, the discourse degenerates into mere *ipse dixits* and *ad hominem* pronouncements.

In an effort, then, to state the assumptions on which this

---

*See Gunnar Myrdal, *Value in Social Theory* (London: Routledge & Kegan Paul, 1958).

volume proceeds, I should like to say that, in my judgment, the object of human society is human welfare—and that welfare in an industrialized age can only be attained through the active intervention of government. I believe, further, that freedom can be endangered from private centers of power as much as from government and that, accordingly, a primary task of the constitutionalist is to protect and maximize human freedoms and human values from any source that may threaten them. Finally, there seems to be a commitment in the United States to scientific and technological development as ends in themselves; a basic task of those in academic life is to take steps to insure that humanistic values will not be lost and that the technocrats will not occupy seats of power unrestrained by law.

The manner in which the Supreme Court has dealt with economic-policy questions has often been recounted. John R. Commons' *Legal Foundations of Capitalism* is the landmark discussion; but Felix Frankfurter's small book on the commerce clause is still rewarding reading; and there are numerous essays in legal, political science, and economic periodicals that develop aspects of the government-business relationship. (As shown in the text, much of the constitutional law created by the Supreme Court revolves around that relationship.) Students of the Supreme Court, however, have been content to use as almost their sole source of data the written opinions of the Justices; thus, with few exceptions, commentary is basically exegesis of the text of what the Justices have said. Almost no attention has been accorded to the inputs that may influence a Justice or group of Justices; and on the other end of the spectrum, the area of "impact analysis"—empirically determining what difference Court decisions have made on the behavior patterns of businessmen and government officials—is an unmapped continent. Lawyers (and other commentators) seem to believe that the formal statement of the law by the Court is all that matters. Commentary suffers not only from these factors but from lack of a contextual analysis. The important question to ask is this:

WHO makes WHAT *decisions,* HOW, and with what EFFECTS? In this volume, the *who* is the Supreme Court, the *what* the substantive content of decisions. An effort is made to indicate how little is known about the *how* and the *effects.* It is further stressed that the formal statement of law by the Supreme Court must be accompanied by studies developing data about the effective control over decisions (in the present context, of an economic nature). In short, the elementary distinction made by political scientists over who has *formal authority* to make decisions and who has *effective control* over them is almost totally absent from the literature about that august body, the Supreme Court of the United States. In this volume, I have tried to strike a balance between more exegesis upon texts of Supreme Court opinions (there is a plethora of that now) and a more sophisticated view of the High Bench. It should be considered to be a preliminary statement, an outline rather than exhaustive discussion.

Arthur Selwyn Miller

Washington, D. C.
August, 1967

Acknowledgments

A condensed version of Chapter Three appeared in the December, 1966, issue of the *George Washington Law Review;* it is reproduced with permission.

Grateful acknowledgment is made as well to the following publishers for permission to quote from copyrighted works: Harvard University Press (for quotations from Don K. Price, *The Scientific Estate);* Penguin Books (for quotations from Peter d'Alroy Jones, *The Consumer Society: A History of American Capitalism);* and The John Day Company, Inc. (for quotations from Peter F. Drucker, *The Concept of the Corporation,* 1964 edition; copyright © 1946 by Peter F. Drucker).

Contents

1

Corporate America

The history of American constitutional law in no small measure is the history of the impact of the modern corporation upon the American scene. We are still sadly awaiting a comprehensive account of the pervasive influence of corporate enterprise upon our national life, and its judicial aspect is only very partially written in the opinions dealing with constitutional protections claimed for incorporated business.*

INTRODUCTION: WHAT THIS BOOK IS ABOUT

This is an essay in American constitutionalism as it has developed since 1787 with respect to business enterprise. Although the title refers to "American capitalism," to lend sharpness to the discussion, the principal theme revolves around the growth of the corporation as the characteristic and dominant business form and the relationship of Supreme Court decisions to that development. The subject is vast, but the discussion is brief; accordingly, much must perforce be given more in outline form than in exhaustive exposition.†

The United States has been and still is considered to be the capitalist society par excellence. However that term may be defined, its irreducible minimum is a conception of economics *and* politics: private commercial enterprise operating with minimal restraints from government. In purest form, its tenets are two: in *economic* terms, private volition in the

---

*Felix Frankfurter, *The Commerce Clause Under Marshall, Taney and Waite* (Chicago: Quadrangle Paperbacks, 1964), p. 63. The book was first published in 1937 by the University of North Carolina Press.

†Footnotes have been kept to the minimum. Extensive bibliographies may be found in most of the works cited.

allocation and distribution of resources and in investment decisions; and in legal (hence *political*) terms, freedom of contract and the "negative, nightwatchman" theory of the state. However, this nation is not now and never was purely capitalistic. (Probably no nation ever follows pure theories of politics. They tend to reflect felt necessities, with the theory coming later as a description of what has taken place rather than what should take place. Certainly this would seem to be true for the United States.) A thread of aid to business, government providing a protective umbrella for the growth of business accompanied by some regulatory measures, may be seen throughout American history—although the pattern is uneven and highly discontinuous. In many respects, change has been at least endemic in the government-business symbiosis, whereas in other respects, certain long-range trends, permitting at least tentative conclusions, seem clearly discernible.

In any event, the proposition that commercial enterprise should be basically private was true in 1787, when the Constitution was written, and remains valid today. Even though the line between public and private activity—and thus between public and private law—is blurred and always has been blurred, the bedrock fact is that the means of production and distribution (that is, the economy) have been and are in private hands. This does not mean that the state (here equated with government) does not exercise considerable influence over business decisions; as will be shown, the clear trend has been in the direction of greater governmental intervention in decisions at one time considered to be solely the concern of business leaders. The relationships between government (the shorthand term for the collectivity called "society")* and business (the shorthand term for the myriad of commercial decisions) make up the basic theme around

---

*Obviously, a distinction must be made between "government," "the state," and "society" and would be in a comprehensive analysis and exposition. See Carl Joachim Friedrich, *Man and His Government: An Empirical Theory of Politics* (New York: McGraw-Hill Book Company, Inc., 1963). For present purposes, however, the terms will be used roughly synonymously.

which this monograph is written, with specific focus on the role that the United States Supreme Court has had in the development of that symbiotic association.

The exposition first looks to history and the series of Supreme Court decisions that have had importance in setting the constitutional and legal milieu in which business has operated. The Court has acted in different ways in different periods of history. For example, the three-quarters of a century in the post-Civil War era—from 1865 to about 1940—reveals one set of judicial attitudes, whereas the quarter-century since 1940 indicates another type of response from the High Bench. Further, still another judicial reaction may be seen in the period prior to the Civil War. In brief, the trend since 1787—with a hiatus in the post-Civil War period—has been toward increased governmental participation in business decisions. At the same time, the corporate form of business proliferated and was consolidated.

Supreme Court decisions possibly had a marked, albeit immeasurable,* role to play in the development of the government-business relationship. The history (1787-1940) will be traced in Chapter Two. Chapter Three will be concerned with the "constitutional revolution of the 1930s" and its implications. What will be called the "Positive State" will be described and analyzed. Emphasis here will be on a changing posture—a lessening influence—of the Supreme Court in economic-policy matters.

The remainder of the book will be devoted to: (1) Discussion of the need for theory, both descriptive and prescriptive, concerning the constitutional position of the

---

*Although much has been said about the power of the Court—about "government by judiciary"—very little is in fact known about the *actual* impact of judicial decisions. This monograph, as well as other commentaries on the work of the Court, should be read in light of the fact that there is almost a complete lack of empirical data showing what connection there is between judicial decision and individual or group attitudes and behavior. See Arthur Selwyn Miller, "On the Need for 'Impact Analysis' of Supreme Court Opinions," *Georgetown Law Journal*, LIII (1965), 365. This is not to say that the Court does not have power; no doubt it does. But at best that power varies with the issue being decided. No attempt is made herein to assess the impact of Court decisions on the economic order.

corporation. The problem has become urgent with the burgeoning of the corporate form of doing business and the fundamental change in the character of government. Ancient doctrines and principles require rethinking. (2) Delineation of emergent problems, principally those revolving around the multinational corporation and the concept of economic planning. (3) Finally, it will be suggested that the American polity has moved past the point where the Supreme Court makes (as it once did) basic economic decisions, and that the locus of power vis-à-vis the economy is now in the avowedly political branches of government and, of these, in the Presidency (viewed institutionally rather than personally).

No attempt will be made to discuss the basic assumption on which much of this exposition rests, namely, that the Supreme Court Justices can and do make policy—"legislate" —in their constitutional decisions. It is far too late to believe that constitutional decisions are babies brought by judicial storks. Modern scholarship has convincingly demonstrated that the Court is a part of the governmental process. The question, accordingly, is not *whether* the Court makes policy or should make policy, but *when, in what instances, how much,* and *to what effect?** Furthermore, as is amply proven by the history of the antitrust laws, the Court has a policy-making function in the interpretation of statutes. Perhaps this is of a somewhat lesser degree than when the Constitution is being construed; still, it is a fatuous dream to think that any statute can be drawn so as to exclude the need for interpretation. As Bishop Hoadly said many years ago, "Whoever hath an absolute authority to interpret any written or spoken laws, it is he who is truly the Lawgiver to all intents and purposes, and not the person who first wrote or spoke them."

Approaching the government-business symbiosis from

---

*See Martin Shapiro, *Law and Politics in the Supreme Court* (New York: The Free Press, 1964); Arthur Selwyn Miller, "Some Pervasive Myths About the United States Supreme Court," *St. Louis University Law Journal*, X (1965), 153; Samuel Krislov, *The Supreme Court in the Political Process* (New York: The Macmillan Co., 1965).

the perspective of the United States Supreme Court provides an especially useful way of seeing the interplay of Constitution, statutes, and the common law in the unfolding of the American economy. Insight is gained not only into the manner in which the Court operates, but also into how other segments of government have acted. Writing in 1924, the late John R. Commons asserted that the Supreme Court operated as "the first authoritative faculty of political economy in the world's history."* That was during the heyday of naysaying on legislative programs designed in part to ameliorate the harmful effects of the Industrial Revolution. Commons was correct for the time in which he wrote, but his insight no longer reflects reality.

From the standpoint of capitalism or, more specifically, the American business community, the growth of the corporation as the characteristic and dominant form of enterprise provides a basis for selecting Supreme Court decisions. In large part, the history of American capitalism (and indeed, as Felix Frankfurter said, of American constitutionalism), is concerned with the manner in which the corporation has waxed both large and strong. It dominates the economy, even though in the 1960s economic enterprise is fairly evenly divided between the *corporate* sector, which controls production and much of distribution, and the *service* sector, defined as "wholesale and retail trade; finance, insurance, and real estate; and general government." In 1965, the National Bureau of Economic Research could report that "the U.S. is now a 'service economy'—i.e., we are the first nation in the history of the world in which more than half of the employed population is not involved in the production of food, clothing, houses, automobiles, and other tangible goods."† Even with that important development, however, the corporation is by far the most significant type of economic enter-

---

*John R. Commons, *Legal Foundations of Capitalism* (Madison: The University of Wisconsin Press, 1924), p. 7.
†Victor Fuchs, "Some Implications of the Growing Importance of the Service Industries," in *The Task of Economics* (Forty-fifth Annual Report of the National Bureau of Economic Research, Inc., 1965), pp. 5-7.

prise; it has more influence on the manner in which American institutions develop than, perhaps, any other single type of organization (save, possibly, government). Indeed, the service sector of the economy is in large extent molded by what corporations do.

CORPORATE AMERICA

To say that the business corporation is the characteristic and dominant form of nongovernmental action in the modern American economy is to state an obvious truism. Corporations are pre-eminent in American society, challenged only by government and, in lesser part, by trade unions. The largest of them straddle the continent and make this nation a common market in fact; but many small businesses are also corporate. Of course, it is not the only way of doing business, for many partnerships and individual enterprises exist, but it is by far the most important. "The corporate system," economist John Kenneth Galbraith has asserted, "is all but coterminous with mining, communications, public utilities and manufacturing—in short, the largest part of economic life."* He could also have listed the giant chains that dominate parts of retailing and could have added "corporate" agriculture, the corner grocer and the individual farmer having in large part been superseded by gigantic combines.

For that matter, other corporate organizations exist—if one defines the term broadly to mean a collective way of conducting affairs—for this country is experiencing an organizational revolution. In this sense, universities and trade unions, churches and veterans' legions, farmers' organizations, and even some of the professions (for example, medicine and law) exhibit a tendency toward organization; as such, they may validly be called a part of the American corporate system. (The individual qua individual counts for little in this scheme of things; he is important only as a member of a group or groups. Individualism is a myth in modern Amer-

---

*John Kenneth Galbraith, "Economics and the Quality of Life," *Science*, CXLV (1964), 117-8.

ica.*) However, the focus here is on the *business* corporation only—that form of collective endeavor that is concerned with commerce in all its forms.

Corporate business is so widespread today that one might be pardoned the belief that it has always been so, that this is the natural order of affairs. Brief reference to history shows the contrary; the corporation, although not unknown in early American history, was relatively rare and relatively small. It was not until the twentieth century that corporations proliferated and became large, strong, and pervasive. The organizational revolution is a latter-day development, although its roots doubtless lie deep in Anglo-American history.

Furthermore, corporate America is a society that gets its tone from and whose economy is dominated by a rather small number of giant enterprises. Not more than four to five hundred corporations, to take *Fortune* magazine's annual listing, are the economic entities that set the pace for the remainder of the economy. Called "corporate concentrates" by Adolf A. Berle and "factory communities" by Peter Drucker, these organizations—for example, General Motors, General Electric, General Dynamics—have so altered social conditions that neither constitutional, that is, political, nor economic theoreticians have yet been able to construct viable descriptive or analytic models or to assimilate the modern corporation into political or economic theory (hence, into constitutional theory). The corporation, thus, is a constitutional anomaly, a creature that cannot be understood in terms of three-hundred-year-old political theory from John Locke or even in terms of later theory from Thomas Jefferson. The classical economic theory of Adam Smith, whose *Wealth of Nations* (published the same year as the Declaration of Independence) does not consider this development, is also inadequate.†

---

*This is a fact, not the statement of a value judgment or normative preference; however much it may be deplored, it cannot be gainsaid. How much the situation today differs from the past is debatable; for most Americans, individualism likely was never very high on the scale of preferred values.
†"The pretence that corporations are necessary to the better government of the trade, is without foundation."—Adam Smith [*The Wealth of Nations* (New York: Modern Library, Inc., 1937), p. 129.]

The same may be said for the underlying theory of the American Constitution, which assumes that only two entities—the individual natural person and government—exist or are important. By making no provision for collective activity (the corporation, the trade union, the political party, among others) classical political theory is now outmoded. Some insights may be gained, to be sure, from Locke, Jefferson, and Smith and from the institutionalized framework of the Constitution of 1787, but they are partial at best and are to be viewed as precursors or progenitors of the present and not as factual descriptions—not even as prescriptions of preferred institutions. The past, at best, is prologue to a radically different public order.

The United States today is a corporate society rushing ahead pell-mell with advancing technology and populated by people many of whom have belief-systems based on long-vanished social conditions. In substance, those belief-systems postulate an individualistic economy and law, predicated on the bedrock principles of private enterprise and freedom of contract and on the assumption that the power exerted by the units of society is roughly coequal. That these notions no longer reflect reality is the essential lesson to be learned from the advent of corporate America. (How real they actually were in the past is also debatable; it may well be that they existed mainly as ideals rather than as descriptions of societal actuality.)*

A MODEL OF THE CORPORATION

What is a corporation? is a question not easily or quickly answered, save on a superficial level. Since 1886, it has been considered to be a "person" (but not a "citizen") in constitutional law, which means that General Motors is equated with John Doe in the eyes of the law. This, as will be argued

*Compare John P. Roche, *The Quest for the Dream* (New York: The Macmillan Co., 1963) with Don K. Price, *The Scientific Estate* (Cambridge, Mass.: Harvard University Press, 1965) and William Withers, *Freedom Through Power* (New York: The John Day Company, 1965).

in a subsequent chapter, may be entirely proper insofar as giving the corporation the protections of the Constitution is concerned, but it does not meet the need insofar as theory is concerned. The corporation is obviously more than a person, however characterized in law. Immortal (at least, almost so), powerful, and invisible, it is a disembodied "economic man," a collective organism with drives and purposes of its own transcending those of any segment of the constellation of interests that make it up. Two decades ago, economist-lawyer Walton H. Hamilton in characteristically colorful language said: "The legal make-believe that the corporation is a person, the ingenuities by which it has been fitted out with a domicile, the elaborate web of 'as-ifs' which the courts have woven,—have put corporate affairs pretty largely out of the regulations we decree." The corporation, he said, unlike real persons has "no anatomical parts to be kicked or consigned to the calaboose; no conscience to keep it awake all night; no soul for whose salvation the parson may struggle; no body to be roasted in hell or purged for celestial enjoyment." No one can lay "bodily hands upon General Motors or Westinghouse . . . or incarcerate the Pennsylvania Railroad or Standard Oil (N.J.) with all its works."*

In the traditional and still orthodox view, the corporation is an entity with only *one* kind of interest: the property of its stockholders. But it is not that simple, quite possibly because the concept of property itself is not simple; it is as difficult to define property as it is to define the corporation.†

A corporation, of course, is a property interest. But it is much more; just as property itself is a congeries of interests, so the corporation may be said to be a bundle or constellation of disparate interests. These interests go far beyond the stockholder. The type of definition, then, that is required

---

*Walton H. Hamilton, *On the Composition of the Corporate Veil,* as quoted in Richard Eells and Clarence Walton, *Conceptual Foundations of Business* (Homewood, Ill.: Richard D. Irwin, Inc., 1961), pp. 132-3.
†The difficulties of defining property are discussed in *American Law Institute, Restatement of Law of Property,* I (1936), chap. i.

is sociological, not legal and not economic.* Viewed as a social organism, a collectivity, the corporation may be said to consist of the following elements:

The security holders—Those who supply the capital represented by the capital stock, the corporate bonds, and other corporate financial obligations. The common stockholders, in the conventional wisdom, are the owners of the company. But, since the Berle and Means landmark study in 1934, it has been widely, albeit not uniformly, conceded that those who own do not control; the power to control is in the hands of the second of this listing of members of the corporate community, the board of directors and managers. It should also be noted that the stockholder does not own the corporation either; what he owns, or, in legal terms, has a property interest in, is a share of stock, a transferable piece of paper that at best is a claim on dividends if those who control decide to distribute some of the corporate assets.

The corporate managers—Those who control but who do not necessarily own. Included are members of the board of directors and of the managerial hierarchy.

Rank-and-file employees—Often these are the members of the trade union. They are to be distinguished from the managerial class and the white collar worker who is not a member of the union.

Union managers (or leaders)—To an immeasurable yet marked extent, the officers of the union may be set aside as a separate segment of the corporate community. In their relations to the rank-and-file workers, they may be analogized to corporate management and its relationship to the shareholders.

---

*As to the latter, economist Andreas G. Papandreou has said: "The economist . . . [retains] his scheme of an acting individual agent, even in the case of the firm, which may legitimately be regarded as a 'collective' of some sort. . . . The economist has not evolved a theory of conscious cooperation." (Andreas G. Papandreou, "Some Basic Problems in the Theory of the Firm," in Bernard F. Haley [ed.], *A Survey of Contemporary Economics* [Homewood, Ill.: Richard D. Irwin, Inc., 1952], p. 183.) The same may be said of lawyers. See, however, the seminal study by Adolf A. Berle, Jr. and Gardiner C. Means, *The Modern Corporation and Private Property* (New York: The Macmillan Co., 1934).

The foregoing lists four elements of the *internal* order of the corporate community. Although exceptions doubtless exist, these four disparate interests are sufficiently pervasive to permit generalization as those inside the corporation. There are, in addition, four segments outside the corporation, having arms reaching into and continuing transactions with the internal elements. This quartet of interests, constituting the *external* order of the corporate community, includes:

Suppliers to the corporation—Those enterprises, many of them corporations themselves, that provide logistic support to the corporation in the making of its final products; they also may supply services to the corporate community.

Dealers of the corporation—Those who retail the products of the corporate community; to be seen perhaps in purest form in the automobile industry.

Consumers of the products—The individual members of the public; the buyers in the market.

The public generally—This is what might be called the public interest or the interest of society generally in the activities of the corporate community. It is not necessarily the arithmetical sum of all the individual interests within the nation; as will be developed, it at times is a transcendent interest.

Although it is true that one or more of these elements may be missing in any given corporation, nevertheless the model seems generally valid. Thus, although a corporation such as Lockheed Aircraft Company has only one important customer and no dealers, it is more than likely that a large corporation will have economic transactions and legal relations with all of the four external segments.

Those transactions and relations, together with the reciprocal relationships internal to the entity, make up an amorphous collectivity, an organism built around a principle of organization for production and operating in accordance with a general concept of cooperation. This model is useful because it enables one to perceive the enterprise as more than a device for doing business, but rather as a new thing that must be considered in new terms. As a New York court put it several decades ago, the corporation is "more nearly a method than a thing"; or, as observed in a leading treatise on corporation finance:

> The legal attributes of the corporation are mere accidents of historical development; they do not describe the corporation as we understand it; nor do they give us any clue to its social and economic significance in our modern industrial society. The human institution of marriage may be described as a legal contract, for under the convenient caption of a contract the jurist would group marriage, the corporation, and house-to-house delivery of milk. An agreement of two people to live together gives no more understanding of marriage as a vital present-day institution than the filing of certain papers with the Secretary of State gives an understanding of the corporation as a present-day institution.
> . . . The corporation is an institution and its reality lies not in legalistic definitions but in the part the corporation plays in the complex balance of forces that constitutes the economic world of the present time. What we are interested in, if we try to define a corporation, is its function, as an institution—and a very important and significant institution—in our contemporary economic life. This is not a question of law, but of the meaning of the thing as it now exists in the economic life of the twentieth century.*

The model is useful also because it enables one to select from the mass of Supreme Court (and other governmental) decisions those that deal with the corporation not as a person or an individual, but that touch and concern one or more of the eight disparate elements of the corporate community. Thus, to mention only three examples, certain decisions relate to labor (the rank-and-file employees), others to corporate dealers, and still others to the public at large (the public interest). In other words, a complete analysis of the Supreme Court and the corporation (or American capitalism) would

---

*Arthur Stone Dewing, *The Financial Policy of Corporations* (5th ed.; New York: The Ronald Press Company, 1953), Vol. I, pp. 16-7.

require mention of the legal and politico-economic relationships between society generally (that is, the government) and the eight units of the corporate community. However, in this monograph, principal attention will be accorded to three of those units: corporate management and its power of private decision; the rank-and-file employees and the protection accorded them by statute; and the public generally (or protection of the public interest by government, principally through the medium of facilitative economic planning).

THE POVERTY OF THEORY

However the corporation is defined—the suggested model is merely an adumbration of an adequate definition—it is clear that the growth of these collective economic organizations (with other groups) poses a critical constitutional question. The American Constitution was a product of an era when the corporation, although not nonexistent, was relatively rare. Fewer than three hundred existed in 1800; the economy, such as it was, consisted of small shops, small enterprises, and agriculture. The organizational revolution had not yet taken place, even though Alexis de Tocqueville could note in *Democracy in America,* published in 1835, that Americans were a nation of "joiners." From the standpoint of the economist, "the functioning of the modern corporation has not to date been adequately explained or, if certain explanations are accepted as adequate, it seems difficult to justify."* In the light of constitutional theory—and thus of political economy, since constitutional law is made up of juristic theories of politics and economics—the corporation presents an intermediate social group between the individual and government; it has wrenched historical constitutional theory in much the same manner as classical economics has been scuttled. In the political theory of Locke and the other philosophers of the Enlightenment, those whose ideas pro-

*Edward S. Mason, "Introduction" to Edward S. Mason (ed.), *The Corporation in Modern Society* (Cambridge, Mass.: Harvard University Press, 1960), p. 4.

vided the intellectual milieu out of which the Constitution
was born, no such intermediate organization was contemplated. The Constitution limits government in favor of individuals, a notion based on the unstated assumption that
individuals live and act as autonomous units. No provision
was made for the pluralistic social group.

But, however much it may run against the myth, the
autonomous individual does not exist as such. The individual
spends his life as a member of groups and is socially significant only as a member of a group—whatever his significance
may be with respect to the Infinite. The Protestant Ethic,
which extolled the merits of hard work, thrift, and rugged
individualism, has been replaced by the Social Ethic: "that
contemporary body of thought which makes morally legitimate the pressures of society against the individual. Its major
propositions are three: a belief in the group as the source of
creativity; a belief in belongingness as the ultimate need of
the individual; and a belief in the application of science to
achieve the belongingness."* The Constitution to the contrary notwithstanding, American society is not composed of
atomistic individuals acting as such. This is an age of collective action.

The constitutional problem posed by the organizational
revolution is that of fitting the group (the organization, in
the present case, the corporation) into an ancient Constitution that made no provision for it. We are confronted with a
condition, as President Grover Cleveland was wont to say,
and not a theory—a condition that cries out for theoretical
treatment. Writing in 1819, in the well-known Dartmouth
College Case, Chief Justice John Marshall described a corporation as

> . . . an artificial being, invisible, intangible, and existing
> only in contemplation of law. Being the mere creature of
> law, it possesses only those properties which the charter of
> its creation confers upon it, either expressly, or as incidental
> to its very existence. . . . Among the most important are

*William H. Whyte, Jr., *The Organization Man* (New York: Simon and
Schuster, Inc., 1956), p. 5.

immortality, and, if the expression may be allowed, individuality; properties by which a perpetual succession of many persons are considered the same, and may act as a single individual.*

In the century and a half since then, the corporation, although still an individual in contemplation of the law, has become a collective organism wielding such immense social power that it has been and can be validly termed a "private government." As such, it presents problems of governance not dissimilar from problems confronting political theorists in thinking about public government. The essential problem is one of legitimacy. As Adolf A. Berle has put it,

> Whenever there is a question of power there is a question of legitimacy. As things stand now, these instrumentalities of tremendous power [the giant corporations] have the slenderest claim of legitimacy. This is probably a transitory period. They must find some claim of legitimacy, which also means finding a field of responsibility and a field of accountability. Legitimacy, responsibility, and accountability are essential to any power system if it is to endure.†

But this poses certain questions: Responsible to whom? Accountable to whom? In what manner? In a very real sense, corporate power is not responsible or accountable to anyone, except in a very broad and ambiguous way. Controlled by managers who at one time were assumed to be responsible to the stockholders but who act, according to Berle, as "an autonomous self-perpetuating oligarchy," corporations exist as decentralized centers of economic power, as feudal entities within the body politic. If the question of responsibility and accountability is to be answered, as indeed it must, required will be a resolution of the relationship of the corporation to all its component parts, both internal and external. In large part, this may involve, as will be argued, constitutionalization of the corporation, by which is meant that its functions, powers, and procedures will be prescribed in accordance with

---

Dartmouth College v. *Woodward,* 17 U.S. 518 (1819).
†Adolf A. Berle, Jr., *Economic Power and the Free Society* (New York: The Fund for the Republic, Inc., 1957), p. 16.

the enduring values of a democratic polity as developed through the legal process. Constitutionalization through the creation and imposition of external norms of corporate behavior may well be in a state of becoming. Judicial decisions, congressional statutes, and presidential actions, as will be shown, together are creating a common law of corporate constitutionalism. The poverty of theory concerning the corporation is in process of being rectified; its "legitimacy," to use Berle's term, is being worked out in the myriad transactions between the units of *public* government and *private* government. A symbiotic relationship between government and business—sometimes called a partnership—is evolving.*

In viewing the relationship between judicial decisions and American capitalism, one essential point should be underscored: the factor of change, which is a social constant and which makes history an uncertain guide to the future. In less than two centuries, the nation has been vastly altered, particularly in the creation of a unified, but not uniform, society. Or, as the sociologist W. Lloyd Warner has said, "The whole American society is rapidly growing into one *primary* community, in which corporations along with other complex hierarchical structures play their significant and necessary roles. Change is built into the very nature of this social system. . . ."†

The point is crucial in tracing the development since 1787 of the government-business relationship. Social change is a constant—and this means that the legal relations of the corporate community, in both its external and internal senses, are themselves in a continuing process of change. This has an important by-product with respect to the intellectual task necessary in analyzing and describing the flow of events

---

*A perceptive essay on the need for a theory of government-business relations is that of Robert A. Dahl, "Business and Politics: A Critical Appraisal of Political Science," in Robert A. Dahl, Mason Haire, and Paul F. Lazarsfeld, *Social Science Research on Business: Product and Potential* (New York: Columbia University Press, 1959), pp. 3-44. See also Dow Votaw, *Modern Corporations* (Englewood Cliffs, N.J.: Prentice-Hall, Inc., 1965).

†W. Lloyd Warner, *The Corporation in the Emergent American Society* (New York: Harper and Row, 1962), p. v.

since 1787, namely, that one must think in terms of trends and of evolution rather than of equilibrium or of a static system. The enduring principles must be identified, those that prevail over the ebb and flow of transient events. When this is done, one is able to discern some attitudes that have been consistently held since the formation of the nation. It is to this that we turn in Chapter Two.

Before doing so, however, one further aspect of change should be emphasized: the rate of social change is increasing; time, in effect, has been telescoped. For many reasons, perhaps the most important of which is the scientific-technological revolution, we are in a period of cataclysmic social change —a condition that seems likely to continue. Ralph E. Lapp put the point this way: "No one—not even the most brilliant scientist alive today—really knows where science is taking us. We are aboard a train which is gathering speed, racing down a track on which there are an unknown number of switches leading to unknown destinations. No single scientist is in the engine cab and there may be demons at the switch. Most of society is in the caboose looking backward."* Dean Don K. Price of the Harvard Graduate School of Public Administration has made much the same point in this manner: ". . . the main lines of our [public] policy, over the long run, are likely to be determined by scientific developments that we cannot foresee, rather more than by political doctrines that we can now state."† If for "political" we read "political and legal"—for public law is the marriage of law and politics— then it may readily be seen that the received wisdom of the past (the law, however enunciated) is at best an uncertain guide to the future. Nevertheless, changes have to be anticipated—and managed—if the enduring values of a democratic polity are to be preserved. A considerable part of that management will be effected in the myriad transactions that make up the government-business partnership.

---

*Ralph E. Lapp, *The New Priesthood: The Scientific Elite and the Use of Power* (New York: Harper and Row, 1965), p. 29.
†Price, p. 186.

2

Constitutional Doctrine and the Consolidation of Corporate Power

Economic doctrines have never as much influenced the making of American economic policy as have political and constitutional considerations. The reason why the whole of American economic policy looks so incoherent—with mercantilist, socialist, liberal, or autarkic elements all living happily side by side—is that political balance rather than economic consistency has been the more powerful drive.*

INTRODUCTION

The United States, as President Calvin Coolidge opined, is a business-oriented society. Business as an institution is all-pervasive; the dominant nongovernmental social grouping, its values and preferences influence or overpower others, not excluding government itself. No other social class even approximates that of the businessman in power and prestige. Furthermore, as has been set forth in Chapter One, American business is dominated by the corporation—that economic collectivity that is a center of wealth and power and that sets the tone and often the details of the remainder of the business community—even though the service aspects of the economy now outweigh in number of employees the productive and distributive. These overmighty economic sovereignties, these units of neofeudalism, these centers of economic

---

*William Letwin, *A Documentary History of American Economic Policy Since 1789* (paper ed.; Garden City, N.Y.: Anchor Books, 1961), pp. xxix-xxx.

power, are at once the characteristic institution of the day and the culmination of decades, even centuries, of legal and economic history.

That development has been and is reflected in both private and public law. Our attention here is directed principally toward the latter, but it is appropriate at the outset to note lines of development in the former as well. Private law, that is, the law that governs the relations between individuals (natural and corporate), was and still is the analogue of the American economic system. Thus, the laws of contract and of property, to take two main categories, have had an evolutionary development since the beginning of the nation in the late eighteenth century. Private law was based on an individualistic concept.

Contract law provides apt illustration; it is the analogue, probably the product of free-enterprise capitalism—the legal machinery necessary for an economic system which relies on free exchange rather than command for the allocation of resources.* In a free society all law is ultimately based on contract, that is, derived from choices freely made by responsible individuals. That, at least, was (and is) the ideal, epitomized in Sir Henry Maine's famous dictum of a century ago: ". . . the movement of the progressive societies has hitherto been a movement from Status to Contract,"† a statement dubious when made and that since has been resoundingly repudiated. Contract, combined with the system of property, was in the final analysis a moral as well as legal concept. As Professors Friedrich Kessler and Malcolm Sharp have put it:

> A system of free contract did not recommend itself solely for reasons of sheer expediency and utilitarianism; it was deeply rooted in the moral sentiments of the period in which it found strongest expression. The dominant current of belief inspiring 19th century industrial society—and

---

*See Friedrich Kessler and Malcolm Pitman Sharp, *Contracts: Cases and Materials* (Englewood Cliffs, N.J.: Prentice-Hall, Inc., 1953), p. 2.
†Sir Henry Maine, *Ancient Law* (New York: E. P. Dutton & Co., Inc., 1917), p. 100. (The book was first published in 1864.)

open society—was the deepfelt conviction that individual and cooperative action should be left unrestrained in family, church, and market and that such a system of *laissez faire* would not lessen the freedom and dignity of the individual, but would secure the highest possible social justice. The representatives of this school of thought were firmly convinced, to state it somewhat roughly, of the existence of a natural law according to which, if not in the short run then at least in the long run, the individual serving his own interest was also serving the interest of the community. Profits, under this system, could only be earned by supplying wanted commodities, and freedom of competition would prevent profits from rising unduly. The play of the market, if left to itself, would, therefore, maximize net satisfactions and afford the ideal conditions for the distribution of wealth. Justice within this context has a very definite meaning. It means freedom of property and of contract, of profit making and of trade. The preestablished harmony: of a social system based on freedom of enterprise and perfect competition sees to it that the private autonomy of contracting parties will be kept within bounds and will work out to the benefit of society as a whole. Freedom of contract, within this cultural framework, like all freedom, is not an end in itself; it is only valuable as a means to an end: "the liberation of the powers of all men equally for contributions to a common good."*

If that, in essence, was the theory of nineteenth-century individualism and of a laissez-faire economy, it was never fully realized—and, of even greater importance, it was soon undercut by two complementary developments: (1) the marriage of technology to entrepreneurship to produce within the economy large, collective, bureaucratically managed enterprises, and (2) the employment of the legal system, legislative as well as judicial, to provide a protective umbrella for the development of corporate economic enterprise.

Our attention in this chapter is directed toward the highlights of the judicial aspects of this historical movement; these began early in the nineteenth century and reached an

---

*Kessler and Sharp, p. 4. The source of the short quote at the end of this passage is given as Green, *Liberal Legislation and Freedom of Contract,* 3 Works (1888), pp. 365, 372.

historic turning point about 150 years later—in the so-called constitutional revolution of the 1930s. The development of science and technology through business activity—that is, the coming of the Industrial Revolution to the United States— is an oft-told tale that need not be repeated here. One facet, however, merits iteration: the factor of change and its bearing on constitutional law.

With change being a built-in constant of the social order, largely because of scientific and technological developments, a crucial problem is to adapt a static document—the Constitution of 1787 with its few amendments—to the successive exigencies of the American experience. This has been accomplished, to put it briefly, by a tacit recognition that the timeless verities of the Constitution are in fact susceptible of being given different content in different periods in history. The words remain the same, but their meaning changes; a person has a good legal mind and will make a good constitutional lawyer when he can grasp and assimilate that simple, yet profound fact. Chief Justice Marshall in 1819 gave early expression to the concept in these oft-quoted words: "We [the Supreme Court] must never forget that it is a *constitution* we are expounding." By that, Marshall, the chief architect of the judicial exegesis of the basic constitutional text, apparently meant that the Constitution was to be given an expansive reading, one permitting (in that instance) a sweeping enlargement of the powers of the central government and the diminution of state power to control economic activity. The Chief Justice did not indicate why the contrary result of limiting the powers of the federal government was not equally tenable, particularly at that time when fear of central power was rife. But the Justices over the years have been content merely to put their opinions in an ostensibly logical form with relatively little regard for the consistency or merit of their logic. Further, the Constitution was "intended to endure for ages to come and, consequently, to be adapted to the various crises of human affairs."* For Marshall,

---

McCulloch v. *Maryland,* 17 U.S. 316, at 407, 415 (1819).

this meant that the powers of Congress, set forth in Article I of the Constitution, were not to be given a narrow, dictionary meaning, but were to gather content as the exigencies of the future unfolded. The powers of the central government were to be sufficient to the need—as the Supreme Court saw the need. The Constitution was not a static, lifeless document, but a dynamic and growing instrument of governance.

The Marshallian view of the evolutionary nature of the Constitution, coupled with his other assertion in the seminal Marbury *v.* Madison,* that it is emphatically the province of judiciary to say what the law is, that is, to interpret the document, has prevailed throughout the Court's history. For several decades (1890-1937), to be sure, succeeding Justices failed to find the same warrant that Marshall did for expansion of governmental power. But even then, through the employment of one device or another, they were able to locate new doctrine and new principle to be applied in particular cases. Outstanding in this development, as will be shown, was the identification of "substantive" due process in the procedural concept that had twice been set out in the fundamental text. The Constitution in their hands remained one designed to endure—but by limiting, not expanding, the powers of government. The reversion to Marshall's idea that power is sufficient to the need has produced the constitutional revolution of recent decades, one characterized by judicial approbation of an accelerating enlargement of areas of official concern and cognizance. Much of this took place within the framework of economic policy, as the balance of this chapter will indicate.

The Constitution always has been considered by its judicial interpreters to be more than a collection of timeless and immutable political verities. To them, it is a "living" document, one sufficiently flexible to be adaptable to the

*1 Cranch 137 (1803). This case launched judicial review of acts of Congress; it is the rock upon which subsequent judicial power rests. The Constitution, of course, does not provide for such power, but its successful assertion in the Marbury Case and the ensuing history have made the power utterly clear.

social problems of different periods of history. Thus, while it may in fact merit Gladstone's effusive label of "the most wonderful work ever struck off at a given time by the brain and purpose of man," it is only because of an inherent adaptability that permits flexibility of interpretation that it has lasted and is extant. Otherwise, it would not only be remarkable, it would be impossible, for a document drafted in the social milieu of a weak collection of agricultural "sovereignties" struggling for existence against Europe's established powers and against the wilderness to maintain viability when that nation has been transformed into an urbanized, industrialized society exercising immense power the planet over. We live today in a "new society" under an old Constitution with built-in provisions for growth.

While a number of observers, including Chief Justice Earl Warren, have asserted that the Constitution is an evolving document, we have never been told much more than that. The concept of the "living Constitution" has never been explained in detail so as to indicate how far it goes and what it means. At most, that concept has been employed by various Justices to justify overruling precedent, changing a line of doctrine, or engrafting a new interpretation upon a constitutional clause. Illustrations are easily found: What "commerce" means, for example, with respect to the powers of Congress is a question which over the years has received varying interpretations from the Supreme Court. That evolution has, in fact, been cyclical; the early expansive Marshall decisions are cited to buttress conclusions reached in and subsequent to the 1940s, after an intervening hiatus of narrow interpretation.

The idea of the "living" Constitution is a justification for adaptation of the basic document to fit new social conditions. The words remain the same—they are both timeless and ambiguous—but their content changes. As Justice Oliver Wendell Holmes might have put it, a word in the Constitution is not a crystal, transparent and unchanging; in the more important, interpretable parts, the constitutional words are the skins of the living thoughts that change with the times and as society changes. Put another way, the Constitution has survived because it has been so adaptable as to permit adequate resolution of the problems faced by succeeding generations and because the Court has acted as a continuing constitutional convention to make those adaptions. The wisdom of the Founding Fathers, in this respect, consisted in the insertion of ambiguity in the fundamental law rather than in the precisely delineated provisions also set out. And that wisdom has been augmented over the years by the activities of the Supreme Court, which have permitted the Constitution to survive. By acting to update the Constitution, it has preserved the document while allowing the urgent tasks of government to be accomplished. As Woodrow Wilson said in 1908, "Whether by force of circumstance or by deliberate design, we have married legislation with adjudication and look for statesmanship in our courts." That statesmanship, although carried out with some deviation, has been in many respects the instrument of preservation, the Constitution being (as Wilson said), "not a mere lawyers' document," but rather "the vehicle of a nation's life."*

It is only by seeing the Constitution as a living instrument of governance, and the Supreme Court as the motive force behind constitutional change, that the decades of American constitutional history up to 1937 can become meaningful. That century and a half from 1787 to 1937 was characterized, so far as American capitalism was concerned, with the Court helping to construct a protective legal umbrella under which business enterprise could and did flourish. Of even more importance, corporate enterprise could wax strong and prosperous. The development may be seen by highlighting three Supreme Court figures—John Marshall, Roger Taney, and Stephen Field. What they built lasted—both in an economic and a legal sense.

---

*Woodrow Wilson, *Constitutional Government in the United States* (New York: Columbia University Press, 1908), p. 157.

THE PATTERN IS SET: MARSHALL AND TANEY

Writing in 1924, economist John R. Commons maintained that the United States Supreme Court occupied "the unique position of the first authoritative faculty of political economy in the world's history."* Judicial theories of property, liberty, and value, enunciated in the cases that litigants brought to the Court, established the legal framework within which business was conducted during the nineteenth and early twentieth centuries. What Commons asserted was even earlier seen by the perceptive Alexis de Tocqueville, who in 1835 noted that scarcely an important question of public policy arose in the United States that did not sooner or later become a judicial question.†

The history of American capitalism may be traced through a series of landmark Supreme Court decisions. In doing so, however, one should heed the admonition of economist William Letwin that,

> The path that economic policy follows in its historical development is sinuous and obscure. To trace all its convolutions is an immensely difficult task. Faced with it, historians fall back, as they must, on simplifying notions. Instead of mapping all the meanderings of the real path, scholars try to match it, however roughly, with ready-made patterns. The professional tool kit of economists and historians contains a few basic patterns that are thought to be generally useful for dealing with economic policy. They bear such names as laissez-faire, socialism, mercantilism, communism, and welfare state.‡

To bring some semblance of order into the mass of raw historical data, one must, in other words, have some sort of conceptual or descriptive model to follow. For present purposes this is accomplished by dividing the 150 years from the drafting of the Constitution in 1787 to the crossing of

---

*Commons, p. 7.
†As will be shown in Chapter Three, de Tocqueville's proposition today states at best a half-truth, the rise of the executive to enhanced power having had as a by-product a diminution of power in the judiciary.
‡Letwin, p. xiii.

the constitutional watershed of 1937 (described in Chapter Three) into halves: first, the period to the Civil War, in which a general theme of an economic policy aimed at encouraging the internal growth of the nation's economy was pursued by way of subsidy and buttressed by favorable judicial decisions; and second, the change from subsidy to regulation in the post-Civil War period, during which the Supreme Court staved off adverse regulation in large part. The year 1937 has been called a constitutional watershed, but it should be kept in mind that the roots of the new economic order ran far back into American history.

The basic emphasis of government, the avowedly political as well as judicial branches, may be summed up in the hypothesis that the legal system was used to encourage and protect business enterprise. Direct governmental subsidies, monetary and otherwise, were one form of such encouragement. Judicially, the law as it evolved during the nineteenth century helped reduce the risk of doing business. The development took two forms: in private law, principally the law of torts—that is, civil wrongs—doctrines of contributory negligence, the fellow-servant rule, assumption of risk, and similar judicially created rules, all served to minimize the costs of doing business by making it difficult for workers injured while at work to recover damages against their employers; second, constitutional law—again, judicially created—preserved liberty of contract and property and insulated commercial enterprise from adverse regulation. Here, again, the evolution was twofold. On the one hand, the Supreme Court cut away the remnants of mercantilism so as to create a national common market; this took place during the first period (1787 to the Civil War), with the Court, in briefest terms, eliminating or severely limiting state regulation of interstate commerce. On the other hand, during the second, post-Civil War period, the Court used the due process clauses of the Fifth and Fourteenth Amendments* to strike down both

---

*Fifth Amendment (1791) applicable to the national government: No person shall be "deprived of life, liberty, or property, without due process of law;

state and federal legislative measures regulatory of business transactions.

The business of the United States has always been business. Peter d'Alroy Jones has put the matter in effective focus in these terms:

> Private business enterprise played a large part in the settlement of the Atlantic seaboard of North America in the seventeenth century, and the British government played only a small part—smaller even than that played by the governments of continental Europe in the earlier settlement of New Spain, Brazil, and New France. Virginia's colonization, for instance, was conceived in business terms—was in fact planned and executed by a joint-stock company, organized rationally as an economic enterprise for profit, a capital investment by a private corporation. . . . All of this is not to claim that economic motivation and organization is a full and ample "explanation" or even most of what there is to say about the early settlement of North America. Venture capital and the technique of joint-stock business enterprise take the historian only so far. . . . From the point of view of the historical evolution of America's wealth, however, the role of joint-stock business in colonial settlement is of prime significance.
>
> A complex of forces drove men to New England's rocky shores in the 1620s; but here too their formal organization, like that of the Virginia settlers, was corporate. In the "middle colonies" even the "proprietors" of Maryland, the Carolinas, New Jersey, and Pennsylvania acted more as free-enterprising land speculators than like feudal aristocrats.*

It was thus in the context of a businessman's world that the fifty-five men later to be canonized in the nation's hagiology as the Founding Fathers met in Philadelphia in 1787 to revise the Articles of Confederation. They did more than revise;

---

nor shall private property be taken for public use without just compensation." Fourteenth Amendment (1868) applicable to state governments: "Nor shall any state deprive any person of life, liberty, or property, without due process of law; nor deny to any person within its jurisdiction the equal protection of the laws."
*Peter d'Alroy Jones, *The Consumer Society: A History of American Capitalism* (Harmondsworth, Middlesex, England: Penguin Books, Ltd., 1965), pp. 12-3.

they produced the Constitution, a charter of government that, although couched in nebulous terms that have made necessary the ensuing decades of exegesis, was in basic thrust a movement toward strengthening the authority of the national government. It "also served to remove some of the most basic inhibitions on economic growth. By destroying internal tariffs, the federal Constitution secured internal free trade and created a large, unified domestic market that was to be one of the secrets of American material success."* That statement by a historian is not wholly accurate. What the Constitution did was place the power to regulate interstate and foreign commerce among the powers expressly granted Congress, while simultaneously denying to the states the power to impose internal tariffs.† In addition, Congress obtained the sole right to coin and regulate the value of money.

It was one thing to put these vague terms in a Constitution, however, but quite another to insure that the notion of "one common market" would be followed. It took the astute interpretation of the commerce clause,‡ by the courts dominated during the first six decades of the nineteenth century by Chief Justices Marshall and Taney, to translate the Delphic phrases of the fundamental law into operational reality. The Constitution does not interpret itself; neither do decisions follow logically from it. The problem of putting contemporary meaning, in the context of specific cases, into ancient constitutional language is not easily solved. There are no ready-made solutions to the abrasive problems of the human condition that, by the peculiarities of the American system, are presented to the Supreme Court for resolution. These problems, as Justice William O. Douglas has said, are "delicate and imponderable, complex and tangled. They require at times the economist's understanding, the poet's insight, the executive's experience, the political scientist's

---

*Jones, p. 37.
†Art. 1, sec. 8, 9, 10.
‡"The Congress shall have power . . . to regulate commerce with foreign nations, and among the several states, and with the Indian tribes." (Art. 1, sec. 8, cl. 3.)

understanding, the historian's perspective."* They are the continuing problems of governance, the resolution of which calls for statesmanship of the highest order, statesmanship, to be sure, subject to the limitations of the judicial process, but statesmanship nevertheless. The Supreme Court unavoidably must operate as a national policy maker in its constitutional (and even its statutory) interpretations.

Knowledge about the Court and its operations has been expanded in recent years; but even so, there are still a number of beliefs about the high tribunal and its activities that may, when viewed coolly and dispassionately, be considered mythical. Four such beliefs merit some attention at this point in order to be able to understand what the Supreme Court did in the nineteenth century:

1. The Supreme Court is to be equated with any other court of law.

2. The intention of the Founding Fathers can guide contemporary decision-making.

3. Decisions can be logically deduced from the Constitution.

4. The Justices can be passionless vehicles for discovering and applying the law.

All of these are questionable, if not outright invalid.†

The notion that the Supreme Court can and may be equated with an ordinary court of law derives from the failure of lawyers and political theorists to assign the Court its real role in the American system. By pretending that the Court is simply a court of law, it becomes easier to parse decisions and easier to ignore the part that the High Bench plays in the decisional structure of government. Morris R. Cohen, a philosopher who was as keen a student of law as this country has produced, appears to be much closer to the mark when he states in 1936: "We cannot pretend that the

---

*William O. Douglas, "The Supreme Court and Its Case Load," *Cornell Law Quarterly*, XLV (1960), 401, 414.

†See, for more comprehensive discussion, Arthur Selwyn Miller, "Some Pervasive Myths About the United States Supreme Court," *St. Louis University Law Journal*, Vol. X (1965), 153.

United States Supreme Court is simply a court of law. Actually, the issues before it generally depend on the determination of all sorts of facts, their consequences, and the values we attach to these consequences. These are questions of economics, politics, and social policy which legal training cannot solve unless law includes all social knowledge."* The Supreme Court, in short, is concerned with formulating and promulgating juristic theories of politics.

In like manner, the view that present-day interpretation can be accomplished by finding out what the Founding Fathers thought (or might have thought had they thought about the problem at issue) is a myth. It is true that the Justices use (and abuse) history in writing opinions, but this is because opinions must be written in language familiar to lawyers. For a Justice openly to disavow history, or any other of the accepted ways of reasoning to conclusions, would be to jeopardize the Court's position by harming its image as a dispassionate purveyor of pre-existing law.

Whether the filiopietistic notion that the intention of the Framers can be the basis for the determination of present cases is a question that raises at least two others: (a) To what extent can such an intention be determined with respect to any important question of the day? (b) Even, however, if such an intention can be determined, is it relevant? The short answer to the first of these corollary questions is that the Framers gave only generalized prescriptions, in those clauses of the Constitution subject to litigation, and that they had no specific intent concerning the precise issue before the Court in any case since then. The answer to the second depends upon an answer to the more basic question: What are the proper ingredients of a constitutional decision? No one has satisfactorily answered that question. The essential question is one of interpretation. It arises whenever an authoritative text exists over a period of time. In smallest form,

---

*Morris R. Cohen, *Reason and Law* (1950), pp. 83-4. Pagination from Collier Books paper edition, 1961; the essay from which the quotation was taken first appeared in 1936.

perhaps, it may be seen in the routine legal instruments like contracts and wills and conveyances. Of broader and more general importance are statutes and other rules of generalized application (e.g., some administrative rules). Constitutions are even broader and more abstract. The legal problem in each instance tends to differ, although judges have not been careful in distinguishing the problems. Much loose language may be found in judicial opinions concerning such matters as effectuating the intention of the parties. The language is just that—loose—and nothing more. For it seems obvious that if intention must be searched for, it is likely the parties did not have a specific intention in the first place. The same may be said for statutes and for constitutions. Language about intention then may be said to be either a cloak for other, unstated, reasons, or it is added to an opinion because lawyers are familiar with it and accordingly feel more comfortable with it.

What may be said about legal documents is also true of any other written instrument or text which exists over a period of time and which must be applied in differing situations. The most obvious is the sacred literature of the various religions of the world—the Bible, the Talmud, the Koran come immediately to mind. Here, too, the "intention of the Framer" is of paramount importance; but here, too, that intention may be obscure and unascertainable. Moreover, the idea of intention as a determinant of present-day decisions rests upon the fallacy that words have a single, undeviating meaning good for all times and places. The teaching of semantics and syntactics is to the contrary.*

Similarly, decisions are not logically deducible from the Constitution. The myth that they can be inheres particularly in those who take a simplistic view of the fundamental law. Only by employing the most transparent of fictions can, say, the relationships between the units of the federal system be determined from the division of powers between central

---

*See, for example, C. K. Ogden and I. A. Richards, *The Meaning of Meaning* (New York: Harcourt, Brace and World, 1923).

and local governments. So, too, with the separation of powers—and with any of the great generalities of the Constitution, including the meaning of commerce and of due process
of law. The framework of government, the generalized statement of powers and limitations, provides at best a point of
departure—not irrelevant, to be sure, for one must not fall
into the trap of what Cohen called "nihilistic absolutism,"
but merely a datum from which reasoning to a conclusion
may proceed. The difficult problem is how that should take
place. The suggestion here (to be expanded later) is that the
Justices are as much or more interested in the social impact
of their decisions as they are in pre-existing law. The constitutional terms are vessels, empty when Marshall came on
the bench, into which he could pour, if not all he wished,
at least much of it. The vessels, after almost two centuries
of interpretation, no longer are empty, but still the Justices
today have choices to make—they can exercise discretion—in
coming to decisions. In doing this, they depend less upon con-
ceptualized formulae than upon "correct appreciation of
social conditions and a true appraisal of the actual effects of
conduct.* (But on these they make guesses; as will be discussed in Chapter Six, they have no institutionalized means
of discernment.)

Allied to the foregoing myths about the Supreme Court
is the further idea that Justices are passionless vehicles for
discovering and applying "The Law." It is seen in many
forms and contexts. The ancient notion of a "government of
laws and not of men" embodies the assumption that the
"law" can rule without intervention of human hand or
mind. Judges do not merely discover the law. Enough is now
known about the nature of law and about the nature of the
thinking processes of judges to be able to conclude that
they, too, carry their biases and prejudices—what Justice
Holmes called his "can't helps"—with them. This does not
mean that a justice is consciously biased; but it does mean

---

*Robert H. Jackson, *The Struggle for Judicial Supremacy* (New York: Random
House, 1941) p. 44.

that he cannot escape his background and heredity. Judges are human, the "cult of the robe" to the contrary notwithstanding. What can be expected from them has been well stated by Justice Felix Frankfurter:

> It is important to appreciate the qualifications requisite for those who exercise this extraordinary authority [of judicial review], demanding as it does a breadth of outlook and an invincible disinterestedness rooted in temperament and confirmed by discipline. Of course, individual judgment and feeling cannot wholly be shut out of the judicial process. But if they dominate, the judicial process becomes a dangerous sham. The conception by a judge of the scope and limits of his function may exert an intellectual and moral force as much as responsiveness to a particular audience or congenial environment.*

Earlier the Justice had, in a celebrated exchange with his colleague, Justice Hugo Black, maintained,

> We may not draw on our merely personal and private notions and disregard the limits that bind judges in their judicial funtion. . . . To practice the requisite detachment and to achieve sufficient objectivity no doubt demands of judges the habit of self-discipline and self-criticism, incertitude that one's own views are incontestable and alert tolerance toward views not shared. . . . These are precisely the prcsuppositions of our judicial process. They are precisely the qualities society has a right to expect from those entrusted with ultimate judicial power.†

Whether all, or even most, of the Justices live up to these statements of the nature of their official duty cannot be stated with any exactitude. Little is known about the actual thought processes of individual Justices. All we know is what they choose to tell us—and that lies mainly in the opinions they write to explain the results reached in individual cases. Whether the opinion reflects what went on in the individual Justice's mind is at best dubious, for most opinions are in

---

*Felix Frankfurter, "John Marshall and the Judicial Function," in Arthur Sutherland (ed.), *Government Under Law* (Cambridge, Mass.: Harvard University Press, 1956), p. 21.
†*Rochin v. California*, 342 U.S. 165, 170-72 (1952).

fact "negotiated" documents. They are the product of a process of bargaining among members of the Court and represent what is acceptable.* It is a fallacy to believe that the opinion can tell anything definitive about the "true" or "real" reasons why a result was reached—if for no other reason than that modern psychology teaches that no one can know with certainty what motivates him to reach a certain decision. Judges do not differ from other humans in this regard, except that their formally written opinions are all that is available, and it is to these that most constitutional scholars turn when writing commentary upon the Supreme Court. The point to be emphasized is that the source material is not adequate to give even a reasonably complete explanation. Perhaps it is for this reason that, even after millions of words have been written about hundreds of years of adjudication, there is still no intellectually satisfying description of the manner in which judges operate. It is even probable that most lawyers cannot give an adequate explication of the judicial decision-making process.

What has been said thus far is prologue to a brief delineation of the Supreme Court's treatment of economic-policy matters in the two three-quarter-century periods up to 1937. It is an oft-told tale. The essential problem during the first period revolved around the extent to which state governments could regulate business enterprise or otherwise intervene in the conduct of business affairs. Despite the powers over commerce and other economic matters granted to Congress, there was little federal activity of a regulatory nature. The principal way in which the national government exercised its economic policy was through the tariff, deliberately protective of domestic industry. In fact a subsidy, it was matched by many other interventions in favor of business. "If one includes all the activities of government [state and federal], and takes into reckoning all the costs, one must conclude," says one economic historian, "that an economic policy, aimed

---

*See Walter F. Murphy, *Elements of Judicial Strategy* (Chicago: The University of Chicago Press, 1964).

particularly at encouraging the internal growth of the nation's economy, was pursued with great energy and at considerable expense."* This early form of paternalism has been repeated throughout American history; its present-day form might be called the rich man's version of the welfare state—as compared with the poor man's version (aid to dependent children, medicare, and so forth).

Direct governmental assistance through legislative action was matched by judicial aid, during the tenure of Chief Justice Marshall. Reference to a few landmark decisions will show the pattern; they include Fletcher *v.* Peck (1810), Dartmouth College *v.* Woodward (1819), Brown *v.* Maryland (1827), and (most important of all) Gibbons *v.* Ogden (1824). There are others, of course, but these will suffice; they indicate, in the words of Mr. Justice Robert H. Jackson in 1949:

> Our system, fostered by the Commerce Clause, is that every farmer and every craftsman shall be encouraged to produce by the certainty that he will have free access to every market in the nation, that no home embargoes will withhold his exports, and no . . . state will by customs, duties, or regulations exclude them. Likewise, every consumer may look to the free competition from every producing area in the nation to protect him from exploitation by any. Such was the vision of the Founders.†

Marshall, in short, believed that interstate commerce—business activity, in general—should be free from the restraints imposed by state and local governments. His decisions so hold. In so doing, this meant that business activity was not regulated at all, for the federal government was entirely quiescent insofar as restraints are concerned. The Supreme Court under Marshall acted as a nationalizing influence, building the open economy and one large common market. As Justice Jackson put it in 1941, the Court had to act because state interferences with interstate affairs "are individ-

---

*Letwin, p. xxi.
†*Hood* v. *DuMond,* 336 U.S. 525 (1949).

ually too petty, too diversified, and too local to get the attention of a Congress hard pressed with more urgent matters. The practical result is that in default of action by [the Court] they will go on suffocating and retarding and Balkanizing American commerce, trade and industry."* The aid to industry, combined with the reluctance of Congress to regulate and the judicial invalidation of state attempts to regulate commerce created the favorable climate for the development of large corporate enterprise—for which science and technology later provided the technical means for such growth.

One reason why the Constitution was written anew, rather than merely revising the Articles of Confederation, was to protect existing property rights. To that end, not only the due process clause (later to become the chief instrument for such protection), but the obligation of contracts clause was inserted in the Constitution: ". . . no state shall . . . pass any . . . law impairing the obligation of contracts. . . ."† Its purpose was to counteract "the ignoble array of legislative schemes for the defeat of creditors," which arose out of the economic distress of debtors following the American revolution.‡ Fletcher *v.* Peck and the Dartmouth College Case§ early set the tone of judicial protection of vested rights, laws impairing the obligation of contracts being thought, in Madison's words, to be "contrary to the first principles of the social compact, and to every principle of sound legislation. . . ." In Fletcher *v.* Peck, Chief Justice Marshall upheld the right of an innocent purchaser of property transferred fraudulently by the Georgia legislature in 1795 over the attempt by the next legislature to annul the grant. His conclusion is worth quoting in full:

> It is, then, the unanimous opinion of the court, that, in this case, the estate having passed into the hands of a purchaser for a valuable consideration, without notice, the state of

---

*Duckworth v. *Arkansas,* 314 U.S. 390 (1941).
†Art. 1, sec. 10, c. 2.
‡This history (and the quotation) may be found in the more recent case of *Home Building & Loan Association* v. *Blaisdell,* 290 U.S. 390 (1934).
§10 U.S. 87 (1810); 17 U.S. 518 (1819).

> Georgia was restrained, either by general principles which
> are common to our free institutions, or by the particular
> provisions of the Constitution of the United States, from
> passing a law whereby the estate of the plaintiff in the
> premises could be constitutionally and legally impaired
> and rendered null and void.*

The opinion is noteworthy not only for its holding that a
subsequent legislature was bound by even the fraudulent
acts of a former, but for its reasoning; note the reference to
"general principles which are common to our free institutions." By language such as this, the Chief Justice gave historical warrant for the Court later (as we will see) finding
general principles, mainly freedom of contract, in the due
process clauses. (The practice—of finding general principles
or new rights—has continued to the present day and shows
few signs of diminishing.) Mr. Justice Johnson, concurring in
Fletcher, used even stronger language; in the only example
where a Supreme Court Justice maintained that the Supreme
Being could be bound, he asserted: "I do not hesitate to
declare that a state does not possess the power of revoking
its own grants. But I do it on a general principle, on the
reason and nature of things: a principle which will impose
laws even on the deity. . . ."† The Supreme Court has been
audacious at times—but never again in articulating restraints
on the deity; much later, the Court, speaking through Mr.
Justice William O. Douglas, flatly stated that "we are a religious people whose institutions presuppose a Supreme Being,"‡
but that is a different proposition.

Marshall's mention of "general principles . . . common
to our free institutions" helps make Fletcher of enduring
importance as an example of judicial decision-making, even
though the obligation of contracts provision is of little present-day importance in constitutional litigation. So, too, with
the famous Dartmouth College Case, in which the Court held
that a royal charter granted to the College in 1769 could not

---

*10 U.S. 87 (1810).
†*Idem.*
‡*Zorach* v. *Clauson,* 343 U.S. 306 (1952).

subsequently be altered by New Hampshire; the charter, according to Chief Justice Marshall, was a contract within the meaning of the Constitution, and, accordingly, its "obligation" could not be "impaired." The major effect of the decision, in the words of one scholar, was the establishment of "a precedent for the immunity of business-corporation charters from state control."* That may be a fair assessment of a decision surely not commanded by the Constitution and, as Marshall admitted in his opinion, "not in the mind of the Convention" when it adopted the contract clause. (Even in 1819, in other words, the intention of the framers was ignored when the Justices found it desirable.) The two decisions lay the groundwork for later constitutional interpretations having the effect of providing a protective legal milieu in which business activity could flourish. Professor Mendelson takes a harsher view:

> Conservative tradition insists that by putting the sanctity of "contracts" above other considerations of ethics and public welfare, Marshall and his associates promoted economic stability. Would it not be more accurate to suggest rather that they encouraged the flagrant corruption of state politics and reckless waste of natural resources that marked the nineteenth century. Surely judicial protection of fraud in the Yazoo land scandal [the Fletcher Case] paved the way for the Robber Barons and their Great Barbecue at the expense of the American people.†

(One might add that a third view is possible: that the decisions in fact made little or no difference in the course of business endeavor or exploitation of the continent. Certainly, neither prevented state control of corporations through reservations in their charters *if* the state authorities wanted to do so; the point is that they did not want to regulate or control in the period before the Civil War, and, when regulation was finally attempted after the Civil War, the Court found other

---

*Wallace Mendelson, *Capitalism, Democracy, and the Supreme Court* (New York: Appleton-Century-Crofts, Inc., 1960), p. 24.
†Mendelson, pp. 24-5.

means—due process—to deal with it. In other words, by then the corporation had become established and, as today, subject to little or no control from state authorities via the charter.)

Whatever conclusion one draws from the decisions of the Marshall Court, it should be noted that they are key foundations to what Edward S. Corwin called "the basic doctrine of American constitutional law": the Doctrine of Vested Rights. Through the operation of the doctrine, "the problem of harmonizing majority rule with minority rights, or more specifically, republican institutions with the security of property, contracts, and commerce"* was resolved by the Supreme Court. However, the strict Marshallian construction of the contract clause was soon ameliorated; in 1837, the Supreme Court then headed by Chief Justice Roger Taney held that the contract clause should not be construed to prevent a state from taking action necessary to protect the vital interests of the public. In Charles River Bridge *v.* Warren Bridge,"† the Court held that the grant of a franchise to operate a toll bridge did not mean that the state could not make a grant to another corporation to build a competing bridge that would soon operate without toll. It took another century, however, for the contract clause so to diminish in importance that today it has little or no significance, having been submerged in the all-embracing concept of due process of law, which, as will be seen, means that the express terms of the Constitution—". . . no state shall . . . pass any . . . law impairing the obligation of contracts . . ."—have had a judicially created qualification of reasonableness inserted in them. The key case is Home Building & Loan Association *v.* Blaisdell,‡ validating Minnesota's moratorium law enacted during the Great Depression.

To the two contract cases of Marshall should be added a

---

*Edward S. Corwin, "The Basic Doctrine of American Constitutional Law," in Alpheus T. Mason and Gerald Garvey (eds.), *American Constitutional History: Essays by Edward S. Corwin* (New York: Harper and Row Torchbooks, 1964), p. 25. (Professor Corwin published the essay in the *Michigan Law Review* in 1914.)
†36 U.S. 420 (1837).
‡290 U.S. 398 (1934).

trio of other important decisions that had the effect of eliminating state regulation of business activity and protecting property: Gibbons *v.* Ogden, Brown *v.* Maryland, and McCulloch *v.* Maryland. In each, moreover, the Chief Justice furthered the *national,* as distinguished from the *local,* interest. Marshall's decisions were "nationalizing" in impact; they helped create the legal climate that, within decades, aided the birth and growth of huge national combines—the "trusts"— the latter-day examples of which dominate the economy and warp historical political lines. McCulloch clearly shows this, for in that case Marshall at once *invalidated* a state tax on a bank incorporated by the federal government and *validated* the exercise of congressional power. The latter was accomplished through invention of the doctrine of implied powers, thereby greatly enlarging federal power. Decisions such as this laid the groundwork for the vastly increased number of activities by the central government—an ironic twist, because Marshall's "conservative" opinions have been used in recent decades to uphold "liberal" legislation!

For such a purpose, McCulloch and Gibbons have been particularly useful, the former for the doctrine of implied powers and the latter for its expansive reading of the meaning of the commerce clause. Gibbons involved a somewhat different question from the contract cases (where it was vested private interests versus public interests), for at issue was a valuable right granted by New York to operate a monopoly in steamboats between New York City and New Jersey. The monopolist obtained a state court injunction against a person violating his right by using steamboats enrolled and licensed under an act of Congress. Marshall seized the opportunity to write an opinion that stands today as the great landmark regarding congressional power over commerce; after a hiatus between 1890 and 1937, Gibbons is cited since 1940 as precedent for current exercises of congressional power. Marshall's nationalizing decisions provide some of the authority, for example, for upholding Title II of the Civil Rights Act of 1964 as well as for other broad sweeps of regulation.* What in ultimate effect Marshall thus did was to politicize economic regulation and to take it out of the hands of the judiciary—another ironic twist.

Gibbons and Brown, the former particularly, are accordingly noteworthy for their longevity; but they are also worthy of study for the manner in which the Chief Justice reasoned to his conclusions. Marshall altered his methodology to suit the case at hand. In Marbury *v.* Madison, for example, the case that established the principle of judicial review, he approached the problem of interpretation of the Constitution as if it were a simple legal instrument—a contract or a will—of private parties, whereas in McCulloch, Gibbons, and Brown he took an expansive view of the document he was construing and approached it as the vehicle of the nation's life rather than a mere lawyer's document. In the Brown decision, a license tax on importers was invalidated, both because it contravened the constitutional prohibition on state import taxes (Art. I, sec. 10) and because it impinged on Congress's power under the commerce clause.

Marshall was writing on a *tabula rasa;* his opinions are classic examples of creative decision-making by a judge who knew what he wanted and how to go about it. His decisions mark the triumph of the views of Alexander Hamilton—the movement from mercantilism (state regulation of economic life) and the formation of an open economy based on a national market. This was a remarkable achievement but one that should not be attributed to the Supreme Court as prime mover. Marshall's court helped by cutting away adverse state regulation of business, but probably of more importance were the affirmative governmental acts to stimulate economic growth:

> Despite the prevailing orthodoxy, government intervention
> in economic life was supported by leading political figures

---

*The Civil Rights Act was upheld in *Heart of Atlanta Motel* v. *United States,* 379 U.S. 241 (1964) and *Katzenbach* v. *McClung,* 379 U.S. 294 (1964). See Robert L. Stern, "The Commerce Clause and the National Economy, *Harvard Law Review,* LIX (1946), pp. 645, 883, for an insightful discussion of the later treatment of the commerce clause. See also Chapter Three, below.

and public policy took the form of local, state, and federal
subsidization of the transportation revolution, federal creation of two national banks, and manipulation of the
economy through Treasury fiscal operations, the deliberate
use of tariffs to divert the allocation of resources into desired lines of development, and government subsidies to
certain industries (fishing, small arms, and, at a state level,
agricultural bounties on grain and silk production).*

The myth to the contrary notwithstanding, government intervention in business affairs—to *help*, be it noted, not to
regulate—was the norm of early American history. Never has
laissez faire been used as a means of prohibiting aid to business. What the Supreme Court did by way of eliminating
adverse state regulation of commercial affairs was buttressed,
moreover, by state courts using common-law doctrines to out-
law budding movements of workers to organize into trade
unions. In all of these ways—plus, of course, a virgin continent filled with natural resources and a burgeoning science
and technology enabling new industries to flourish—the Ham-
iltonian system became fact. When in the McCulloch Case
the validity of the Second United States Bank was sustained
and rendered immune from control by state governments, it
could and did contribute heavily to stable economic growth:
"By upholding specie payments for its own notes and cajoling
the state banks to do likewise, it encouraged the creation of
a stable national currency. By using capital raised in the
East as a basis for its business in other sections of the nation,
the Bank made credit and currency available where it was
most scarce. Finally, the Bank gave speedy and economical
loans to the federal government in time of need."†

But what the Court did *not* do may be of even more importance than what it did accomplish. For assertion of the
power of judicial review by the Supreme Court in 1803
was followed in ensuing decades by the Court looking
almost entirely to the acts of *state* governments; it was not

*Jones, p. 99.
†Jones, p. 106.

until 1857, in the case involving Dred Scott, that the Court again invalidated a federal action as contrary to the Constitution. This meant that affirmative federal (and state) actions designed to enhance economic growth—the tariff, for example—got no judicial cognizance. (They still do not.) American capitalism, in other words, owes more to the avowedly political branches of government than to the judiciary for its early development. Whether the economy would have grown as it did *without* positive programs of government assistance is a question that history cannot answer. What is known is that economic growth did take place, government did affirmatively help, and the Supreme Court participated in the development by striking down adverse state regulations. The conclusions to be drawn from this state of affairs are not self-evident, although it may be fairly said that business enterprise in this country has never been wholly private. "The line between private and public action is blurred, and always has been blurred. . . ."*

For whatever reason—and, to repeat, history gives no convincing answers—the corporation, by the time that Marshall left the Court in 1836, had become a key institution in American life. The transition from small business to big business, from single proprietor to collectivity, and (eventually) from capitalist to bureaucrat was well under way by the time that Attorney General Roger B. Taney succeeded John Marshall as Chief Justice of the Supreme Court of the United States. Taney brought different preconceptions and viewpoints to the center seat on the High Bench; he was a Jacksonian in belief and in politics. One of President Jackson's most trusted advisers, he brought the anti-economic-privilege predilections of Old Hickory to the Court. Taney, moreover, believed in judicial restraint and in the operation of democracy through the legislative processes; he was a forerunner of those like Justice Felix Frankfurter who, a

---

*Eugene V. Rostow, *Planning for Freedom: The Public Law of American Capitalism* (New Haven, Conn.: Yale University Press, 1959), p. 366.

century later, in different times and on different issues, took a similar position of the limited nature of judicial review. Finally, he wanted to maintain, although he was not successful in so doing, that the commerce clause did not in and of itself prohibit state laws regarding business—as the Court viewed the need for such prohibitions. He was not willing, in other words, to accept the Marshallian pronouncements in Gibbons *v.* Ogden and Brown *v.* Maryland.

But what Marshall and his colleagues wrought was built on a firm socio-economic foundation, and Taney could not turn the clock back to the *status quo ante*. The 1850s, in the words of economic historian Stuart Bruchey, "saw a phenomenal increase in incorporation, with nearly half of all corporations chartered between 1800 and 1860 appearing in that decade."* Accordingly, whatever reservations or misgivings reflective of the Jacksonian philosophy Taney may have had about corporations, they were not adequate to stem the tide toward the (private) collectivization of American business. Bruchey asserts that Taney adhered to a view of "corporate egalitarianism," by which he meant the "ideal of publicly sponsored free competition in the interest of community welfare. His essential contribution was so to adjust constitutional law to the needs of the corporation as greatly to stimulate its use in business."† The cases of particular interest are Charles River Bridge *v.* Warren Bridge (1837), Bank of Augusta *v.* Earle (1839), Cooley *v.* Board of Wardens (1851), and Swift *v.* Tyson (1842). In these decisions, the Chief Justice provided an intellectual bridge between the nationalism of Marshall and the laissez-faire posture of the post-Civil War Court dominated by Justice Stephen J. Field. It was Taney's fate to usher in the corporate age, even though, before he came to the Court, he held strong disapproving views of corporate power: "It is a fixed principle of our political institutions," he said in 1833, "to guard against the

---

*Stuart Bruchey, *The Roots of American Economic Growth, 1607-1861: An Essay in Social Causation* (New York: Harper and Row, 1965), p. 139.
†Bruchey, p. 137.

unnecessary accumulation of power over persons and property in any hands; and no hands are less worthy to be trusted with it than those of a moneyed corporation."*

The Charles River Bridge Case is of interest mainly because it ameliorated the doctrine of vested rights that Marshall had so carefully erected in Fletcher *v.* Peck and the Dartmouth College Case. He strictly construed legislative grants in the interests of the entire community:

> The whole community are interested in this inquiry, and they have a right to require that the power of promoting their comfort and convenience, and of advancing the public prosperity, by providing safe, convenient, and cheap ways for the transportation of produce and the purposes of travel, shall not be construed to have been surrendered or diminished by the State unless it shall appear by plain words that it was intended to be done. . . . While the rights of property are sacredly guarded, we must not forget, that the community also has rights, and that the happiness and well-being of every citizen depends on their faithful preservation.†

Thus the state of Massachusetts could validly grant a competing franchise for a toll bridge over contract-clause objections of the first grantee. Of particular interest for any student of the Court is the manner in which judges can approach the same type of factual situation and come to diametrically opposite conclusions; this puzzles those who believe in a "government of laws and not of men" but not those who recognize that the law is in fact far more uncertain than it at times appears. Put another way, the Charles River Bridge Case is a prime example of the manner in which legal principles tend to travel in pairs of opposites and how judges have to exercise what Holmes called "the sovereign prerogative of choice" between conflicting principles in most cases that reach decision on the merits. This appears to be true

---

*From Taney's *Report from the Secretary of the Treasury on the Removal of Public Deposits from the Bank of the United States,* 23d Cong., 1st Sess. (1833), Senate Doc. 2, I, 20; quoted in Mendelson, p. 36.
†11 Peters 420, 549-50 (1837).

for all appellate courts, but it is valid beyond peradventure for the Supreme Court of the United States.*

But if Taney was able to water down some of the rigidities of Marshallian doctrine in the contract-clause cases, he found himself largely circumscribed from altering affairs as far as the commerce clause was concerned. The key cases are Cooley and Earle.† The former has more present-day interest; it is still cited by the Supreme Court in recent opinions, whereas the latter is mainly of interest for the historian. It is not even mentioned in some recent casebooks used for law-school instruction in constitutional law.

Both continued the judicial interest in a *national* economy, as compared with the Balkanizing tendencies of some states, Earle by giving legal recognition to the fact that corporations have the same capacity to do business outside their home state as within and Cooley by enunciating the classic doctrine that the very type of business might preclude state regulation by "imperatively demanding a single uniform rule. . . ." In short, the two cases enhanced the growth of corporations; and this is so even though Taney was careful in Earle not to call the corporation a citizen within the privileges and immunities clause of the Constitution. Article IV, Section 2 reads: "The citizens of each state shall be entitled to all privileges and immunities of citizens in the several states." Taney was able thus to circumscribe the constitutional rights of corporations, while at the same time stimulating its use by permitting its operation nationwide. He rejected the applicability of the citizenship clause to the corporation not because the Constitution demanded such a result, but because, as Felix Frankfurter put it, "he chose to deny, by reason of his economic and political outlook, the enhancement of strength that such constitutional protection would give."‡ Little did he know that, a few decades

---

*For discussion, see Arthur Selwyn Miller, "On the Choice of Major Premises in Supreme Court Opinions," *Journal of Public Law*, XIV (1965), 251.
†*Cooley* v. *Board of Wardens*, 53 U.S. 299 (1851); *Bank of Augusta* v. *Earle*, 13 Peters 519 (1839).
‡Frankfurter, *The Commerce Clause*, p. 65.

later (1886), the Court would assume without argument that corporations were persons within the meaning of the due process clause of the Fourteenth and Fifth Amendments.

What the Earle Case meant is that corporations could freely send their agents into other states and enjoy the protection of the laws of the other states but that those states were free to legislate against their entry. (Not that many states so wanted; then, as now, competition reigned among states to attract industry.) It was not until 1877 that the important corollary was added to the Earle doctrine that a state cannot exclude nor unduly burden a corporation from another state in doing interstate commerce;* all that Earle permits—and still does—is for a state to refuse entry to a foreign corporation wanting to do *intra*state commerce. That is the law; the economics makes the law seem absurd—states want to attract business (that is, corporations) rather than repel it. So Earle is of antiquarian interest, but Cooley is not. In that famous case, one in which Taney silently concurred in the opinion of Justice Curtis, further nationalizing tendencies in judicial decision-making may be seen:

> Now the power to regulate commerce, embraces a vast field, containing not only many, but exceedingly various subjects, quite unlike in their nature; some imperatively demanding a single uniform rule, operating equally on the commerce of the United States in every port; and some, like the subject now in question, as imperatively demanding that diversity, which alone can meet the local necessities of navigation.
>   . . . *Whatever subjects of this power are in their nature national, or admit only of one uniform system, or plan of regulation, may justly be said to be of such a nature as to require exclusive legislation by Congress* [italics mine].†

Accordingly, it was the Court presided over by Chief Justice Taney, but not Taney himself, who enunciated the doctrine since known as the Cooley rule (in the italicized portion). It fits with Marshall's nationalizing opinions, aids corporate growth, and, again, puts the Court in the forefront of articu-

---

*So held in *Pensacola Tel. Co.* v. *Western Union Tel. Co.*, 96 U.S. 1 (1877).
†53 U.S. 299, 319 (1851).

lating economic policy via constitutional interpretation. The power to regulate commerce, in other words, in the absence of congressional action carries with it the negative implication that certain business activities—as determined by the Court—cannot be regulated by the states. As with the Marshall opinions, Cooley is echoed in modern times. Said a majority of the Court in 1945: "For a hundred years it has been accepted constitutional doctrine that the commerce clause, without the aid of Congressional legislation, thus affords some protection from state legislation inimical to the national commerce, and that in such cases, where Congress has not acted, this Court, and not the state legislature, is under the commerce clause the final arbiter of the competing demands of state and national interests."* The "national interests" have been in a nationwide economy, and the Court in such cases as Cooley helped provide the favorable climate for the burgeoning of corporate enterprise.

One might ask why the Court took it upon itself to articulate these national interests when the Constitution gave the power to regulate commerce to Congress. Congress did little or nothing before 1887 to protect interstate commerce against state legislation designed to favor local interests; in that year, it enacted the Interstate Commerce Act. Followed three years later by the Sherman Antitrust Act, the period marks the first significant federal legislative regulation of interstate commerce. It is a fascinating, albeit unrewarding, exercise to speculate on what type of economy would have emerged in this country had the Supreme Court not ruled as it did. Holmes apparently thought it made a great difference; in an oft-quoted statement he asserted: "I do not think the United States would come to an end if we lost our power to declare an Act of Congress void. I do think the Union would be imperilled if we could not make that declaration as to the laws of the several states. For one in my place sees how often a local policy prevails with those who are not trained to national views and how often action is taken that embodies what

Southern Pacific Company v. *Arizona*, 325 U.S. 761 (1945).

the Commerce Clause was meant to end." At best, however, that is an *a priori* statement made by one who could only have proceeded on the assumption that what the Court decided made a difference as to the nature of the economy. But that we do not know or at best can only guess at, even though, as Felix Frankfurter has said:

> The raw material of modern government is business. Taxation, utility regulation, agricultural control, labor relations, housing, banking and finance, control of the security market —all our major domestic issues—are phases of a single central problem: namely, the interplay of economic enterprise and government. . . . In law . . . men make a difference. It would deny all meaning to history to believe that the course of events would have been the same if Thomas Jefferson had had the naming of Spencer Roane to the place to which John Adams called John Marshall, or if Roscoe Conkling rather than Morrison R. Waite had headed the Court before which came the Granger legislation. The revolution of finance capital in the United States, and therefore of American history after the Reconstruction period, would hardly have been the same if the views of men like Mr. Justice Miller and Mr. Justice Harlan had dominated the decisions of the Court from the Civil War to Theodore Roosevelt's administration. There is no inevitability in history except as men make it.*

But, despite the fervent statement of Frankfurter, one can say with equal certainty that men are scarcely free to make history; *their* actions, including Supreme Court Justices, are very probably as compelled by drives and forces over which the individual has no control as they are of the operation of his free will. Furthermore, the Frankfurter assertion is based on the assumption that law, however articulated (by court or legislature), can alter social conditions. Scholars are far from agreement on that score; the argument has raged for centuries, so whether—to employ William Graham Sumner's phraseology—"stateways" can change "folkways" is as

---

*Felix Frankfurter, *Law and Politics: Occasional Papers of Felix Frankfurter*, ed. Archibald MacLeish and E. F. Pritchard, Jr. (paper ed.; New York, Capricorn Books, 1962), p. 62.

yet an unanswered question. Accordingly, the Court, taking it upon itself to make the series of nationalizing decisions it did prior to the Civil War, *may* have made a difference, but, with deference to Holmes and Frankfurter, one cannot say with certainty. It may be only lawyers' conceit and American pride in its unique contribution to the science of government—judicial review—that perpetuates the belief. Finally, despite Frankfurter, it is far from self-evident that history has meaning.

THE RISE AND FALL OF ECONOMIC DUE PROCESS

The power of the Supreme Court to impose its will on the nation received what is probably its most severe test in the post-Civil War period ending in 1937. During that time, to put the matter as briefly as possible, the High Bench, under the leadership of Justice Stephen J. Field and of such luminaries of the American bar as Roscoe Conkling,* constructed principles of laissez faire and read them into the Constitution to protect both individual *and* corporate economic activity from adverse governmental regulation. With few exceptions—to be noted shortly—these principles prevailed until the constitutional revolution of the 1930s, until, that is, the rise of the "Positive State" during the past three decades. The history, again, is familiar; it needs only brief restatement.† A few landmark cases will indicate the development: Munn *v.* Illinois (1877), the Slaughterhouse Cases (1873), Allgeyer *v.* Louisiana (1897), Lochner *v.* New York (1906), Muller *v.* Oregon (1908), Adair *v.* United States (1908), and Coppage *v.* Kansas (1915). There are many others, of course,

---

*See Benjamin R. Twiss, *Lawyers and the Constitution* (New York: Russell & Russell, Inc. 1962; first published in 1942 by Princeton University Press). The book is a fascinating account of the influence of the legal profession on the course of constitutional decisions.

†See Commons, *Legal Foundations of Capitalism,* for a perceptive study of this history from the standpoint of an economist. Commons wrote in the 1920s and did not anticipate what happened during the 1930s and 1940s, but his work, although hard going, still merits attention.

but these will suffice to trace the development of government by judiciary in economic matters, with its exceptions in the public utility cases and the aberration in Muller *v.* Oregon.

These cases deal with the government-business symbiosis. They have, to the extent that they place limitations on regulation of business affairs, been repudiated in recent years and are thus of historical interest only. The period began with Munn *v.* Illinois and the Slaughterhouse Cases, which *upheld* regulation, and ended with the principles of those cases in effect being re-enunciated. Laissez faire, as the Supreme Court explicated it, was a legal principle of fundamental importance; the Court put forward a theory of political economy predicated on a notion of individualism, finding it in the natural law and the writings of the philosophers of the Enlightenment. But they did it at the very time that individualism became an anachronism, when, as John D. Rockefeller later put it, "large-scale organization had revolutionized the way of doing business and when individualism had gone, never to return."* The Court did it, ironically enough, in an intellectual atmosphere in which the name of Adam Smith was high on the list of saints; but Smith wrote his *The Wealth of Nations* in 1776 and decried the tendency toward incorporation. Moreover, laissez faire was a moral principle; poverty and failure were equated with sin, wealth and business success with virtue. The general philosophical views have since been labeled "Social Darwinism," the chief exponents of which were Herbert Spencer and William Graham Sumner.†

The history of the three-quarters of a century between the Civil War and 1937 may be seen as a contest between the judiciary and the legislature; on a philosophical level, it may be viewed as a struggle between rugged individualism and a rising tide of equalitarianism. Munn *v.* Illinois provides apt illustration and serves as a point of departure. Could busi-

---

*Quoted in Allan Nevins, *John D. Rockefeller* (New York: Charles Scribner's Sons, 1940), I, 622.
†See Richard Hofstadter, *Social Darwinism in American Thought* (rev. ed.; Boston: Beacon Press, 1955) for a classic account of the philosophical temper of the age.

ness call on the Supreme Court so to interpret the Constitution as to invalidate the onslaught of legislation regulating prices charged by the corporate monopolies? The answer first given was "no," at least for those businesses "affected with a public interest." The Court echoed Chief Justice Marshall in Gibbons *v.* Ogden (1824) when he said, in another context of course:

> We are now arrived at the inquiry—What is this power? It is the power to regulate; that is, the power to prescribe the rule by which commerce is to be governed. This power, like all others vested in Congress, is complete in itself, may be exercised to its utmost extent, and acknowledges no limitations, other than are prescribed in the constitution. . . . The wisdom and the discretion of Congress, their identity with the people, and the influence which their constituents possess at elections, are, in this, as in many other instances, as that, for example, of declaring war, the sole restraints on which they have relied to secure them from its abuse. They are the restraints on which the people must often rely solely, in all representative governments.*

The Munn Case is noteworthy for several reasons—for beginning the constitutional concept of "business affected with a public interest" (although it is probable that Chief Justice Waite did not think in the limiting terms that concept later acquired), for asserting the primacy of the legislature over the judiciary in questions of price regulation of businessmen (in this instance, a partnership, not a corporation), and for a dissenting opinion of Mr. Justice Field that foretold the shape of things to come. Munn & Scott, the partnership, claimed that their conviction for operating a grain elevator without a license and at rates higher than the law allowed intruded on a field of commercial regulation belonging to Congress, and, of more importance, violated their rights of free enterprise protected by the Fourteenth Amendment. The majority of the Court disagreed. In a famous opinion, Chief Justice Waite asserted:

---

*9 Wheaton 1 (1824).

[Property] does become clothed with a public interest when used in a manner to make it of public consequence, and affects the community at large. When, therefore, one devotes his property to a use in which the public has an interest, he, in effect, grants to the public an interest in that use, and must submit to be controlled by the public for the common good, to the extent of the interest he has thus created. He may withdraw his grant by discontinuing its use; but, so long as he maintains the use, he must submit to the control.

Applying these ideas to the situation at hand, Waite then concluded that,

Certainly, if any business can be clothed "with a public interest, and cease to be *juris privati* only," this has been. It may not be made so by the operation of the Constitution of Illinois or this statute, but it is by the facts.*

Who, then, court or legislature, is to have the final word on the determination of what is a reasonable compensation for utility services (as in Munn)? The answer drew on English history and gave it constitutional sanction:

In countries where the common law prevails, it has been customary from time immemorial for the legislature to declare what shall be a reasonable compensation under such circumstances. . . . The controlling fact is the power to regulate at all. If that exists, the right to establish the maximum of charge, as one of the means of regulation, is implied. . . .

We know that this is a power which may be abused; but that is no argument against its existence. *For protection against abuses by legislatures the people must resort to the polls, not to the courts* [my italics].†

As with the earlier Marshall opinions, Munn has a modern counterpart. Professor Robert G. McCloskey has shown in a perceptive essay on the rise and fall of economic due process that the Court now says—probably finally—that it is not its affair to decide whether economic legislation "offends the

*94 U.S. 113, 126, 132 (1877), pp. 126, 132.
†94 U.S. 113, 126, 132 (1877), pp. 133-4.

54   *Constitutional Doctrine and Corporate Power*

public welfare" and also that "debatable issues as respect business, economic, and social affairs" are for legislative decision.*

Thus it is that the Allgeyer-Lochner-Adair-Coppage line of decisions, which highlighted the post-Civil War period, has now been repudiated. They are important not for what they say as present-day doctrine, but because they constitute the most blatant attempt at judicial economic government ever attempted in this country. Erected as a principle of eternal truth was freedom of contract—something not mentioned in the Constitution but found by the majority of the Court in the late nineteenth century in one of the most remarkable feats of judicial law-making this nation has seen. If Munn and the Slaughterhouse Cases reveal the initial judicial attitude following the Civil War, perhaps the turning point came in 1886 when what Taney had refused to do in Earle—call the corporation a citizen—was in effect accomplished by denominating the corporation a "person" within the meaning of the Fourteenth Amendment.† This important point was settled by Chief Justice Waite telling counsel in oral argument that the Court would not hear argument on it since all the Justices were of the opinion that corporations were persons within the purview of the amendment. The ramifications have been considerable, for this almost casually accepted notion was the basis for corporate protection of liberty and property against violations of due process of law—but a process of law that had no historical antecedent. And it happened only thirteen years after the Court had said, in the Slaughterhouse Cases, in which it was alleged that the Fourteenth Amendment was contravened by Louisiana granting a monopoly in New Orleans for slaughtering animals, "We doubt very much whether any action of a state not directed against the negroes as a class, or on account of their

*See Robert G. McCloskey, "Economic Due Process and the Supreme Court: An Exhumation and Reburial," *The Supreme Court Review*, (1962), 34. Professor McCloskey cites *Day-Brite Lighting* v. *Missouri*, 342 U.S. 421 (1952) and *Williamson* v. *Lee Optical Co.*, 348 U.S. 483 (1955).
†*Santa Clara County* v. *Southern Pacific Railroad Co.*, 118 U.S. 394 (1886).

race, will ever be held to come within the purview of this
provision [equal protection]. It is so clearly a provision for
that race and that emergency, that a strong case would be
necessary for its application to any other. . . ."* One of the
ironies of American history is the way in which an amendment designed to aid freed slaves was employed to protect
corporate enterprise. True it is that the amendment—slowly
at first, with a rush in recent years—has been used to further
the legal status of the Negroes, but that development was
far overshadowed by the furtherance of the cause of the
"robber barons" during the late nineteenth and early twentieth centuries. What the Court had said in 1877 about the
primacy of the legislature in regulatory matters became, by
1890, the supremacy of the judiciary.† Stephen J. Field, who
had dissented in Munn, had, within thirteen years, swung a
majority of the Court to his view.

SUBSTANTIVE DUE PROCESS

History is replete with ironies. Not the least of these in
the American past is the way in which the Supreme Court—
American courts and the legal profession generally—during
the post-Civil War period "placed itself between the public
and what the public needed and helped to protect individuals who did not need protection against society, which did
need it."‡ Not only individuals, of course, but also "persons"
—those artificial persons called corporations—got protection
which, as centers of economic power, they did not need
against laborers and others who did need it. This was done
in the name of liberty—liberty of *contract,* even though the
Constitution does not mention such a liberty—by the Justices importing into the due process clause limitations on the
substance, as distinguished from the procedure, of govern-

---

*83 U.S. 36 (1873).

†See *Chicago, Milwaukee & St. Paul Railway* v. *Minnesota,* 134 U.S. 418
(1890).

‡Sidney Fine, *Laissez Faire and the General Welfare State* (paper ed.; Ann
Arbor: The University of Michigan Press, 1964), p. 164. See also Roscoe
Pound, "Common Law and Legislation," *Harvard Law Review,* XXI (1908),
403.

mental action. The result was substantive due process, a remarkable invention that changed judicial review from a seldom used, innocuous power to one of the most (outwardly) awesome powers of government. It is now no longer viable as far as economic matters are concerned, but it is very much alive with regard to other issues.*

To trace the threads of development through the tangled skein of history is possible only by finding, after the fact, regularities and uniformities that may not have existed. If one pays attention only to the Supreme Court's decisions, it is fairly easy to find these threads. The cases, although often written in the turgid prose of lawyers, are clear as far as results are concerned; but what was behind them, by way of social context and the individual philosophies of the Justices, is quite another matter. Nevertheless, in the period following the Civil War we may see that marriage of technology to entrepreneurship which (by drawing on favorable legal principles and a legal profession the leaders of which were the minions of the entrepreneurs) produced the now-familiar large industrial enterprises. There was, in short, the rise of the collective power of capital, of business enterprise, all done in the name of an individualism that—again, an irony—had vanished. Corwin relates the matter well:

> [The doctrine of vested rights and the doctrine of freedom of contract] . . . especially when they are projected against the social environment in which they respectively arose, are two quite different things. Ownership as a source of control over others is another thing; and as the prerogative of the great corporations dealing with unorganized workingmen, ownership—ordinarily an absentee ownership—is obviously of the latter description. Moreover, while corporate ownership was expanding, opportunities for personal acquisition were contracting.†

---

*For example, the Fourteenth Amendment's due process clause now incorporates, by Supreme Court decisions, all of the substantive liberties of the First Amendment: speech, press, assembly, right of petition; it even includes the separation of church and state concept imbedded in the "no establishment of religion" clause of that amendment.

†Edward S. Corwin, *Liberty Against Government* (Baton Rouge: Louisiana State University Press, 1948), p. 180.

At the time, then, of the flowering of the great trusts or corporations came the close of the frontier; at the time when the Supreme Court was extolling the merits of freedom of contract and of laissez faire, whatever social conditions might have made them possible had vanished. By 1900 the new doctrine was firmly entrenched; Mr. Justice Field, the great dissenter of the 1870s, had triumphed. The agrarian and populist revolt of the late nineteenth century had been neatly undercut by the High Bench. The victory was of relatively short duration, to be sure, but was not without some lasting effects; the synthesis that is emerging from a century of government-business jousting is the mixed economy, not one of the grand alternatives of laissez faire, on the one hand, or of socialism, on the other.

Allgeyer, Lochner, Adair, Coppage—that line of cases of the early age of industrial America in which the Supreme Court failed to recognize that necessitous men are not free men—established the doctrine of freedom of contract, enunciated as well as any place in the Adair Case by Mr. Justice Harlan. He relied on Allgeyer and Lochner as establishing that "liberty of contract . . . cannot be unreasonably interfered with." The Court equated the right of an employee to quit his employment with "the right of the employer, for whatever reason, to dispense with the services of the employee," and ruled that legislation that "disturbs that equality is an arbitrary interference with the liberty of contract which no government can justify in a free land."* (The opinions of the Court during that period are singularly devoid of rational reasons for the decisions. Here, as at other times, the Court decides by issuing conclusions. This, it may be said, is normal—then, now, and throughout Court history.) Accordingly, labor legislation forbidding discrimination by employers for union activity by employees was invalid as violative of substantive due process. The Court considered the power of the individual worker to be equal to the power of the employer—even though that employer

---

*Adair v. United States, 208 U.S. 161 (1908).

was a collectivity, a corporation, and a person in law only by application of a transparent legal fiction—an assumption that is difficult to explain except on grounds of wilful blindness or, perhaps, of a complete lack of knowledge of the facts of industrial life. Whatever conclusion one draws on that question—and here, again, history provides only dim clues—perhaps the off-bench statement of Mr. Justice Samuel F. Miller provides as good a hint as any: "It is vain to contend with judges who have been at the bar the advocates for forty years of railroad companies, and all the forms of associated capital, when they are called upon to decide cases where such interests are in contest. All their training, all their feelings are from the start in favor of those who need no such influence."* So, too, the dissenting opinion—one of his most famous—of Mr. Justice Holmes in the Lochner Case indicates what the Court was doing; it is worth quoting at some length:

> This case is decided upon an economic theory which a large part of the country does not entertain. If it were a question whether I agreed with that theory, I should desire to study it further and long before making up my mind. But I do not conceive that to be my duty, because I strongly believe that my agreement or disagreement has nothing to do with the right of a majority to embody their opinions in law. It is settled by various decisions of this court that state constitutions and state laws may regulate life in many ways which we as legislators might think as injudicious, or if you like as tyrannical, as this, and which, equally with this, interfere with liberty to contract. Sunday laws and usury laws are ancient examples. A more modern one is the prohibition of lotteries. The liberty of the citizen to do as he likes so long as he does not interfere with the liberty of others to do the same, which has been a shibboleth for some well-known writers, is interfered with by school laws, by the post office, by every state or municipal institution which takes his money for purposes thought desirable. The 14th Amendment does not enact Mr. Herbert Spencer's Social Statics. The other day we sustained the Massachusetts vac-

---

*Quoted in Charles Fairman, *Mr. Justice Miller and the Supreme Court* (Cambridge, Mass.: Harvard University Press, 1939), p. 374.

cination law. . . . United States and state statutes and decisions cutting down the liberty to contract by way of combination are familiar to this court. . . . Two years ago we upheld the prohibition of sales of stock on margins, or for future delivery, in the Constitution of California. . . . The decision sustaining an eight-hour law for miners is still recent. . . . Some of these laws embody convictions or prejudices which judges are likely to share. Some may not. But a Constitution is not intended to embody a particular economic theory, whether of paternalism and the organic relation of the citizen to the state or of *laissez faire.* It is made for people of fundamentally differing views, and the accident of our finding certain opinions natural and familiar, or novel, and even shocking, ought not to conclude our judgment upon the question whether statutes embodying them conflict with the Constitution of the United States.

General propositions do not decide concrete cases. The decision will depend on a judgment or intuition more subtle than any articulate major premise. But I think that the proposition just stated, if it is accepted, will carry us far toward the end. Every opinion tends to become a law. I think that the word "liberty," in the 14th Amendment, is perverted when it is held to prevent the natural outcome of a dominant opinion, unless it can be said that a rational and fair man necessarily would admit that the statute would infringe fundamental principles as they have been understood by the traditions of our people and our law. It does not need research to show that no such sweeping condemnation can be passed upon the statute before us. A reasonable man might think it a proper measure on the score of health. . . .*

Although Holmes would have reached a different result from that of the majority in Lochner, he did it on the grounds that the Constitution was not written to encompass any particular economic theory. He, too, as with his colleagues in the majority, did not see—at least, he did not articulate—what has since become obvious: that the great disparity in bargaining power between employer and employee made liberty of contract a mockery. The entire Court at that time did not recognize that the *collective* nature of economic en-

---

*Lochner v. New York, 198 U.S. 45 (1905).

deavor had created an entirely new social milieu in which ancient doctrines of individualism and of freedom had to operate. They failed to see that freedom could be limited by centers of economic power—the corporation—as well as by government. It was not until after the Second World War that the first, halting recognition of the dimension of "private" economic governments surfaced. (See the discussion in Chapter Four.)

If the dissenting opinion of Holmes is the classic statement against what Commons called "due purpose of law," as distinguished from "due procedure of law,"* then the Allgeyer Case similarly sets forth the meaning of the new doctrine:

> The liberty mentioned in the [Fourteenth] Amendment means not only the right of the citizen to be free from physical restraint of his person, but the term is deemed to embrace the right of the citizen to be free in the enjoyment of all his faculties; to be free to use them in all lawful ways; to live and work where he will; to earn his livelihood by any lawful calling; to pursue any livelihood or avocation, and for that purpose to enter into all contracts which may be proper, necessary, and essential to his carrying out to a successful conclusion the purposes above mentioned. . . . His enjoyment upon terms of equality with all others in similar circumstances of the privilege of pursuing an ordinary calling or trade, and of acquiring, holding, and selling property is an essential part of liberty and property as guaranteed by the Fourteenth Amendment.†

The difficulty with that formulation is, at this date, wholly obvious: calling a corporation a person is a convenience, not a fact, and to equate the power of the natural person with the artificial person is utterly fallacious. Furthermore, it is one thing to protect individuals from despotic government by executives, which was one of the reasons for the Constitution, but quite another for the Court (oft-times by a mere 5-4 majority) to interpose itself between the public will as reflected in legislative action to further the general welfare. All of this

---

*Commons, p. 333.
†*Allgeyer* v. *Louisiana,* 165 U.S. 578 (1897), p. 589.

was done in the name of *individual* liberty! In effect, the Court said to the laborers, those who wanted maximum-hour and minimum-wage legislation and prevailed on legislators to enact it, that they had to be "free" whether they wanted to or not—and whether they could or not. The now obvious failure to see that freedom can be limited by centers of power other than public government was a predilection of the majority of Supreme Court Justices that could not last, simply because it was absurd. To say to a worker that he could not combine into unions to protect himself against the overmighty economic sovereignty of the corporations is, by any criterion, palpable nonsense. Why, one is forced to ask in sheer exasperation, if capital (businessmen) can combine into collective organizations, could not labor do the same? But it was not until 1937 that the Supreme Court may be said to have agreed with that simple proposition.

The tendency in the United States toward equality, early noted by de Tocqueville, had by 1900 become sufficiently strong, however, that the Court could not invalidate all efforts of legislatures to rectify imbalances in economic power. Its power, whatever it was (little is known about it), was never complete. Some countervailing tendencies in judicial decisions may be seen in the early twentieth century; Holden *v.* Hardy and Muller *v.* Oregon provide illustrations. In legal terms, the contest was between valid exercises of the police power and the limitations against government embedded in due process or, as Commons put it, "due purpose" of law. Holden sustained a state-imposed eight-hour day for employees in mines and smelters,* while in Muller the Court upheld Oregon's statute regulating the length of time women could work, basing its decision on special considerations relating to women.† The same result was obtained in Bunting *v.* Oregon,‡ a case noteworthy for the successful argument of

---

*169 U.S. 366 (1898).
†208 U.S. 412 (1908).
‡243 U.S. 426 (1917).

the man who, twenty years later, was to become Mr. Justice Felix Frankfurter. Drawing on the technique of factual documentation of the deleterious effect of long hours of work on the health of women, Frankfurter borrowed from Louis D. Brandeis who, a decade earlier, had argued the Muller Case and launched the use of "the Brandeis Brief." Under this technique, the Court is provided with socio-economic data—nonlegal information—to show a factual basis for the need for legislation.

These cases, however, are aberrations; they reveal that the principle of substantive due process had begun slowly to erode about as soon as it had been created out of the whole cloth by the intellectual heirs of Mr. Justice Field. The pro-business attitude of the Supreme Court and other organs of government may be seen in other ways. Two instances should suffice to indicate the situation: first, the judicial handling of the antitrust laws enacted by Congress, and second, the manner in which a new technique of government—the independent regulatory commission—was dealt with. Both reveal, again, how corporate power became solidified at a time when individualism was the prevailing shibboleth and when legislatures were beginning to be concerned with the growing influence of such economic collectivities.

ANTITRUST DECISIONS

The Sherman Act (1890) was a Congressional attempt to enforce competition, that is, freedom of contract, on a business community that was rapidly seizing the benefits of combination and collaboration. It states in terse "constitutional" language that *"every* contract, combination in the form of trust or otherwise, or conspiracy in restraint of trade . . . is . . . illegal. . . ." The emphasis is supplied for the purpose of noting that Congress had stated its intent in stark and apparently unmistakable terms. This posed, then, a problem of interpretation. Does *every* mean *all?* For the lay mind, perhaps so, but for the legal mind. The Supreme Court

Justices, in the early cases interpreting the Act, split on whether it applied only to "unreasonable" restraints of trade; thus in United States *v.* Trans-Missouri Freight Association* the Court divided 5 to 4 and by that bare majority held that *every* meant *all.* That was in 1897; in 1911, that 5 to 4 had not only been overturned, it had all but vanished. In the famous case of Standard Oil Company of New Jersey *v.* United States,† the Court by an 8-to-1 majority enunciated the "rule of reason" as applying to the statute—as casual and as important a piece of judicial legislation as has ever been promulgated by the highest tribunal. What the rule of reason means, in final analysis, is that the Court is to say which contracts or combinations or conspiracies in restraint of trade are proscribed by the Sherman Act; and that has meant that the Court, since 1911, has been making decisions in this area without ever announcing clear principles by which they determined reasonableness in a given situation.

Here, then, is a classic situation of judicial government, but with a basic difference from what has been seen above. This is a matter of statutory and not constitutional interpretation, which means that what the Court decides can be "overruled" by Congress if it so desires. Ultimate power, in other words, lies in the avowedly political branches of government. This means, as will be shown in Chapter Three, that, with the coming of systematic economic legislation by Congress, the attention of the business community slowly concentrated on influencing the course of political decisions; a quarter of a century after the Standard Oil Case, the Court no longer operated as a faculty of political economy. The power of the Court, at its peak in the early years of the twentieth century, has diminished since then to a position of relative insignificance in economic-policy matters. This is not to suggest that the Court is wholly without power, but simply that its eminence has vanished.

It would be an instructive exercise, if such were possible,

---

*166 U.S. 290 (1897).
†221 U.S. 1 (1911).

to attempt to measure the impact of the Supreme Court's opinions in Sherman Act and other antitrust laws on the nature and structure of the American economy. Quite possibly, what the Court has done has had a considerable influence, but that no one can tell with any certainty. What can be said without contradiction is that the economic combines of today, three-quarters of a century after enactment of the Sherman Act, are immensely larger and wield far greater power—economic and political—than the trusts of the late nineteenth century that led to the Act.* The congressional effort to enforce competition has not been very successful. What might be hypothesized with greater validity is that the business community has recognized that discretion is better than audacity in combining and monopolizing; accordingly, in many industries there seems to be a tacit understanding—although probably not an express agreement—for the leaders in the industry not to harm one another unduly. Automobiles provide a good illustration; for General Motors, with its resources, could probably monopolize the entire industry. Probably it is fear of public reaction, seen in such statutes as the Sherman Act, that prevents this. In other words, there is unannounced collaboration—sometimes more than that, as the electrical conspiracy cases in the early 1960s indicate†— among the oligopolies that control what Adolf A. Berle has called "the American Economic Republic."‡

By judicial interpretation, then, the Sherman Act has become at best a sheathed sword in the government's arsenal, dependent for its force both on a Supreme Court that is dominated by Justices who are enforcement-minded—which has seldom been the situation—and on the vagaries of what the Department of Justice might do by way of bringing prosecutions. No matter what Congress may say, the courts or the

---

*See William Letwin, *Law and Economic Policy in America: The Evolution of the Sherman Antitrust Act* (New York: Random House, 1965), and Rostow, pp. 272-316.

†See Clarence C. Walton and Frederick W. Cleveland, Jr., *Corporations on Trial: The Electric Cases* (Belmont, Calif.: Wadsworth Publishing Co., Inc., 1964).

‡Adolf A. Berle, *The American Economic Republic* (New York: Harcourt, Brace & World, Inc., 1963).

administration might, and often do, alter what seems to be the plain legislative command. Aggressive enforcement of the Sherman Act and other antitrust laws has not been a hallmark of twentieth-century administrations, save for sporadic exceptions (as during the time that Thurman Arnold was in charge of the Antitrust Division of the Department of Justice).* Those charged with bringing suits seem by and large more interested in the inconsequential economic relationships than in staying the growth of mammoth business. The result is clear; big business is here, here to stay, for better or for worse. One can deplore or applaud the development, but the tendency is to accept it—if for no other reason than the famous retort to a lady's remark that she "accepted the universe": "By gad, she had better!"

What happened during the history of the Sherman Act in the hands of its judicial and administrative interpreters may be analogized to what took place after Congress enacted the Interstate Commerce Act of 1887. By that statute, which was the first time the national legislature attempted to *regulate* interstate commerce in the sense of putting restraints on it, railroads and joint rail-water transportation were made subject to the ostensible control of the Interstate Commerce Commission: on rates, on pooling, and on methods of administration. The question for the railroads was whether to attack this regulation as an invasion of the liberty guaranteed by due process of law. To this question, they received some sage advice from Richard Olney, Attorney General under President Cleveland, advice that has since been followed for the Interstate Commerce Commission and other regulatory agencies. Said he, in response to a letter from a friend who was president of a railroad:

> My impression would be that looking at the matter from a railroad point of view exclusively it would not be a wise thing [to try to get the ICC abolished]. . . . The attempt would not be likely to succeed; if it did not succeed, and were made on the ground of the inefficiency and uselessness

*See E. W. Hawley, *The New Deal and the Problem of Monopoly* (Princeton, N.J.: Princeton University Press, 1966).

of the Commission, the result would very probably be giving it the power it now lacks. The Commission, as its functions have now been limited by the courts, is, or can be made, of great use to the railroads. It satisfies the popular clamor for a government supervision of railroads, at the same time that supervision is almost entirely nominal. Further, the older such a commission gets to be, the more inclined it will be found to take the business and railroad view of things. It thus becomes a sort of barrier between the railroad corporations and the people and a sort of protection against hasty and crude legislation hostile to railroad interests. . . . The part of wisdom is not to destroy the Commission, but to utilize it.*

A sager or more prescient analysis of the independent regulatory commission would be difficult to find. For what Olney counselled and foresaw is, by and large, what has occurred for most, if not all, of the commissions. They are in a close relationship with the industries they ostensibly regulate. Often, it seems, the commissions are as much, or perhaps more, interested in looking to the welfare of the regulated than in protecting the public or consumer interest. The pattern is far from conclusive, but it is at least a working hypothesis that Olney's advice has been borne out by history.† As in the antitrust situations, the Supreme Court stepped in to insure that administrative determinations under the Interstate Commerce Act would not operate to harm the railroads (that is, corporations whose prices could be regulated by public commission). In the famous decision in Smyth *v.* Ames,‡ the Court affixed a "rule of reasonableness" to the actions of the Interstate Commerce Commission. The tale is well told by Benjamin Twiss in his classic study of the influence of the American bar on the course of constitutional decision-making, *Lawyers and the Constitution.*

---

*Quoted in Louis L. Jaffe, *Judicial Control of Administrative Action* (Boston: Little, Brown & Co., 1965), p. 12.

†See Marver H. Bernstein, *Regulating Business by Independent Commission* (Princeton, N.J.: Princeton University Press, 1955). Professor Bernstein's thesis is disputed by Louis L. Jaffe in "Book Review," *Yale Law Journal,* LXV (1956), 1068.

‡169 U.S. 466 (1898).

Said Twiss, summarizing activities of lawyers in the late nineteenth century, the contention "that railroads were entitled to reasonable profits was won in 1898, in the case of Smyth *v.* Ames, which has been more prolific of legalistic elaboration and judicial and administrative headaches than any other decision in public law."* As with the antitrust laws, the Court assumed the power of giving meaning to congressional statutes.

The Sherman Act and the ICC situations provide instructive guidance concerning a number of important matters: (1) The growth of corporate power has taken place despite legislative attempts to slow it down or halt it entirely; (2) the Supreme Court was active in diminishing the impact of such statutes; (3) the American business system, by the twentieth century having become corporate in leadership and its characteristic nature, has close and continuing relationships with the regulators in government; (4) the American bar was largely business oriented; (5) the regulatory statutes at the turn of the century, some of which were at first declared invalid by the Supreme Court, display a rising tide of equalitarianism, which peaked in the New Deal of the 1930s, and the resulting synthesis produced what in the next chapter will be called the Positive State; and (6) there was the beginning of a shift in the role of the Supreme Court from making ultimate constitutional decisions in economic-policy matters to deciding questions of statutory interpretation. All these and more attest to an incontestable fact: that, by the early twentieth century, corporate power had become so solidified in the American social structure that corporations had come to seem part of the natural order of things.

CONCLUSION

"Political balance rather than economic consistency," Professor William Letwin asserts (in the headnote to this chapter), has been more important in the development of

---

*Twiss, p. 77.

the American economy and of the structure of American capitalism. That political balance *apparently* has been influenced by the course of Supreme Court decisions. We have noted the early opinions of the Courts presided over by Chief Justices Marshall and Taney; attention has also been paid to the rise and fall of economic due process. The corporate form was given early life during the pre-Civil War period and grew to "gianthood" after that War and during the first half of the twentieth century. The Court under Marshall struck down adverse state legislation in the interest of a national economy; so, too, did some of the Taney Court's most important decisions. After the Civil War, the Supreme Court aided business enterprise and its growth by invalidating regulatory attempts by both the state and national legislatures and also, when such statutes were upheld, by severely limiting their impact.

It was this activity that economist John R. Commons wrote about in his classic *Legal Foundations of Capitalism,* a book that, although it shares with other works by economists a turgid and difficult writing style, nonetheless clearly points up the fact that the Supreme Court for a brief period articulated some economic policy in the nation. This was done by rendering decisions in cases brought before it by litigants, principally businessmen, who sought from the High Bench the protection of constitutional limitations. Those limitations the Justices found in the delphic phrases of the Constitution; in so doing, they had to create law, as it were, out of the whole cloth. Nothing in the Constitution expressly commanded the results reached in any of the decisions discussed in this chapter—or, for that matter, in the long history of the government-business relation. The Court, in short, had a creative task of bringing meaning to the terse constitutional terms. In this task, there was and is no prescribed method of operation, no conventional wisdom to which the Justices may revert in reaching their decisions.

Whether a causal connection exists between Supreme Court decisions—that is, the constitutional law promulgated by the highest court—and social change (in this instance, the changing nature of the economy) cannot be stated with any exactitude. Perhaps the political economy of the American people would not have been markedly different today had the Supreme Court never existed—or, at least, had it never assumed the role of giving content to the meaning of the Constitution. But, whatever the reason and doubtless they are multiple, by the mid-twentieth century, the organization had become dominant; the corporation in all its complexity had become not only the economic entity par excellence, but was being treated as though it were a political body and hence susceptible to political types of questions.* No doubt the Supreme Court had a part to play, however immeasurable it may be, in this development. Its decisions concerning economic questions (other questions, also) in final analysis are judicial utterances of politico-economic theories. At the very least, it may be said that the Court was not unfavorable to business and corporate growth. But neither, for that matter, were other governmental organs, state or federal, legislative or executive. At the time, anti-business elements managed to push through legislation that appeared to hamper business activity, but these, when not invalidated by the Supreme Court, may have had little long-term significance.

Corporate America—so labeled by Professor Andrew Hacker—is the culmination of almost two centuries of constitutional history. Of possibly greater significance, it is the result of the marriage of science and technology to entrepreneurship—to capital—which had as its central thesis a theory of organization. The consequence has been the growth of pluralistic social groups of many types, of which the business corporation may be only one, but, if so, the most important.† In briefest terms, the development has

---

*Andrew Hacker, "Introduction," to Andrew Hacker (ed.), *The Corporation Take-Over* (New York: Harper & Row, 1964), p. 1.
†See Kenneth E. Boulding, *The Organizational Revolution* (New York: Harper & Row, 1953); Sheldon Wolin, *Politics and Vision* (Boston: Little, Brown & Co., 1960), chap. x.

meant that economic life has become politicized. We are witnessing in this nation a slow but steady drift toward the fusion of economic and political power, made possible, according to Dean Don K. Price, by science and technology. "Science," Price says, "is beginning to alter the basic relation of political and economic power. . . ."* In many respects, the new relationship has already made traditional notions of conservativism, liberalism, and radicalism obsolete. The old labels are political, and economic attitudes are changing. It is one of the ironies of history that the opinions of Chief Justice John Marshall, by present notions a conservative, are employed by the modern Supreme Court to uphold liberal legislation. Price aptly states another change in radicalism and conservativism:

> Science, by helping technology to increase prosperity, has weakened the kind of radicalism that comes from a lack of economic security. But science has helped to produce other kinds of insecurity: the fear of the new kind of war that science has made possible, the fear of rapid social and economic change, and the fear that we no longer have a fixed and stable constitutional system by which to cope with our political problems. And these fears are breeding a new type of radicalism.
>
> The new radicalism is ostensibly conservative. It springs in part from the resentment men feel when their basic view of life is unsettled—as medieval man must have felt when he was asked to think of a universe that did not revolve around the earth, or as some physicists felt a generation or two ago when their colleagues began to talk about relativity and indeterminacy. The new conservative radicalism has a fundamentalist faith in the written Constitution, and the high priests of that faith seem to have desecrated it. The Supreme Court has applied relative policy standards in place of fixed rules of precedent; but worse still it has admitted into its system of thinking not only the moral law as revealed in tradition, but arguments from the sciences, even the behavioral sciences.†

---

*Price, p. 24.
†Price, p. 163.

The "new economics" thus is accompanied by the "new politics," as will be seen in Chapter Three; and this in turn has generated the need for theory. For true it is that the modern corporation, as economist Gardiner C. Means has said, "has undermined the preconceptions of classical economic theory as effectively as the quantum undermined classical physics at the beginning of the twentieth century."* Accordingly, Americans will have to learn the contours and the details of a new political economy—a new constitutional order—that has already appeared and that seems likely to solidify in the future. Corporate power has become consolidated but so, too, has governmental power.† It is that duo of new facts of the social order that we now turn.

---

*Gardiner C. Means, "Collective Capitalism and Economic Theory," in Hacker (ed.), *The Corporation Take-Over,* p. 67.
†See Eli Ginzberg, Dale L. Hiestand, and Beatrice G. Reubens, *The Pluralistic Economy* (New York: McGraw-Hill Book Co. Inc., 1965).

3

Constitutional Revolution
Consolidated: The Rise
of the Positive State

The first principle of the law for the control of the economy is that the
government is responsible for the general level of employment. Twenty-five
years ago even the idea was not taken seriously. . . . For better or for worse,
the idea has disappeared that the state can be but a passive spectator while
booms alternate unpredictably with busts. . . . American law, like the law
of other capitalist democracies, has accepted the view that prolonged
depressions and inflations threaten the fabric of society
far too gravely to be tolerated.*

INTRODUCTION

In the long constitutional history of the United States, a
few—a very few—landmarks stand out with particular clarity. One surely is Marbury *v.* Madison, the case that launched
judicial supremacy in constitutional matters and thereby
immersed the federal judiciary deeply in politics. Another is
the Civil War, an episode that settled in blood that this nation was truly a union and that settled in law that *raison
d'état* was an operative principle of the American constitutional order; when followed by the Civil War Amendments,
it ushered in a new constitutional system the contours of
which are still being traced. A third is the rise and fall of
economic due process in the fifty-plus years before 1937,

---
*Rostow, pp. 10, 12.

which, as has been seen in Chapter Two, climaxed the period of attempted economic government by judiciary. Finally, there is the rise of "positive" government—the Positive State —during the past three decades, epitomized by enactment by Congress of the Employment Act of 1946.

Others may suggest additional landmarks. For example, the Sherman Antitrust Act of 1890 has had and still has significance for the structure of the American economy. And during the past score of years, a growing tendency by the Supreme Court to expand the Fourteenth Amendment's equal protection clause is noteworthy, principally in the areas of ethnic relations and in legislative apportionment. So, too, is the burgeoning nationalization of the human rights and liberties encapsuled in the Bill of Rights, protected (in form at least) since 1791 against federal action but only in recent years against state action. These, of course, are of great importance and would merit close attention in any comprehensive exposition of American constitutional history. For present purposes, however, attention is focused on the coming of the Positive State, an event that may ultimately overshadow most of the other prominent constitutional landmarks.

In briefest terms, the Positive State is a shorthand term for the express acceptance by the federal government—and thus by the American people—of an affirmative responsibility for the economic well-being of all.* It involves a societal shouldering of a duty to take action to create and maintain

---

*The extent of that responsibility is revealed in a news account in August, 1966, that one of every three adults in the United States "has come to depend for part of his income on a regular check from Uncle Sam." —*Washington Post*, August 18, 1966, p. K4. Each month checks are sent to 34 million individuals. This will rise to 40 million by 1970. Millions more, of course, get part or all of their income indirectly from the federal Treasury—by working for private companies with federal contracts or by being beneficiaries of state and local welfare programs partly financed by federal funds. In addition, large numbers benefit by occasional disbursements; for example, a farm-crop payment, a government research grant, or a medicare payment. Some of the problems of this development are delineated in Charles A. Reich, "The New Property," *Yale Law Journal*, LXXIII (1964), 733.

minimal conditions within the economy—of economic growth, of employment opportunities, of the basic necessities of life. The notion of a constitutional duty of government itself illustrates a new departure; although, as we have seen, there were many interventions in aid of business and commercial activity prior to the modern era, these were fundamentally different from the proposition that a governmental duty exists to aid all of the people. Although having only a statutory base the Positive State can be said to connote a basic constitutional alteration. Exemplified in a broad range of programs, federal and state, it is the American version of the welfare state.* Because of certain invidious connotations placed on the word "welfare" (usually by those who have it but who decry the desire of others for it), the term "the Positive State" has been selected. That term suggests, in addition, the basic posture of government and, accordingly, has the merit of being somewhat more descriptive than other labels (for instance, the Welfare State, the Social-Service State, the Public-Interest State, the Administrative State, the Security State). In this chapter, the contours of the Positive State are traced, with emphasis on the impact that the development has had for the American economic system—that is, for American capitalism.

The Positive State received its charter in 1946 when Congress enacted the Employment Act, surely one of the most important legislative actions ever taken in American constitutional history. In form a statute and thus outwardly not of the dignity of a constitutional precept, it nonetheless overshadows most, if not all, of the true constitutional amendments. Written in constitutional language—that is, language

---

*At least three levels of welfare exist: (1) for those in disadvantaged circumstances and those who benefit from what are usually called welfare programs—such as medicare, Social Security, unemployment compensation, aid to dependent children, and so on. This is the poor man's version of the welfare state. (2) The rich man's version is made up of those who get far larger benefits from tax benefits (such as depletion allowances in extractive industries) or from salaries paid while performing government contracts and other similar programs. (3) The intellectual's version consists of research grants, contracts to nonprofit corporations, and so on.

of high-level abstraction with little particularity or precision in prescription—the act should be considered as making
constitutional law, but by Congress and not, as is the usual
situation, by the Supreme Court. Its enactment has brought
about a radically different government-business symbiosis
from that which existed in the post-Civil War era down to
the late 1930s.* Often mislabeled the Full Employment Act,
its purpose may be found in its preamble:

> The Congress declares that it is the continuing policy and
> responsibility of the federal government to use all prac-
> ticable means consistent with its needs and obligations and
> other essential considerations of national policy, with the
> assistance and cooperation of industry, agriculture, labor,
> and state and local governments, to coordinate and utilize
> all its plans, functions, and resources for the purpose of
> creating and maintaining, in a manner calculated to foster
> and promote free competitive enterprise and the general
> welfare, conditions under which there will be afforded use-
> ful employment opportunities, including self-employment,
> for those able, willing, and seeking to work, and to promote
> maximum employment, production and purchasing power.†

That pronouncement culminated the New Deal in politics
and the constitutional revolution of the 1930s; it ushered in a
new posture of government vis-à-vis the economy. With it came
conscious guidance of the economy, not at once to be sure, but
incrementally, so that by 1965 the *London Economist* could
herald an "unrecognized economic revolution." And with it
came a spate of Supreme Court decisions dealing with the
corporation, decisions that, after the breakthrough of the
1930s that placed the constitutional imprimatur on the eco-

---

*There are some, it may be appropriate to note, who maintain that making
constitutional law, other than by amendment, is solely a judicial function.
But surely that is an attenuated view of the law-creating process, for
Congress and the President can at times create constitutional law as well.
The custody of the "Ark of the Covenant of our Fathers," as the American
Bar Association once called the Constitution, is as much within the province
of the avowedly political branches of government as it is that of the
Supreme Court.
†For an exposition of the meaning of the act in law and economics, see
Rostow, *Planning for Freedom: The Public Law of American Capitalism.*

nomic policies of Congress, radically altered the role of the Supreme Court. No longer does the High Tribunal make the ultimate determinations in questions of political economy; power over *those* decisions has been ceded to the political branches of government. No longer, in other words, does it exercise its naysaying power as *constitutional* interpreter in an effort to stem the tide of economic equalitarianism. Rather, it operates in the essentially different milieu of statutory interpretation—to carry out the stated purpose of Congress in economic-policy matters. Although this does not mean that the Court has wholly abdicated its creative proclivities in politico-economic issues, it does mean that those activities are both circumscribed in scope and, more importantly, always subject to possible reversal by Congress. Furthermore, the critical question of judicial expertise in questions of political economy is being asked with increasing insistence. The new doctrine and the new posture of the Supreme Court is the burden of this chapter. Since the nature of government is important to the business community, the main features of the Positive State are outlined.

THE HISTORY

A look, first, at some precursors—a scattered group of decisions antedating 1937 and the constitutional watershed crossed then—is desirable. For this, as has been seen in Chapter Two, one may go back to Munn *v.* Illinois (1877) and the flowering of the public-utility concept. Even during the heyday of laissez faire, the Supreme Court held *some* regulation of business permissible. In the main, those enterprises said to be "affected with a public interest" were subject to governmental restraints in that certain decisions of corporate management were (ostensibly) subject to official intervention and supervision. The businesses so affected were, by and large, those that historically were considered to fit a peculiar class of natural monopolies and other enterprises for which the market did not operate. The public-utility limitation on businesses subject to the regulatory powers of government received its death blow in 1934 when the Supreme Court decided in Nebbia *v.* New York* that price-fixing of milk by New York was valid. Since that time, there is no closed category of businesses that may be regulated; (the decision as to whether to regulate is political, not judicial) (that is, not constitutional). As the Court said in 1955: "The day is gone when this Court uses the Due Process Clause of the Fourteenth Amendment to strike down state laws, regulatory of business and industrial conditions, because they may be unwise, improvident, or out of harmony with a particular school of thought. . . . We emphasize again what Chief Justice Waite said in Munn v. State of Illinois, . . . 'For protection against abuses by legislatures the people must resort to the polls, not to the courts.' "†

The decline and fall of the public-utility concept is familiar history. Well-known also are the few cases decided prior to 1936 and 1937 that were the harbingers of a new doctrine: principally Muller *v.* Oregon,‡ decided in 1908, in which the Court upheld Oregon's regulation of work hours for women (the case is famous for the first use of the Brandeis Brief, a technique of argumentation employed by the man who was to become Mr. Justice Louis Dembitz Brandeis, whereby the Court was furnished with a collection of social and economic data designed to show the adverse consequences of long hours of labor on the health of women); Blaisdell *v.* Home Building & Loan Association§ in which Minnesota's mortgage moratorium law, passed in the depths of the Great Depression, was held valid over impassioned dissenting opinions; and Norman *v.* Baltimore & Ohio Railroad,‡ sustaining the exercise of Congressional power over the monetary system in a manner that invalidated contractual obligations to pay the principal and interest on bonds

---

*291 U.S. 502 (1934).
†*Williamson* v. *Lee Optical of Oklahoma,* 358 U.S. 483 (1955).
‡208 U.S. 412 (1908).
§290 U.S. 398 (1934).
‡294 U.S. 240 (1935).

in "gold coin of the United States equal to the standard of weight and fitness" at specified dates.

The Norman decision, part of a group of cases known as the Gold Clause Cases, is particularly useful in providing a transition from the older judicial attitude to that which is now taken for granted. Robert H. Jackson, in a book written while he was Attorney General (he was later to become a Supreme Court Justice), has related how astonished Europeans were that American monetary and economic policy could be dependent on the result in a lawsuit between private parties over a difference of $15.60 (the amount in litigation in the Norman Case); "Why," he was asked, "should lawyer-judges be supreme over the national parliament, the President, the Treasury, and the whole government in a matter so vital to economic life?"* It may have been a tacit recognition that judicial policy-making in economic matters was incongruous that helped lead the Court quietly (and doubtless finally) to withdraw from making *ultimate* economic decisions. This was begun in earnest within three years after the Gold Clause Cases—but, it is appropriate to note, only over an outraged dissenting opinion by Mr. Justice McReynolds in those cases; he asserted that "loss of reputation for honorable dealing will bring us unending humiliation; the impending legal and moral chaos is appalling"—as classic an example of a clouded judicial crystal ball as can be found in the nearly four-hundred volumes of *United States Supreme Court Reports.*

The breakthrough came in the 1937 decision in West Coast Hotel Co. *v.* Parrish† and peaked later that year when Court opinions validated the National Labor Relations Act and the Social Security legislation. The period of 1934-37 saw the apotheosis of judicial intransigence; the majority of a badly divided Court systematically outlawed the core of

---

*Robert H. Jackson, *The Struggle for Judicial Supremacy* (New York: Random House, 1941), pp. 94-104.
†300 U.S. 379 (1937).

President Roosevelt's New Deal, while simultaneously knocking out similar examples of state legislation. Particularly noteworthy were the decisions that invalidated the National Recovery Act and the Agricultural Adjustment Act, both key facets of the Roosevelt program and both found to violate the Constitution.

Then came the 1936 national election in which the American people swept Roosevelt back into the presidency with a well-nigh unanimous electoral vote. With the election and its aftermath, of which the Rooseveltian attempt to "pack" the Supreme Court is of special interest, came a new judicial voting alignment. (The drive to pack the Court, it should be noted, was not without precedent; shortly after the Civil War, President Grant succeeded in adding two justices to the then seven-member Court and, in so doing, got a reversal in the Legal Tender Cases.) FDR lost the court-packing battle, but he won the campaign and perhaps the war, for beginning in 1937 judicial vetoes became acquiescence in socio-economic questions. Badly wounded in the struggle, which was the center of public attention in 1937, the Court, without announcement and without fanfare, dropped its laissez-faire stop sign and erected in its place a placard of permissiveness. That attitude still prevails and doubtless will continue—subject only to judicial intervention over the *manner* of regulation but not *whether* regulation can take place. In lawyers' language, the Court looks to the procedure and not the substance of economic policy-making; it thus has apparently been won over, so far as economic questions are concerned, to the viewpoint of Justice Oliver Wendell Holmes: "About seventy-five years ago [he once said to Justice Stone] I learnt that I was not God. And so, when the people . . . want to do something I can't find anything in the Constitution expressly forbidding them to do, I say, whether I like it or not, 'Goddammit, let 'em do it!' " The "let 'em do it" philosophy is so pervasive that, since 1937, the Court has invalidated only one minor state action that regulated the economy,* a period of judicial abnegation all the more astonishing when compared to the several decades before that date. The only exception to that proposition may be the Steel Seizure Case of 1952,† striking down presidential seizure of the steel mills during a labor strike; but even there the Court did not deny that Congress could have taken over the industry, and more, the long-range importance of the case for the nature of presidential power is dubious. Further, the Court has stretched the economic clauses of the Constitution so as to validate their use for regulation of basically noneconomic matters, principally in the area of race relations. In other words, once the Positive State was given the judicial imprimatur, Congress and the President could validly use their new *economic* powers to effect *social* changes as well. The power of the purse, backed up by the enormous assets of the Treasury, which, with the advent of the income tax, became the chief recipient of the tax dollar, is being employed today in a number of programs in which business is regulated to accomplish both economic *and* social goals.

To summarize, when Congress enacted the Employment Act in 1946 and thus gave the Positive State its express charter, it at once ended the constitutional revolution of the 1930s and inaugurated a fundamentally new government-business relationship. The Supreme Court helped this development by rendering a series of decisions updating the Constitution. The first, grudging approval was given to the "new economics" in the early 1930s (Nebbia, Blaisdell, Gold Clause); that trickle became a flood by the early 1940s: in United States *v.* Darby and Wickard *v.* Filburn.‡ In Darby, the Court upheld the Fair Labor Standards Act of 1938 in which Congress, among other things, prohibited the

---

*See *Morey* v. *Doud,* 354 U.S. 457 (1957). It is worthy of note that the basis for the decision was equal protection, not due process as had been the case in the period leading up to 1937.

†*Youngstown Sheet & Tube Co.* v. *Sawyer,* 343 U.S. 579 (1952).

‡*United States* v. *Darby,* 312 U.S. 100 (1941); *Wickard* v. *Filburn,* 317 U.S. 111 (1942).

shipment in interstate commerce of goods produced by child
labor; in so doing, it expressly overruled Hammer *v.* Dagen-
hart,* thereby at one stroke displaying the new permissiveness toward economic regulation and revealing once again
the evolutionary nature of the Constitution. In Wickard,
the farm assistance program was extended to a farmer whose
wheat had only an indirect and remote connection with interstate commerce. These (and allied) cases opened the flood-
gates wide enough to give constitutional approbation to
systematic regulation of any aspect of business affairs that
government (federal or state) might want to undertake.

However, it would be a mistake to maintain that the
Court *caused* these constitutional changes, although some
weighty opinion may be cited in support of that precise proposition. For example, Mr. John C. Satterfield, former president of the American Bar Association, asserted in 1962 that
"fundamental changes are being made in our form of government by judicial decisions." Such a view does not com-
port either with history or with an accurate understanding
of the role of the United States Supreme Court in the
American polity. That Court, rather than being the *cause*
of constitutional change, is the *instrument* through which
the basic document has been and is being updated—a far
different proposition from the pronouncement of Mr. Satterfield. Much more important—in fact, of the most profound
significance—in the process of constitutional change are the
social conditions within the nation that have been altered
so fundamentally since 1787.

Frederick Jackson Turner, the eminent historian, said
in 1920: "Behind institutions, behind constitutional forms
and modifications, lie the vital forces that call these organs
into life and shape them to meet changing conditions."
Among these "vital forces" are the urbanization of American society, the scientific-technological revolution, the rapid
growth of population, the creation of a nationwide business
system dominated by a few enormous corporations, the grow-

---

*247 U.S. 251 (1918).

ing interdependence with other nations brought about by changes in transportation and communication, and the emergence of the United States as the strongest and wealthiest power in history. All these and more dovetail to produce the social conditions that underlie constitutional change. What the Supreme Court has done is to recognize what has taken place, not cause it, and, by acting as what may be called a continuing constitutional convention, to adapt the Constitution to the exigencies of modern life. Had this not been done, it may be said, the Constitution, a document written for the horse-and-buggy days and for a relatively weak agricultural nation, could scarcely do duty almost two centuries later for the colossus that straddles the planet. To assert, as does Mr. Satterfield, that the Supreme Court caused the change simply cannot be supported. True it is that the Court has poured new content into the ancient constitutional phraseology, but this is because, as Justice Oliver Wendell Holmes said in 1920:

> When we are dealing with words that also are a constituent act, like the Constitution of the United States, we must realize that they have called into life a being the development of which could not have been foreseen completely by the most gifted of its begetters. It was enough for them to realize or to hope that they had created an organism; it has taken a century and cost their successors much sweat and blood to prove that they created a nation. The case before us must be considered in the light of our whole experience and not merely in that of what we said a hundred years ago.*

There is a myth to the contrary, of course, perpetuated by such commentators as Mr. Satterfield and even such present-day Supreme Court Justices as John M. Harlan.

This should not be taken to mean, it is emphasized, that the Court is without power, that it is a mere passive instrument. Doubtless it does have some power and does wield some influence over the shape of events. But what is meant

---

*Missouri v. *Holland,* 252 U.S. 416, 433 (1920).

is that one is hard put to find any instance where *over the years* the Court has ever in fact caused great constitutional change or, put another way, where the Court has ever been able to force its will permanently upon the American people. The examples of the Eleventh and Sixteenth Amendments to the Constitution, the several dozen times that the Court has reversed itself (either expressly or tacitly), the large areas in which it refuses to rule at all, the times when it has supinely bowed to assertion of *raison d'état* by the Executive—these examples and more all point to an ineluctable conclusion: the Court is the instrument and not the cause of change; the Court has power only insofar as it has the force of public opinion behind it. Over the long run, government by judiciary is not possible.

The point is important when one views the operations of the High Bench and the American business system. For the period of, roughly, ✦1890 to 1937, as we have seen, the Court did *try* to impose its will on the nature and character of the American economy. It failed, at least partially, and has been in retreat since in economic questions. (Perhaps the failure was not complete, for Court decisions did maintain a favorable milieu in which the corporation could and did flourish.) The business community knows this, for it no longer places reliance on the Court to help protect its interests. Rather, the American businessman, today as throughout American history, is primarily engaged in attempting to guide the course of *political* decision-making—in Congress and in the congeries of administrative agencies that are loosely tied together under the rubric of the executive branch of government. Parenthetically, the attempt to judicialize administration, through the establishment of the independent regulatory commission, has now been proved invalid. The coming of economic planning by the avowedly political organs of government (Congress and the President) has been accompanied by a marasmus of the concept of the independent commission, manned by experts, who would impartially decide questions of business regulation. This point, as well as others, is a characteristic of the Positive State; it should be placed in perspective with other characteristics of the new constitutional order.]

THE POSITIVE STATE IN ACTION

The Supreme Court having constitutionalized the Positive State in the series of legitimizing decisions since 1937, certain significant consequences followed. Although still in the process of being worked out, enough is known even now to enable one to trace the contours of the new posture of government.

1. Most fundamental, perhaps, is the change from a Constitution of *limitations* to one of *powers;* or as Edward S. Corwin termed it, "a Constitution of powers in a secular state." The American Constitution was drafted by men who feared despotism and who fragmented governmental power to avoid it; basically, the Charter of 1787, particularly with respect to the national government, was a set of limitations. The core principle was that the central government had only those powers specifically delegated to it, mainly in Article 1. Even when the Supreme Court added the concept of implied powers in 1819, the general posture was one of limitation, the apotheosis of which was reached in the judicial attempt to establish a laissez-faire government in the late nineteenth and early twentieth centuries. Summed up in the Jeffersonian idea that "that government is best which governs least," limited government held sway until the advent of the New Deal in the 1930s.

The notion of limitation became, with seeming abruptness, one of power, even duty, on the part of government to take action. It was not so abrupt as it appeared, for what took place in the post-1937 period can only be understood in light of history. Affirmative government, in other words, is part of a process the underlying principle of which is that government in the United States has always been as strong (or positive) as conditions demanded. Chief Justice Charles

Evans Hughes gave apt expression to the new concept in his opinion in the bench-mark case of West Coast Hotel Co. *v.* Parrish, particularly in these words:

> The principle which must control our decision is not in doubt. The constitutional provision invoked is the due process clause of the Fourteenth Amendment governing the States, as the due process clause in the Adkins case governed Congress. In each case the violation alleged by those attacking minimum wage legislation for women is deprivation of freedom of contract. What is this freedom? The Constitution does not speak of freedom of contract. It speaks of liberty and prohibits the deprivation of liberty without due process of law. In prohibiting that deprivation, the Constitution does not recognize an absolute and uncontrollable liberty. Liberty in each of its phases has its history and connotation. But *the liberty safeguarded is liberty in a social organization which requires the protection of law against the evils which menace the health, safety, morals, and welfare of the people. Liberty under the Constitution is thus necessarily subject to the restraints of due process, and regulation which is reasonable in relation to its subject and is adopted in the interests of the community is due process* [my italics].*

This statement, of the greatest importance particularly in the italicized sentences, changed the nature of liberty under the Constitution and ushered in the Positive State. Recognition was given to the view that liberty could be infringed by forces other than government and, of even more importance, that those other forces may require the affirmative intervention of government to counteract them. Corwin put it this way: "From being a limitation on legislative power, the due process clause becomes an actual instigation to legislative action of a levelling nature."† Individuals, as well as government, could now be limited by due process. In economic terms, the power of the state could countervail the power of private collectivities. And of even more significance, as Chief Justice Hughes said, due process does not mean only

---

*300 U.S. 379 (1937).
†Corwin, p. 161.

liberty against government, it also can be used by government to restrain the liberty of some in the interests of the community. The "requirement" (Hughes' term) of the protection of law against the evils that menace the welfare of the people may not be judicially cognizable in the historical and orthodox sense that an individual may bring an action in court to force its fulfillment. But that is of lesser importance than the judicial recognition—the harbinger of the later congressional action in the Employment Act of 1946—of a responsibility of government to take action. The Positive State, in other words, is the responsible state.

Furthermore, it may well be that the nation is on the verge of recognition of another new concept: that of constitutional duty. The development, for the most part, has taken place thus far within Supreme Court decisions on the Fourteenth Amendment, particularly those relating to Negro rights. But other portents are discernible—for example, in the recent decisions dealing with apportionment of state legislatures. In these as yet scattered decisions may be perceived an effort by the Supreme Court to develop the contours of a concept under which government—that is, governmental officials—are at times required to take certain action. To the extent that such a concept exists, it may be called something new under the constitutional sun, for the charter of 1787 was a set of limitations on government. We now have not only a "Constitution of powers," as Corwin put it, but also a "Constitution of affirmative duties." These are as yet largely inchoate, but a clear signal of one future development in constitutional law is in that direction.*

2. "Democracy," Professor Frank H. Knight recently said, "has assumed the task, enormously more difficult than enforcing a law known to all, of deciding what the law ought

---

*See Arthur Selwyn Miller, "An Affirmative Thrust to Due Process of Law?," *George Washington Law Review,* XXX (1962), 399. One of the clearest indications of the new development came on October 10, 1966, when the United States Court of Appeals in the District of Columbia ruled that patients committed to mental hospitals after criminal trials have a constitutional right to "adequate treatment," and cannot be merely confined to the hospital. (See *Washington Post and Times Herald,* October 11, 1966, p. 1.)

to be and making any changes called for."* In present context, with the coming of a Constitution of powers, the American democracy now has assumed the task, immensely more difficult than merely umpiring the private decisions and disputes in the market, of deciding what economic policy ought to be and of taking action to effect necessary changes. Put another way, *the second noteworthy feature of the Positive State is the advent of a system of economic planning by the federal government.*

The American system of planning is, as economist Gardiner C. Means calls it, "facilitative"; it involves basic reliance on the private character of economic and commercial enterprise but insists that certain decisions of corporate managers and trade-union leaders be taken "in the public interest." As such, it falls far short of the almost completely planned economies of Communist China and the Soviet Union. Since all economic processes involve the making of decisions, it should be seen at the outset that today those decisions are made in two principal ways: by government authorities who seek to manage the operations of the economy and by the market, through the decisions of enterprises, unions, workers, farmers, investors, and consumers. In all economies, both features exist, although different emphases are given. In the United States, the market is relied on with government making those minimal decisions considered desirable to influence the nature and character of that market—chiefly in the direction of economic growth and employment opportunities. Conversely, communist nations depend mainly on the plan, although some scope is given to free choice by workers and farmers and other individuals. Thus the federal government facilitates economic growth and seeks to control inflation through the use of wage-price guidelines announced periodically by the Council on Economic Advisers to the President. That Council, authorized by the Employment Act of 1946, is the nerve center of the American plan-

---

*Frank H. Knight, "On the Meaning of Justice," in *Nomos VI: Justice* (New York: Atherton Press, 1964), pp. 1-2.

ning operation. But all nations—developed and less developed, private enterprise and state socialist—can be located, as economist Theodore Geiger has said, "somewhere along a continuum which ranges from comprehensive and detailed planning by the national authorities of all significant aspects of economic activity to reliance upon decentralized nongovernmental decision making in accordance with market conditions as influenced by government policies."*

The responsibilities of the Employment Act are implemented by three types of legal and economic arrangements, two of which have relatively long histories. The first, however, is, at least in its present-day scope and intensity, rather novel: the manipulation of fiscal and monetary policy to carry out the broad purposes of the act. This is accomplished by the government and the Federal Reserve system seeing to it that money is spent for goods and services in a volume sufficient to assure high levels of employment without precipitating the pressures of general inflation. Included are tax policies, adjustment of the discount rate, and governmental expenditures ("pump-priming"), which together make up a system of indirect controls of economic activities. By "indirect" is meant that the government is not a participant in the decisions business managers make; what it does is to take action that, in its cumulative impact, alters the milieu in which the businessman operates. Accordingly, it narrows or circumscribes the range of choices that corporate managers may make. Primary emphasis, however, is not to control but to stimulate the market and thus to produce economic growth without the debilitating effects of inflation. It is a somewhat perilous path trod by the government decision makers, one in which there must perforce be a considerable amount of trial and error.

The second and third instruments for carrying out the Employment Act are complementary: on the one hand, the competitive and regulated markets for goods and services,

---

*Theodore Geiger, "Planning and the Market in Economic Decision Making," *Looking Ahead*, XIII, No. 9 (December, 1965), 5.

and, on the other, the labor market in which corporate managers and union leaders are permitted to legislate the rules governing the relationships of business enterprise and labor. The market is a complex system of interaction between business units and consumers and government; it is, as Eugene V. Rostow has noted, an economic order which is also a system of law.* Similarly, the business-labor symbiosis has produced a system of industrial jurisprudence, a sort of common law of the corporate community. In these instruments, as with the first, one essential point is to be noted: activity, whether public or private or, as is so often the case, a combination of both, is aimed at producing what, for want of a better term, can be called the "common good." The techniques through which the Employment Act is implemented, in other words, all aim at maximizing the *general,* as distinguished from the *particular,* interest. True it is that the individual decisions of businessmen and union officers are usually taken in an effort to further their particular or parochial interests without much reference to what the overall social impact might be. But this is accomplished, nay, permitted, by government only because of the assumption (so far, warranted) that these parochial decisions will through the intervention of the cautious guiding hand of government inure to the common good. The "invisible hand" of Adam Smith has been replaced by the visible, albeit indirect, hand of government, which intervenes just enough to create the conditions in the private sector that fulfill the goals of the Employment Act.

In this, it should be noted, the essential change is not that the government is taking action; as has already been seen, throughout American history the government was never quiescent. The change is in the type of action: *from* aid to business and curbing of labor organizational activity *to* minimal controls on business so as to curb the excesses (plus continued aid to business). The business of this nation is still business, to echo President Coolidge, but business ever

---

*See Rostow, *Planning for Freedom: The Public Law of American Capitalism.*

increasingly for the common good rather than for the personal aggrandizement of the latter-day successors of the "robber barons."

3. *Third in this listing of the contours of the Positive State are the changes that have occurred and are continuing to occur in the constitutional framework of government, principally within the two basic divisions of governmental power (federalism and the separation of powers).* Economic planning, it has been said, is the DDT of federalism. That may well be. For planning by government generates a need for unified and perhaps uniform economic policies throughout the nation. That need runs counter to the diversity inherent in federalism; it also is contrary to the fragmentation of power within the national government itself. In both federalism and the separation of powers, in short, may be seen centripetal tendencies leading toward the centralization of official power. No doubt there are causes other than economic planning for this development; after all, planning is more a symptom or a result than a cause. However, for whatever reason, significant constitutional changes have taken place within recent decades—without amendment and without fanfare. In essence, these changes may be summed up in the proposition that political power is being centralized. For purposes of analysis, the twin developments within the divisions of government are discussed; however, it should be emphasized that this third of the listing of facets of the Positive State can be reduced to the one mighty trend toward centralization. Paradoxically, many of the official measures are taken to create conditions permitting the maximization of individual freedom although a simultaneous growth of organization—the organizational revolution—is producing the social conditions that run counter to the exercise of that freedom. (A tacit recognition that business is organized—is corporate—has been made by the Supreme Court, as will be discussed.)

When the decision in NLRB *v.* Jones & Laughlin Steel

Co.* upholding the Wagner labor relations statute was followed soon thereafter by cases validating the Social Security legislation, the constitutional underpinnings for a new form of federalism were created. What had been, at one time at least, "dual federalism," with the states and federal government considered to be roughly coequal in power, now became cooperative federalism, with the central government incomparably the stronger of the two. Harold Laski asserted in 1939: "The federal form . . . is unsuitable to the stage of economic and social development that America has reached. . . . I infer . . . that the epoch of federalism is over,"† a sentiment echoed by Karl Lowenstein: "Experience . . . demonstrates that, whatever strength of tradition and emotional values of political theory federalism is still imbued with, the economic imperatives of the technological state require unified if not uniform economic policies throughout the entire territory and do not brook that kind of economic fragmentation which goes with effective member-state sovereignties."‡ The "sovereign" states, all fifty of them, are anachronisms in the American body politic; like it or not, the political, economic, and technological conditions of the modern era do not permit now, and ever increasingly will not permit in the future, that diversity that is federalism. The formal structure of American government may remain, for political organizations have a way of existing, like vermiform appendixes, long after their functions have atrophied, but the substance and the content will be elsewhere. The *important* decisions of government are made in Washington. A century after the Civil War settled on the battlefield that this is one nation, the development of science and technology, of concomitant

---

*301 U.S. 1 (1937).
†Harold Laski, "The Obsolescence of Federalism." *The New Republic,* XCVIII (1939), 367.
‡Karl Lowenstein, "Reflections on the Value of Constitutions in Our Revolutionary Age," in Arnold Zurcher (ed.), *Constitutions and Constitutional Trends Since World War II* (rev. ed.; New York: New York University Press, 1955), p. 211.

business enterprise, and the deep and irretrievable immersion of the United States in the world community, together weld the nation into a true community (in the sociological sense).

As with federalism, so it is with the separation of powers (a misnomer, it should be noted, for what the Constitution established is a system of separate institutions sharing the same powers—quite a different thing); here, too, the trend has been centralizing—toward the aggrandizement of power in the executive branch. The "administrative state" has arrived, and the locus of power within the national government, if it can be located at all, seems to be within the executive. The consequence has been a relative diminution of power in both the Congress and the judiciary. In 1818, Justice Story could remark that the "Executive has no longer a commanding influence. The House of Representatives has absorbed all the popular feelings and all the effective power of the country." A century and a half later sees the executive (viewed institutionally) as incomparably stronger than the House.

Congress, faced with mounting tasks of government legitimized in the Supreme Court decisions discussed earlier and called the constitutional revolution of the 1930s, obviously could not hope to keep up with the details of administration. As a consequence, delegations of sweeping power were and are being made to a tangled mass of agencies, departments, commissions, and other governmental offices. In net effect, the delegations in the 1930s and 1940s were attempts to establish some sort of regulatory control over segments of the business community. Thus the National Labor Relations Act and the Fair Labor Standards Act dealt with labor relations, the various farm acts with agricultural control, the Social Security legislation operated both as a compulsory pension program and a device to alleviate the perils of unemployment. Further congressional actions of great importance to the business community came in the post-World War II programs designed to deal with the Cold War.

Of these, the national security and space budgets, which run into many billions of dollars annually and which permit administrative action to be taken of great significance to the economy, are probably the most important. As with the delegations of legislative power to the agencies and commissions, so it is with arms and space expenditures; neither gets any sustained Supreme Court scrutiny. When review does take place, in the extremely rare administrative decision that gets appealed to the courts, the agency action is usually upheld. The judicial action is radically different from what it was in pre-1937 days, having changed from constitutional to statutory interpretation. Although this does not mean that the Court does not have a creative function, it emphatically does mean that its power is greatly circumscribed.

Simultaneously, one of the quietest pragmatic innovations in our constitutional history was occurring: Presidential initiative in legislation. This, too, is a recent development, one that may validly be termed a facet of the Positive State, although its roots run back to the eighteenth century. Having its genesis at least as far back as the Budget and Accounting Act of 1921, which required that the executive propose an annual executive budget, presidential initiative in legislation reached a point by 1949 that the legislative program of the President had become a fixed, definite, and comprehensive entity, announced in annual messages and delineated in a set of special messages during each session of Congress. Moreover, the presidential initiative runs to the *substance* as well as to the *financial* aspects of government. In effect, Congress is handed an agenda each year, which they can respond to or react against, modify or ignore, but which by and large sets the outward limits of what Congress does. An important additional aspect of presidential initiative is that the first stage of bill-drafting is accomplished within the executive branch. The original drafts of proposed legislation may and often are modified and amended during passage through Congress, but the important factor to note is that the draft is usually first written within the executive branch and, of perhaps even more importance, the office of the Presidency (more specifically, the Bureau of the Budget) operates as an office of central clearance within the executive. In short, presidential initiative in legislation illustrates a flow of power toward the executive branch and, within that branch, toward the Presidency.

What this "quiet pragmatic revolution" has meant for Congress has been summed up by Professor Samuel P. Huntington in this manner: "The congressional role in legislation has largely been reduced to delay and amendment; congressional activity in overseeing administration has expanded and diversified."* As late as 1885, Woodrow Wilson could observe that "the predominant and controlling force, the center and source of all motive and of all regulative power, is Congress. . . . The legislature is the aggressive spirit."† Today the "aggressive spirit" is clearly executive, both in proposing legislation and in its final content. Best seen perhaps in national defense and foreign policy, the trend is all-pervasive. As to national defense, the House Armed Services Committee put the matter effectively and accurately in 1962 in these words:

> To any student of government, it is eminently clear that the role of the Congress in determining national policy, defense or otherwise, has deteriorated over the years. More and more the role of Congress has come to be that of a sometimes querulous but essentially kindly uncle who complains while furiously puffing on his pipe but who finally, as everyone expects, gives in and hands over the allowance, grants the permission, or raises his hand in blessing, and then returns to the rocking chair for another year of somnolence broken only by an occasional anxious glance down the avenue and a muttered doubt as to whether he had done the right thing.‡

---

*Samuel P. Huntington, "Congressional Responses to the Twentieth Century," in David B. Truman, *The Congress and America's Future* (Englewood Cliffs, N.J.: Prentice-Hall, Inc., 1965), p. 23.
†Quoted by Huntington, in Truman, p. 23.
‡U.S., Congress, House Committee on Armed Services, *Authorizing Appropriations for Aircraft, Missiles, and Naval Vessels*, Report No. 1406, 87th Cong., 2d Sess., 1962, p. 7. See the discussion of the constitutional point in

But if there has been a decline in the *legislative* role of Congress—and all thoughtful students of the Congress agree on this point—at the same time, an increase in its *administrative* role is clearly evident. Needed in the modern state, says Professor Huntington, "are means to control, check, supplement, stimulate, and ameliorate . . . the bureaucracy."* It has now become evident that the judiciary cannot adequately accomplish this task. If control of the bureaucracy is to be done, save in a few spectacular instances, judicial review is too episodic and sporadic, too dependent on the accident of litigation to permit the sustained oversight necessary. Either new institutions must be developed or old institutions must take on new tasks. In this country, we have opted for the latter, and it is Congress that is changing and assuming a new posture vis-à-vis the bureaucracy. The development has several facets. In briefest terms, however, as George B. Galloway has asserted, it is not legislation but control of administration that is becoming the primary function of the modern Congress.

Power abhors a vacuum. Speaking very briefly, government by the legislature *and* the judiciary, in their separate but complementary areas, characterized nineteenth-century America—save only for those periods of emergency (for example, the Civil War) when the President exercised his prerogative and assumed the mantle of power. The posture has dramatically changed in this century; American government has executive hegemony as its most prominent aspect. Failure (abetted by Supreme Court roadblocks) by the states to act and an inability of Congress to act save in broad generalities, accompanied by judicial abdication of ultimate economic decisions, has permitted, even demanded, executive (or administrative) action. In this, the United States is merely following, not leading, a worldwide trend; one is

---

Arthur Selwyn Miller, "Presidential Power to Impound Appropriated Funds: An Exercise in Constitutional Decision-Making," *North Carolina Law Review*, XLIII (1965), 502.
*Huntington, in Truman, p. 24.

hard put, as a result, to find any government in all of the nation-states truly dominated by the legislature or, indeed, in which the legislature is even on a roughly equal position of power with the executive. The epoch of the representative assembly, one is constrained to infer, is over, in the sense of that assembly being the locus of governmental power. It was, in many respects, a creature of the Enlightenment and of the open societies that developed in one rather small geographical area (mostly along the North Atlantic littoral) and that were (are) limited in time to a few centuries at most. Today, the United States is the oldest *continuous* government in the world, and it, too, is following the path of other parliamentary democracies toward executive dominance.

In summary, the Congress of the United States today is only nominally the policy maker, the official norm setter, within the field of its constitutional competence. Effective control, as compared with formal authority, over policy tends ever increasingly to be in the hands of the Presidency. Preservation of the original Constitution's separation of powers helps to make Congress believe that it must and should be the principal source of policy initiatives, of grand designs for national programs, but that is an illusion, an illusion pregnant with frustration. Ultimate constitutional power is *formally* in the hands of Congress, but, in domestic and certainly in foreign policy, its primary impact is not on the subjects and content of legislation but on its timing and details. Effective control is elsewhere.

Congressional power, furthermore, is splintered; it is not one entity, but many; as with the executive branch, it is only seemingly a monolith. Congress, accordingly, is in fact a collection of committees that meet periodically to approve one another's actions.

In net effect, splintering of legislative power into the power of committees (and subcommittees) has given great power to certain individual committee chairmen who can make their weight felt by being able to swing the entire legislative branch behind their decisions. In some instances, a symbiotic relationship has grown up between committees and the administrative agencies over which they have jurisdiction. Note how this operates in the "subgovernment" of sugar:

> Consider the tight little subgovernment which rules the nation's sugar economy. Since the early 1930s, this agricultural commodity has been subjected to a cartel arrangement sponsored by the government. By specific prescription, the sugar market is divided into the last spoonful. . . .
>
> Political power within the sugar subgovernment is largely vested in the chairman of the House Agricultural Committee who works out the schedule of quotas. It is shared by a veteran civil servant, the Director of the Sugar Division in the U.S. Department of Agriculture, who provides the necessary "expert" advice for such a complex marketing arrangement. Further advice is provided by Washington representatives of the . . . producers.*

Observe here a three-sided power structure: the chairman of a House Committee, a high civil servant, and the Washington representatives of the producers. Here in microcosm may be seen (1) the shift in interest of Congress from content of legislation to its administration; (2) the close relationship between high executive officials and key Congressmen; (3) the fragmentation of power within the Congress and within the executive, neither being the monolith many suppose both to be; (4) the operation of a fourth (or fifth or sixth, depending on one's count) branch of government in the policy-making process—the Washington representative, otherwise known as the lobbyist. In all of this, the Supreme Court has little or nothing of importance to say. This is "politics," and despite de Tocqueville's oft-quoted aphorism to the contrary, the issues seldom if ever get into the judiciary.

As seen from the executive point of view, Congress is a "client group," albeit a very special one, not essentially dissimilar from other client groups (such as industry, labor unions, veterans' legions, churches, and the remainder of the pluralistic power centers of the American polity). The

---

*Douglass Cater, *Power in Washington* (New York: Random House, Inc., 1964), pp. 17-8.

executive deals with Congress, both separately in the routine transactions between bureau or agency or department and the appropriate committee or subcommittee and overall through the institutionalized Presidency. The "subgovernment of sugar" mentioned above illustrates the former. The latter characteristic displays *within* the loose collection of feudal entities that constitute the executive branch the same centripetal propensities that are to be seen in the federal system and in the tripartite division of power (separation of powers); a centralizing tendency may thus be seen throughout government. In each of three areas, major constitutional innovations are taking place.

Let us consider very briefly the coming of the "institutionalized Presidency." The office is both one man and many; it is personalized and bureaucratized; it is the Chief Executive and the civil servants (normally of the very highest quality) who make up the Executive Offices of the President. Although no doubt it is accurate, as Richard E. Neustadt has said in his illuminating essay, *Presidential Power,* that the power of the President in mainly that of persuasion and that he looks out from the White House at a collection of "feudalities" within the executive-administrative establishment, there can be no question that he is also a binding force.* "In many spheres of action the executive establishment can scarcely move except as it invokes the President."† He legitimates actions of the public administration, in his constitutional capacity of Chief of State and Head of Government. Slowly but surely, an accretion of power is becoming evident within the Office of the Chief Executive, as yet far from complete. The increased activity of government, in large part since 1900, has carried with it the pressing need for consistency or congruency of policy; where that takes place, when it does (which is far less than some suspect), it is by the little-known and little-sung administrators who man the several offices in the institutionalized Presidency.

---

*Richard E. Neustadt, *Presidential Power* (New York: John Wiley & Sons, Inc., 1960).
†Truman, p. 109.

The need is for coordination of public policy; to the extent that it exists, it is accomplished by staff officers in the office of the President, principally within the Bureau of the Budget.

This does not mean that full coordination occurs; one of the as yet unsolved problems of the Positive State is the lack of consistency in policy. But it does mean that what coordination that does exist is by and large far greater than in the past. Since the enactment of the Budget and Accounting Act in 1921, gathering impetus during the incumbency of Franklin D. Roosevelt, the institutionalized Presidency, beginning with President Kennedy (and perhaps even with President Eisenhower), has become the nerve center of government. A constitutional development of major importance, it at once shows the flexibility of American institutions and the elasticity of the Constitution, for all three of the centripetal movements within government have been accomplished within the framework of the charter of 1787. It is quite remarkable that Americans can simultaneously believe that they live under a written and rigid Constitution, handed down by the wisdom of fifty-five supposedly extraordinary men in 1787, and accept evolution of the document into a form and substance quite different from that envisaged by the Founding Fathers. Perhaps it is not so remarkable, on reflection, for the human mind has a large capacity to hold inconsistent ideas at the same time, but surely it is an outstanding example of the manner in which sacred texts, political or theological, can evolve and take on new meaning as new social conditions emerge.

The final facet of the changing nature of traditional separation of governmental powers may be seen in the federal judiciary, mainly the United States Supreme Court. It has become truistic to assert that the role of the Court has radically altered during the past three decades. Two features of this alteration are particularly noteworthy: (1) as has been noted previously, the shift from *constitutional* to *statutory* interpretation regarding most of the important socio-economic questions of the era, and (2) the emphasis on human dignity, often subsumed under the rubrics of civil rights and civil liberties, as contrasted with the protection of property. Discussion of the latter will be deferred to the next section, on the problems of the Positive State. (We focus now on the change from ultimate decisions over socio-economic matters to those that in form and in fact (although not entirely) are subject to being overruled or reversed by the political branches of government, principally the Congress but also the executive.)

The Court as statutory interpreter may be seen in a discussion built around the Steel Seizure Case of 1952,* even though the decision turned on a constitutional question. Nevertheless, statutes were involved. The case is useful not because of what it decided or its impact, but because (1) it is the most important (putative) judicial limitation on executive powers ever issued; (2) it taught the Chief Executive a lesson—since heeded—to avoid invoking such extraordinary powers when dealing with business and labor and to employ, instead, several lesser sanctions none of which is as potent as seizure but the cumulative impact of which enables the President to prevail; (3) it displays in classic style the inadequacies of the judiciary, both institutionally and with respect to the individual competence of the Justices, in ruling on portentous economic questions. In short, the Steel Case and its aftermath points up the aggrandizement of power in the Presidency at the expense of the other branches. And that is so even though President Truman lost the decision!

The Steel Case erupted when the President ordered seizure of the nation's steel industry during the Korean War following inability of management and labor to agree on a new collective-bargaining contract. The President justified his action not on congressional authorization—he did

---

*Compare Philip B. Kurland, "Guidelines and the Constitution: Some Random Observations on Presidential Power to Control Prices and Wages," in George P. Schultz and Robert Z. Abiler (eds.), *Guidelines, Informal Controls, and the Marketplace* (Chicago: University of Chicago Press, 1966), p. 209.

not, for example, follow the procedures of the Taft-Hartley Act—but on a theory of inherent executive power that enabled him, simply because he was the Chief Executive, to take action considered necessary "in the national interest." Contested by the steel companies in an action brought in a federal district court in Washington, the suit soon reached the Supreme Court. The Court, seeing the urgency of quick action, soon came to a decision. Over a strong dissenting opinion by Chief Justice Vinson, it invalidated the seizure and ordered the mills returned to the corporate owners. Secretary of Commerce Sawyer, against whom the suit was brought,* and President Truman did not contest or defy the decision.

Several lessons may be derived from this minor *cause célèbre*. The case reveals (1) that the judiciary will erect limits to executive power in certain instances; (2) the respect that Supreme Court decisions receive, for the ruling was accepted without question by officials and the public at large; (3) the Justices, in their several opinions, had no clearcut idea of the nature of executive power or of the fundamental government-business question that was at issue; their opinions, taken by and large, may be said to be well-nigh classic examples of judicial futility in grappling with deepseated economic problems; and (4) the executive learned an important lesson, namely, to avoid taking action that would in some way end in judicial decision-making; in other words, the President, since the Steel Case, operates in the labor-management area in ways that do not present issues justiciable before the Supreme Court. In this way, he is enabled to manipulate the political process, to preserve his options, and to achieve his goals. He does not always succeed, but his power is maximized by steering clear of the courts.

Since 1952, the President thus has acted in a much more sophisticated manner with respect to price increases and to

---

*The President, as Chief Executive, is not amenable to an action brought against him personally. Hence, the suit had to be brought against a subordinate officer in whose custody the steel mills had been placed.

the collective-bargaining process. The difference may be seen in the way in which President Kennedy mobilized the forces of the executive branch in 1962 in a direct confrontation with the United States Steel Corporation when that company raised prices after the President believed it had agreed to keep them steady. Using existing statutes, such as the anti-trust laws and military procurement regulations, Mr. Kennedy added the power of public opinion and other non-seizure sanctions. The result was a dramatic rollback of already announced price increases by the steel industry. The point here, among other fascinating aspects of the imbroglio, was that the judiciary (and, indeed, Congress) had nothing whatsoever to say or do; the controversy was settled quickly and with brutal efficiency.

The lesson was clear (and has since been employed by President Johnson in a number of instances): mobilize the awesome resources of the executive branch and bring them to bear on the allegedly erring corporation. In 1965, Mr. Johnson added a new technique to his arsenal: the threatened sale from government stockpiles of aluminum and copper in order to hold the price line in those industries. The presidential action was in accord with his mandate—as he interpreted it—under the Employment Act of 1946; he sought to control economic inflation by keeping price and wage rises within guidelines promulgated by his Council of Economic Advisers.

Institutionally, the judiciary has had nothing to say in this area of presidential government. The Steel Case, cast in this light, seems a lonely and ineffectual attempt by American industry and the Supreme Court to stay the flow of executive power. Greater sophistication in the management of controversy has since eliminated the judiciary. Furthermore, it should be noted that no serious attempt has been made to have Congress act to try to strip the President of his powers—exercised, it should be emphasized, without express statutory authority—which leads one to the conclusion that the American businessman is not wholly uneasy about the new situation. The reason for this relatively calm acceptance of what, by any criterion, are extraordinary powers is itself a fascinating question, but outside the scope of the present discussion. Suffice it only to say that the situation evidences a growing partnership between government and business, a partnership that may likely continue and wax even closer so long as economic growth (and thus profits) continues.

When it comes to judicial exercise of power in economic-policy questions, that power clearly lies wholly within the province of the interpretation of statutes. Antitrust provides a ready illustration, both of the policy-making powers of the Supreme Court and of the increasingly obvious lack of competence on the part of the Justices to make decisions in this area. Other examples lie in judicial review of administrative action—say, by the Federal Power Commission or the Federal Communications Commission. The efficacy of both antitrust and judicial review is itself a debated question, although one may say without fear of contradiction that in both areas the competence of the Justices, and indeed the adequacy of the adversary process itself, are at best dubious. What powers the Supreme Court does have must come within the framework of statutory interpretation. One of the inputs of this process is an evaluation, tacit no doubt, of the reaction Congress might have to a decision that went beyond proper judicial action. Put another way, this means that the power of the Court is circumscribed, simply because it must always have in mind the possibility that it will be reversed by political action. A mere statute, not a constitutional amendment, can do that.

The consequences are fairly clear. On the one hand, there is a situation of judicial reluctance to intrude too far into the decisional process of the public administration. On the other hand, the public administrators themselves have two great powers. First, theirs is the power of initiation—of taking action—which, by and large, is discretionary with them and not subject to judicial review. They can remain quiescent if they so desire. Or they can push ahead, in which event they run the risk of appeal to the courts and an adverse decision. Bureaucracies are not noted for their innovative tendencies; accordingly, that risk is seldom run; it eventuates when some person, natural or collective, is disgruntled by an administrative decision. That does not often happen, given the myriad of such decisions and the fact that the majority of administrative decisions are not appealable to the courts at all. Second, and of perhaps more importance, is the power to interpret a court decision. Supreme Court decisions do not enforce themselves; the Court has no way to insure compliance in the usual case. Hence, it must depend on delegated commands to other officials, political and judicial, to put its edicts into operational effect. Whether this is done depends in great part on whether a given official or his agency feel bound by the decision. Surely, it is accurate to say that a Supreme Court decision involving an appeal from an order of, say, the Federal Power Commission, gets little or no attention in other regulatory commissions or in the departments and agencies of the executive branch.

The clear conclusion to be drawn is that the power of the Supreme Court in economic matters is greatly attenuated; in some respects, it does not exist at all. Economic policy today, insofar as government is concerned, is a result of the play of the political processes—whatever the situation may have been in the past.

4. Next in this listing of characteristics of the Positive State concerns both the nature of law and the role of the judiciary in that State: *the politicization of law and the legal process.* The coming of a bureaucracy, swollen far and doubtless permanently beyond its historical size, has been characterized by sweeping and well-nigh limitless delegations of power to the tangled collection of commissions, agencies, departments, boards, and other administrative organizations. The Positive State is the "administrative state," exemplified by broad discretion in the administrators—whether they are department heads (for example, the Secretary of Defense in many government-contract matters), commis-

sioners of the regulatory agencies, the President himself and his immediate advisers (the office of the Presidency), or most other parts of what was once termed a "headless fourth branch of government" but what may more circumspectly be called the executive-administrative branch.)

Writing in 1962 about the regulatory commissions, Judge Henry J. Friendly maintained "that the basic deficiency, which underlies and accounts for the most serious troubles of the agencies, is the failure to 'make law' within the broad confines of the agencies' charters" and "that once this basic deficiency is remedied, other ills will largely cure themselves; and that shadows and miseries will long be with the agencies if it is not." Judge Friendly's point was that much of the "justified dissatisfaction" with administration is the failure of administrators and others "to develop standards sufficiently definite to permit decisions to be fairly predictable and the reasons for them understood."* The indictment is sound, even though the Judge's remedy may be faulted as being too heavily weighted on the side of making the public administration look like an idealized version of the judiciary. What it means, in brief, is this: administrators, having been invested with broad delegations of power to regulate "in the public interest," have failed to produce workable meanings of that term. In other words, power to regulate in the public interest has given the administrator uncanalized discretion and, of even more importance, has transferred many of the commissions and departments into little political arenas.

During the 1930s, when the Positive State was in process of creation, much attention was paid to "government by expert," by which was meant that the problems of economic regulation could be turned over to administrative agencies that would be manned by experts who would issue objective decisions in the public interest. A more naïve conception of

---

*Henry J. Friendly, *The Federal Administrative Agencies: The Need for Better Definition of Standards* (Cambridge, Mass.: Harvard University Press, 1962), p. viii.

government, in this or any other country, would be hard to come by. What has happened is what Judge Friendly discusses—and which should have been foreseen by even the more myopic of the zealots who plumped for government by expert. It is not that the agencies are unnecessary or should be abolished, but the point is that, by delegating power from Capitol Hill, Congress merely succeeded in transferring the political battleground westerly down Pennsylvania Avenue. We still have "government by expert"—by elite structures—but objectivity is no longer assumed.

Public economic policy, as a consequence, insofar as it is determined administratively (and that is to a very great extent indeed), tends, as has been said, to be the resultant of a parallelogram of conflicting political forces. Government institutions, having become solidified and accepted, are at once the object of that struggle and one of the participants in the contest. The aim is to control the flow of public-policy decisions. Particularistic interests, by energizing political forces, battle for influence in that process. But, at the same time, the agency itself—and government, as an entity—is one of those groups, with drives and interests of its own to further. That "regulation is politics" is asserted by an astute student of the public administration, Professor Marver Bernstein:

> The fraternity of political scientists and public administration experts has increasingly accepted the finding that regulation is a political process. "Politics" is now rightly viewed not only as unavoidable, but as essential to the formulation of policies that bear some rational relation to economic and technological conditions. As one scholarly study concludes: "The mentality which disdains 'politics' and strives for a neutral and technical perfection rejects the very solvents that would reduce the obstructions."*

In effect, Professor Bernstein in that statement echoes Judge Friendly; the political scientist agrees with the lawyer as to the *description*—but they disagree as to the *prescription*.

*Marver Bernstein, "The Regulatory Process: A Framework for Analysis," *Law and Contemporary Problems*, XXVI (1961), 329, 340-1.

Bernstein considers the fact that regulation is politics to be necessary and perhaps even desirable, whereas Judge Friendly thinks that it should be corrected. In this, the Judge restates the age-old plaint about discretion in government and in essence seeks a return to a government of laws and not of men. But, as Charles A. Horsky has said, ours is emphatically a "government of men, not of laws,"* so Judge Friendly's call faces heavy odds, at the very least.

The deeper, more profound meaning of the political nature of regulation (and administration) is the growing politicization of law and the legal process. Law has increasingly become a purposive tool for the furtherance of desired goals rather than a set of interdictory commands limiting the discretion of administrators or canalizing their decisions. If administration is politics, at least at one level—the lower one goes on the bureaucratic hierarchy, the more the administrator is confined by rules and regulations internal to the executive branch (the internal law of administrative procedure)—the received notions, the conventional wisdom about the nature of law, become suspect and require re-examination in the light of the imperatives of the day. Legal scholars have not as yet accomplished this necessary task, but do it they must if ever a philosophical reconciliation of law and politics is to be forthcoming and if ever the administrative process is to receive legitimacy in the American constitutional order. That will be an immense job. Let us look at but one facet of the manner in which the politicization of law has changed the relationships among the three branches of the federal government.

The reference here is to the development of a system of "appellate review" by Congress of certain administrative (and judicial) decisions, principally by members of the business community who believe they have been adversely affected by certain decisions. In essence, the effort is to energize the political processes of Congress so as to overturn,

---

*Charles A. Horsky, *The Washington Lawyer* (Boston: Little, Brown & Co., 1962), p. 68.

reverse, or modify administrative and judicial interpretation of statutes that are considered to be improper—or that interest groups can persuade Congress were improper. Most of the successful reversals by Congress of Court decisions have been in the economic field; in sum, because the task of the Supreme Court in economic matters has shifted from constitutional to statutory interpretation, the business community has been able to go to a higher court of review: the United States Congress. According to Professor Alan F. Westin, "The clear conclusion is that the 'Congressional Court of Appeals' has been primarily, overwhelmingly, an instrument by which large-scale corporations and business associations have overturned Supreme Court rulings since 1944 which have harmed their economic interests."* Much less success has resulted in efforts by others to legislatively overrule the Supreme Court in civil-liberty and civil-rights decisions, although a number of efforts have been made.

The other aspect of the congressional role as ultimate "court of appeals" stems from administrative rulings. Here, one must separate the ordinary citizen who considers himself aggrieved from the large corporate entity. For example, if a person is denied a passport by the State Department, his remedy lies with the judiciary (after he has exhausted whatever administrative appeals he may have). Even so, the institution of the complaint to one's Congressman when an individual believes he has been harmed administratively is a viable, albeit unstructured, means of attaining justice in individual instances—not always, to be sure, but enough to provide a means by which the Congress can serve as a "court of appeals." When to that is added the private bill, the legislation designed to aid a specific individual or individuals, it may be seen that Congress does operate for the private person as well.

Even more striking and possibly of more importance

---

*Alan F. Westin, "Corporate Appeals to Congress from Supreme Court Rulings," Mimeographed paper presented to the American Political Science Association convention, 1962. See Walter F. Murphy, *Congress and the Court* (Chicago: University of Chicago Press, 1962).

is the manner in which the corporate community turns to Congress as a means of circumventing proposed administrative action. For example, when the Federal Communications Commission apparently took the National Association of Radio and Television Broadcasters at their word and proposed to enact into FCC rules the code of ethics on television commercials that had been enunciated by the NARTVB, the reaction of the industry was immediate and effective. But it was not judicial; the proposed rules were not taken to federal court, as one might suppose. Rather, a complaisant Congressman was induced to introduce a bill denying the FCC such powers; that bill was hurried through committee and passed the House of Representatives by an overwhelming vote. At that time, the officials in the FCC saw new light; they hastily rescinded the proposed rules—and there the matter rests at this writing. The television industry used Congress in that instance as a "court of appeals," thus illustrating, at one stroke, the relative impotence of courts and the political nature of regulation.

5. Fifth and last in this listing of prominent features of the Positive State may be stated in the form of a trend: *toward the progressive blurring of what purportedly is public and what supposedly is private in the relationships of government and business.* The development may be seen in a number of ways: the reciprocal participation by business leaders in government decisions and by government officials in business decisions; the dependency of large segments of the business community on government for its economic viability; judicial recognition of the corporate (that is, collective) way of doing business, with a consequent halting beginning toward "public-izing" private business for the imposition of constitutional norms; and the employment by government of private (and certain nonprofit) corporations as administrative devices. In addition, another aspect may be seen in the rise of new concepts of property, largely based on "government largesse," which affects not only business but people at large.

What may be seen here is a trend or a tendency, not an abrupt departure. During the nineteenth century and in the twentieth century before 1937, there were a number of ways in which government and business intertwined. The line between them was never so sharp as laissez-faire theory postulated and as some latter-day spokesmen assert. For example, as long ago as 1913, Woodrow Wilson, in *The New Freedom,* called attention to the influence of business in governmental decisions. Worth quoting are a number of his observations:

> One of the most alarming phenomena of the time,—or rather it would be alarming if the nation had not awakened to it and shown its determination to control it,—one of the most significant signs of the new social era is the degree to which government has become associated with business. I speak, for the moment, of the control over the government exercised by Big Business. Behind the whole subject, of course, is the truth that, in the new order, government and business must be associated closely.
>
> *   *   *
>
> Business is in a situation in America which it was never in before; it is in a situation to which we have not adjusted our laws. Our laws are still meant for business done by individuals; they have not been satisfactorily adjusted to business done by great combinations. . . .
>
> *   *   *
>
> The government, which was designed for the people, has got into the hands of bosses and their employers, the special interests. An invisible empire has been set up above the forms of democracy.*

What President Wilson noted there has since then been changed by the programs of the Positive State. Government and business are, as he said, associated closely—in what might be called a partnership, although who is the senior partner in this symbiotic relationship is as yet uncertain. Wilson suggested that the "special interests"—"Big Business"—were

---

*Woodrow Wilson, *The New Freedom* (New York: Doubleday & Company, Inc., 1913), pp. 24-5, 34-5.

in control, foreshadowing in some respects what his successor in the White House, Dwight D. Eisenhower, said in his farewell message: "In the councils of government, we must guard against the acquisition of unwarranted influence, whether sought or unsought, by the military-industrial complex. The potential for the disastrous rise of misplaced power exists and will persist."* Essentially, what is seen here is the gradual merger of political and economic power. Far from complete as yet, it nevertheless is true that the tendency is all too clear. Government and business are growing closer together. A number of the largest corporations in the nation are dependent on government contracts for their livelihood; so too, for that matter, are a number of the most prestigious universities as well as other nonprofit concerns. There can be little doubt, as a consequence, that, with the proliferation of government, a progressive blurring of the alleged line between public and private is taking place. Economist Robin Marris, writing from England, puts the matter somewhat differently in making what is the same basic point: ". . . The industrial capital of western democracies is no longer divided into two classes, 'public' and 'private,' but rather into three, 'public,' 'private,' and 'corporate.' The corporate sector likes to be described as 'private,' but this may represent no more than a desire to conceal. . . ."†

No doubt, this is a more accurate way of describing the economy: there is purely private activity, there is governmental activity, and there is corporate activity. Although it is indubitably true that larger and larger segments of purely private business and individuals as individuals are bound to government by monetary and other chains, that is only one part and perhaps not the more significant part of the merger of public and private in economic matters. Not only are large segments of the business community dependent on government for their financial viability, those corpora-

---

New York Times, January 18, 1961, p. 22.
†Robin Marris, *The Economic Theory of Managerial Capitalism* (New York: The Free Press, 1964), p. 13.

tions that are either government contractors or are within the Supreme Court's definition of interstate commerce are subject to norms imposed by government through which a number of regulatory programs are advanced. This has been called "administration by contract," and it is valid to state that a substantial portion of the public administration is contracted out to private organizations, profit and nonprofit.* Since most of the contracting activities of the federal government are not subject to court review, the Supreme Court has had little to say about this development—important though it may be. Since Perkins *v.* Lukens Steel Company was decided in 1940,† it has been almost impossible for anyone to contest any federal action taken pursuant to a contract. As a result, private businesses have been used to achieve some of the regulatory ends of government, including nondiscrimination in employment, buy-American legislation, minimum wages and maximum hours, and aid to small business. The system indicates both the relative impotence of the federal courts and the fact that government (political power) and business (economic power) are growing closer together.

Another illustration of the trend may be found in the handful of decisions, possible harbingers of the future, that "public-ize" the corporation through the imposition of constitutional norms. The landmark case here is Marsh *v.* Alabama,‡ in which the Supreme Court for the first and only time in American history directly applied the Constitution to a private corporation. But a number of other decisions in recent years have largely dimmed the line between private and public, so that, whenever any ostensibly private organization is performing a public function (in the eyes of the Court) or has some tie to government, it is subject to the same constitutional restraints as is government itself. The outstanding instances lie in the area of the White Primary

---

*See Arthur Selwyn Miller, "Administration by Contract: A New Concern for the Administrative Lawyer," *New York University Law Review,* XXXVI (1961), 957.

†310 U.S. 113 (1940).

‡326 U.S. 501 (1946).

Cases,* in which the Court brought political parties within the ambit of state action and the Constitution. And in the Sit-in Cases, those that reached the Court after Negroes were arrested for sitting in restaurants and other business organizations, the Court by employing one device or another has struck down the convictions for trespass without simultaneously holding the businesses subject to the Constitution. Only Mr. Justice William O. Douglas of the present Court is apparently willing to go that far.† Furthermore, there is language in some Supreme Court opinions and direct holdings in some state courts that labor unions are, in certain instances, subject to constitutional limitations, particularly in whether they can discriminate in admittance policies on the basis of race, color, creed, or national origin.‡ The clear lesson from this is that the Supreme Court as well as Congress and the executive no longer perceive a sharp division between public and private. When added to this is what Professor Charles Reich of the Yale Law School calls the "new property"§— the largesse distributed in various ways by government— the trend becomes clear for all to see.

Businessmen themselves, or at least some of them, have not missed the development. Witness these statements, the first by Melvin H. Baker, Chairman of the Board of National Gypsum Company and a Vice-President of the National Association of Manufacturers, and the second by Frank N. Ikard, President of the American Petroleum Institute:

> Since the early part of this century we have been developing a new form of public-private society. . . . Call it what you will, the fact remains that this kind of government is here to stay, and those who would accomplish almost anything of public interest must work with the government. I say work "with" it, not "for" it.

*   *   *

There is an old saying that facts have a way of out-running

---

*The leading cases are *Smith* v. *Allwright,* 321 U.S. 649 (1944) and *Terry* v. *Adams,* 345 U.S. 461 (1953).

†See, for example, *Bell* v. *Maryland,* 378 U.S. 822 (1964).

‡Discussed in Arthur Selwyn Miller, "The Constitutional Law of the 'Security State,'" *Stanford Law Review,* X (1958), 620.

§Reich, p. 733.

thoughts. The facts of today's world are such that the old attitudes of many businessmen toward government, and the old attitudes of many government people toward business, are no longer relevant. There can be no longer any question as to whether or not these two groups can or will work together. The vast changes that are sweeping our nation make cooperation a necessity.*

Mr. Ikard went on to say, in as trenchant a statement as has been made by a leading businessman, that "for the foreseeable future, the roles of business and government are indissolubly linked." But this development, as well as some of the others involved in the coming of the Positive State, brings with it a number of unsolved problems, problems that in their sweep and scope present some of the greatest difficulties the American people have had to face.

PROBLEMS ENDEMIC IN THE POSITIVE STATE

We have described some of the features of a new constitutional order, government with a permanent affirmative thrust. It arose not because of some Machiavellian conspiracy of "creeping socialists" bent on subverting the wisdom of the Founding Fathers, but because of certain felt necessities— hydraulic pressures that developed slowly and that found a vent in the Positive State. In this sense, government today is the resultant of social pressures. But in another, very real sense, as has been pointed out, government has assumed profound responsibilities far transcending those of the past. In addition to internal order and national security, the main assumed duty is epitomized in the Employment Act of 1946 —the economic well-being of the American people. But although the Positive State has, in its entirety, helped resolve some of the pressing problems of yesteryear, other and perhaps equally pressing problems have developed. If the price of liberty is eternal vigilance, then the price of good gov-

---

*Baker's statement appears in *The Christian Science Monitor,* July 2, 1959, p. 10; Ikard's may be found in "Where Business and Government Meet," *Petroleum Today,* VII, No. 4 (Fall, 1966), 24-5.

ernment is eternal concern. In this concluding section, some
of the problems endemic in the Positive State are outlined.
Basically they are constitutional problems, but, for purposes
of analysis, two categories are employed: (1) economic and
(2) political. A conclusion that will be reached is that the
problems, for the most part, are not susceptible of judicial
resolution and that, accordingly, they either must be met
within the framework of the political process or new social
techniques must be invented.

ECONOMIC PROBLEMS

There are two main problems of an economic nature:
controlling inflation and achieving internal integration without external disintegration. Obviously, an overlap exists,
but they will be treated separately here. A third possible
problem may be suggested, that of providing employment
sufficient for the entire work force, but since that problem is
not nearly so clear as the others—it is the subject of intense
disagreement and dispute—it will not be discussed.*

1. As to inflation, programs designed to enhance employment opportunities, to provide for economic growth,
and to fulfill the general objectives of the Employment Act
have the tendency, thus far unsolved, of causing inflationary
spirals in the economy. The "voluntary controls" so far imposed by the American system of economic planning have
not yet been able to stem the tide. In the offing, accordingly,
are more stringent economic controls—in prices, in wages,
in monetary affairs. Should they come, there is little doubt
that the Supreme Court would uphold any constitutional
challenge to their validity.

It seems clear beyond peradventure at the time that,
whatever may be the situation elsewhere, the problem of
inflation is endemic in America's managed economy. Its control is dependent on close cooperation among all the important economic power centers of the nation—government, the

---

*For discussion, see Garth L. Mangum (ed.), *The Manpower Revolution*
(New York: Doubleday & Co., Inc., 1965).

corporations, the labor unions, the farmers, to name only the most prominent. Even with the system of voluntary restraints embedded in the guidelines of the Council of Economic Advisers—and there, the voluntariness may be hotly disputed—the price level creeps slowly upward. The unanswered question is whether the spiral can be halted or controlled within manageable boundaries. Only time can give an answer to that.

2. The same may be said for the other economic problem: whether the move toward internal economic integration that is characteristic of the Positive State can be made without suffering external disintegration. In other words, is the Positive State autarchical? The question asks much; space permits only an adumbrated answer.

Governments intervene in the economy for a variety of reasons. Two main types of intervention may be noted, both revolving around the concept of security; those that are taken for national security reasons and those that are taken to enhance the economic well-being (that is, security) of the people. Included in the former are such measures as the following:

Military considerations:　Speaking in 1955, Struve Hensel, an Assistant Secretary of Defense, stated: "To be militarily sound, our foreign economic policy must harmonize two objectives which often conflict. On the one hand, the United States must preserve and nourish a strong industrial base to support our military force. . . . At the same time . . . a new military need has come to the forefront. . . . The United States needs allies and must be prepared to take whatever steps are necessary to attract and hold allies."* That points out the basic dilemma. It has been resolved thus far in favor of maintenance of a strong industrial base. Multilateralism in trade has had to give way to considerations of military necessity. The preservation of American industry, thought

---

*Struve Hensel, "Effect of the Cold War on Foreign Economic Policy," *Vital Speeches*, XXXI (1955), 1097, quoted in Arthur Selwyn Miller, "Foreign Trade and the 'Security State': A Study in Conflicting National Policies," *Journal of Public Law*, VII (1958), 37.

to be indispensable to national security, prevails over an expanded trade program and the lowering of tariff barriers.

Another set of policies, a hangover from the depression of the 1930s, acts in a similar fashion. These are the so-called Buy-American Acts, of which the most important is the Buy-American Act itself; but there are others, including provisions in such legislation as that setting up a public housing program, the rural electrification program, and amendments to the Department of Defense appropriation acts. The unifying thread of these statutes is pure economic nationalism: American funds spent by American governmental agencies must, as a general rule, go to American firms. (It is noteworthy that a number of states also have buy-American policies, designed to keep out foreign imports—but for reasons of economic well-being rather than national security.)

The stockpiling program is another instance of defense autarchy. Still accurate is a statement made in 1955: "The underlying conception seems to be of a continental bastion, relying on no one else to supply . . . [American] needs and those of its surviving friends."*

Still another is the United States maritime policy, which may be characterized as one of a number of postwar commercial policies blatantly running counter to the avowed international economic policy of the United States. The American shipping industry is protected against foreign competition.

Embargoes of strategic materials to potential enemies make up still another set of autarchical foreign economic policies. Not only are American firms prohibited from trading with the Soviets, but efforts have been and are being made to get others within the American orbit also to embargo trade. Not always successful, as witness the shipment of British busses to Cuba, nevertheless the policy is a positive detriment to expansion of trade.

In sum, the main thrust of American economic policy

---

*Raymond Vernon, "Foreign Trade and National Defense," *Foreign Affairs,* XXXIV (1955), 77.

has been to provide both defense and opulence, thus going beyond Adam Smith, who once opined that "defense is more important than opulence" and who, accordingly, was willing to suffer what to him were economic privations in the interests of national security. Trade has become an instrument of national policy and is something more than an institution for the furtherance of those who engage in trading as entrepreneurs. And this is true, even though in recent years the United States has (outwardly) attempted to move toward a system of freer trade. Enactment of the Trade Agreements Act of 1962 and the so-called Kennedy Round of negotiations is one example. But as spokesmen for the underdeveloped nations said in 1964 at the United Nations Conference for Trade and Development, the policies under that situation tend to look at best toward integration among the nations of the "rich man's club"—those along the North Atlantic littoral—and do not necessarily inure to the benefit of the rest of the world. The Positive State is autarchical in its military security policies. (The success of the Kennedy Round, in 1967, may indicate as an eventuality the multinational integration of the North Atlantic community states.)

Economic well-being: In the United States today, policies of both a public and private nature are promulgated for the purposes of insuring minimum income security to individuals and groups. Two examples—those relating to employment and to agriculture—will suffice to show the extent of what is done and the relation to freer trade. Here, again, internal policies designed to further the well-being of individuals and groups work toward external disequilibrium. Nations such as the USA attempt to "export" unemployment; and for various reasons, they continue to aid agriculture at the expense of greater trade from primary producers. At least autarchy is the result.

Beggar-my-neighbor policies may be seen to dovetail employment and inflation problems. "One of the greatest difficulties of Keynesian economics . . . is how to achieve a full employment level of effective demand without precipitating inflation well before that point is reached. If this is a serious problem even in "closed economy" economies, it becomes much more so when internal economies are exposed to external strains."* On the theoretical level, the problem is one of a dilemma that may be stated in this way: External stability multinationally is dependent on the maintenance of internal stability at full employment in the leading countries, chiefly the United States, whereas the maintenance of full employment may require the imposition of controls on external trade so as to minimize outside influence on the economy. In short, external stability depends on internal stability, which in turn may well be achievable only at the expense of external stability.

Whether this is a real problem or not is the subject of considerable controversy among leading economists. The antagonists tend to fall into two main schools; those who decry full employment policies and call for an open international society and those who accept full employment but who tend to slur over the problems of external trade. No one has as yet been able to produce a theory that reconciles the two points of view. While the theorists dispute, the politicians pursue both policies or at least attempt to do so—full employment and multilateral trade.

Although some effort has been made in recent years to liberalize foreign trade, the clear tendency since enactment of the Employment Act of 1946 has been toward economic nationalism.† The difficulties experienced under the Kennedy Round of trade negotiations with the other industrialized nations lead to the conclusion that world-wide trade liberalization will be difficult, perhaps impossible, to achieve. How much of this failure may be attributed to the employment and other welfare policies of the Positive State (in the United States and its counterparts in Western Europe) is the

---

*John Williams, "International Trade Theory and Policy—Some Current Issues," *American Economic Review Supplement*, XLI (1951), 418.
†For fuller discussion, see Miller, "Foreign Trade and the 'Security State': A Study in Conflicting National Policies," p. 37.

question. However, it is to be emphasized that it is not so much welfare or employment policies that may cause modern industrialized nation-states to be nationalistic economically; rather, it is the continuing viability of the corporate entity (as defined in Chapter One), including its productive capacity, that is the goal. Restrictive policies in foreign economic matters have, in other words, far more than employment security as their goal; their goal is the furtherance of the values of all the segments of the corporate community, including not least the overall common good.

Economic nationalism may also be seen in the agricultural policies of the Positive State. As I concluded in another study, "While the United States says that it desires freer trade in its external commercial policy, its agricultural policy uses import quotas and other restrictions in addition to export subsidies. Both the flow in and out of the United States is under substantial governmental control."* In this, the United States does not differ markedly from other industrial powers. One of the major stumbling blocks, for example, in greater economic integration among the nations of the European Common Market has been an inability to resolve differences over agricultural imports and exports. In many respects, the deference accorded farming interests is a heritage from the past, from a time when this nation was in fact an agricultural, small-shop economy dominated by rural interests. The urbanization that has accompanied industrialization is slowly eroding that influence in American public policy. In this respect, the Supreme Court has aided the development through the series of decisions dealing with the apportionment of state legislatures and of the House of Representatives. The "one man, one vote" formula means that urban areas will have ostensible control over the legislatures.†
(Whether this will mean fundamentally different policies emanating from state legislatures is as yet unknown; but what

---

*Miller, "Foreign Trade and the 'Security State': A Study in Conflicting National Policies," p. 56.
†See, for example, *Reynolds* v. *Sims,* 377 U.S. 533 (1964).

it probably does mean, at the least, is that the emphasis on agricultural protection may be diminishing.)

POLITICAL (CONSTITUTIONAL) PROBLEMS

The assumption of profound responsibilities by government, far transcending those of the past, presents political as well as economic problems. These political problems are constitutional in the highest sense of the word and are as important to the government-business relationship as are the economic problems. In fact, the economic problems can only be understood in light of the political order.*

In assuming the new posture vis-à-vis the American people and the economy, government has to some degree taken on a momentum of its own, separate from and greater than the individual interests of the nation. This may be stated another way: The Positive State, as a collectivity, is the hypostatization of the public interest—and the public interest is greater than the arithmetical sum of the private interests of the nation. President John F. Kennedy put the thought in express terms in 1962, in the context of a prior assertion by the Secretary of Labor concerning the public's interest in collective bargaining negotiations. In response to a question at a press conference, the President said:

> These companies are free and the unions are free. All we [the executive] can try to do is to indicate to them the public interest which is there. After all, the public interest is the sum of the private interests and perhaps it's even sometimes a little more. In fact, *it is a little more* [italics added].†

With these words, the President, wittingly or unwittingly, articulated a theory of government basically different from that which historically existed (at least in theory). Within the concept of the public interest as so stated by the Chief Executive may be found both the essence of positive government

---

*We need, in other words, a science or discipline of political economy, one that would merge politics and economics and public law in a common crucible.

†*New York Times,* March 8, 1962, p. 14.

and many of the problems inherent in the new posture of officialdom vis-à-vis the persons and groups of American society. Some of the economic problems have been discussed above, but there are philosophical and political problems as well.

The architectonic problem has already been mentioned: the subtle emergence of an entity (the Public-Interest State) with drives and purposes of its own and with interests that transcend those of the populace, individual and group. The state, as a legal association, exists not only for social utility— as Roscoe Pound said, law exists to provide a "maximum satisfaction of [social] wants felt by different social sections and interests"—but we are beginning to see the emergence of the state with a separate group personality of its own. Not that the development is wholly new; throughout American history, the nation (here equated with the state) has acted to override individual interests when deemed necessary—as in times of emergency, such as war. Thus *raison d'état* is a recognized principle of American constitutionalism, although the Supreme Court may not articulate it in precisely those words.* And we have never hesitated to sacrifice the individual for the good of society and of the state; as Holmes noted, we have never been reluctant to march conscripts to the battlefront with bayonets at their backs. (At the present time, in this Orwellian world, this is being done in the name of freedom!) Furthermore, the doctrine of sovereign immunity, operating in a nation with purported popular sovereignty, provides additional evidence of the historical roots of the notion. What is new, so new that only faint beginnings may be seen and delineated, is the state as a "group-person," to use Gierke's term. The apposite analogy —particularly apt in this volume—is the private corporation, by legal fiction and American constitutional law a person, but a collectivity in fact. Just as the corporation appears to be greater than the arithmetical sum of its parts (share-

---

*See Carl J. Friedrich, *Constitutional Reason of State* (Providence, R.I.: Brown University Press, 1957).

holders, employees, and so forth), the state is "a little more" than the sum of the private interests of society.

This poses critical questions of the highest importance. The essential danger in the state as group-person was pointed out in 1933 by Ernest Barker:

> If we make groups real persons, we shall make the national State a real person. If we make the State a real person, with a real will, we make it indeed a Leviathan—a Leviathan which is not an automaton, like the Leviathan of Hobbes, but a living reality. When its will collides with other wills, it may claim that, being the greatest, it must and shall carry the day; and its supreme will may thus become supreme force. If and when that happens, not only may the State become one real person and one true group, which eliminates or assimilates others; it may also become a mere personal power which eliminates its own true nature as a specific purpose directed to Law or Right.*

Let me be very clear about this. I am hypothesizing an emergent and already visible danger, not suggesting a *fait accompli*. The Positive State is composed of programs and demands, of drives and urges that necessitate at times the submergence of individual and lesser group desires in the name of the common good—the public interest. The Positive State, in Professor Charles A. Reich's terminology, is the "public interest state." As Reich puts it, there is an underlying philosophy uniting the characteristics of the public interest state: "This is the doctrine that the [enormous] wealth that flows from government is held by the recipients conditionally, subject to confiscation in the interest of the paramount state."† He likens this to "feudal tenure," but if so, it is feudalism writ large; the ultimate superior right is in the state, not the feudal lord. Amaury de Reincourt aptly stated the concept in *The Coming Caesars,* an important, albeit neglected, interpretation of this nation's history and future. The

---

*Ernest Barker, "Introduction" to Otto Gierke, *Natural Law and the Theory of Society, 1500 to 1800* (paper ed.; Boston: Beacon Press, 1957), p. xxxiv. (Gierke's work originally appeared in 1913; Barker's translation was made in 1933.)

†Reich, p. 733.

"human society" he envisages there "is not merely an aggregate of separate human individuals; it is an entity in its own right, endowed with a life of its own, a collective life greater and far more lasting than the lives of the separate individuals who belong to it. . . ."*

The development, to the extent that it is or has taken place, is not solely that of the omnipresent and omnipotent state. Far more complex than that, the change that seems slowly to be coming involves the merger of political and economic power (as we have seen). The state thus becomes, in this conception, but one of the dominant societal groups; it is in a symbiotic and interlocking relationship with the "supercorporation." The consequence is that power over the major decisions of public policy is not solely or even principally in the hands of the political officeholders; as Professor Henry S. Kariel has shown, power is shared with the leaders of the major pluralistic power centers of the nation.† Accordingly, the Positive State as a group-person has as an integral part of its structure the corporation (as defined in Chapter One). Since the end of the Second World War, there has developed a system whereby more and more of the *public* administration is delegated to ostensibly *private* groups, profit and nonprofit—corporations, universities, "think tanks" such as the RAND Corporation, and so forth. An external bureaucracy has arisen; its existence exemplifies the close relationship of government to social group and reveals the complexities of the Positive State as a group-person.‡ The state, in other words, shares governmental power with private groups. This, it should be noted, has not presented any serious constitutional question; the Positive State, under prevailing constitutional law, can ramify far beyond the

---

*Amaury de Reincourt, *The Coming Caesars* (paper ed.; New York: Capricorn Books, 1964), pp. 9-10. (The book was originally published in 1957.)

†Henry S. Kariel, *The Decline of American Pluralism* (Stanford, Calif.: Stanford University Press, 1961).

‡Delegation of governmental power to private groups is discussed in Miller, "Administration by Contract: A New Concern for the Administrative Lawyer," p. 957.

ideas of the most gifted of the begettors of the Constitution. For true it is, here as elsewhere, that the fundamental law— the charter of 1787—is a living instrument that grows and changes with the exigencies of the time. Americans like to pretend, of course, that they live under a written Constitution changed only by amendment, but that is about as fallacious a view of this nation's constitutionalism as can be taken.

If the Positive State is a group-person in political theory, that is merely the most portentous (and dangerous) problem of that state. A number of lesser questions obtrude; these are listed with little discussion.

Government by elites: For a number of reasons, not least of which is the complexity of public-policy issues and the distance the people have from the facts and their evaluation, it has become only too evident that the "popular rule" model of governmental decision-making simply does not reflect reality.* Closer to the mark may be the "pluralistic group" model embellished with variations from the "power elite" model. The simplistic view of public affairs epitomized by the popular rule model has been summed up as follows:

> The objective of the popular rule model is to ensure that each and every citizen will participate with equal power in the deliberations of government, and that each will derive more or less equal values and share more or less equally in the maintenance of the system. The ideal image is one consisting of a society composed of individuals, rather than of groups and classes, and one that is motivated by public rather than self-interest. Not only is such a society expected to have little conflict, but what little it does have is expected to be readily handled or resolved through rational argumentation among well-intentioned citizens and with decisions by majority rule. It is assumed rather than stated that the types of political problems which will arise are of a kind that lend themselves to relatively quick and easy solutions. In other words, it is viewed as a simple society

---

*For brief but perceptive discussion of this and other models of the decision-making process, see William C. Mitchell, *The American Polity* (New York: The Free Press, 1962), pp. 73-104.

with a government performing little more than the most elementary functions that self-reliant citizens cannot do for themselves.*

The very statement of such a model is its own refutation. It is a statement of an *ideal* rather than a description of *reality*. Much more accurate, although perhaps not fully descriptive of the complicated governmental structure of the United States, is a combination of the pluralistic group and power elite models.

Theorists of these models view American society as a struggle of power among the centers of decentralized social power groups, including the corporation, the trade union, farmers groups, veterans legions, church organizations. There is debate, but a common core of agreement nonetheless, over the extent to which this struggle for power is, in the first place, controlled by the leaders of the power groups and, in the second place, over the role of government in the process. For present purposes, it is not necessary to mediate this debate; the point sought to be made is much simpler, namely, that there seems to be a large area of agreement among students of the governmental process that the popular rule model of government does not reflect reality and that, accordingly, governmental decision-making tends to be a complex interaction among the affected interest groups of society in accordance with what a specific issue might be. In other words, depending on the issue, the decisions that are produced by the formal structure of government tend to be the resultant of a process of bargaining by interest groups most affected by the proposed decision. In this process, government is both a participant (as the official group) and the object of the bargaining by the private groups. Public policy at best becomes the product of a parallelogram of conflicting political forces.†

---

*Mitchell, p. 75.

†Compare David B. Truman, *The Governmental Process* (New York: Alfred A. Knopf, Inc., 1951) with C. Wright Mills, *The Power Elite* (New York: Oxford University Press, 1956).

Put into constitutional terms, what this means is that *effective control* over decisions is the result of an interaction between government and interest groups; in other words, what may be termed the "living law of American constitutionalism" suggests that public policy is in large part developed by the leaders of the affected interest groups, one of which is government itself. The further point is that *within government*, as well as *within the affected interest groups* with respect to any particular issue, what Robert Michels called the "iron law of oligarchy" seems to be operative. According to this theory, control of a society or of any organization is by those in positions of leadership; oligarchy, in other words, is symptomatic of any bureaucracy or large-scale organization, whether it be public or private. The "iron law" is summed up in these words: "It is organization which gives birth to the domination of the elected over the electors, of the mandataries over the mandators, of the delegates over the delegators. Who says organization says oligarchy."*

Within government, the men of power include not only those political appointees in the top governmental positions, but also the professional civil servants in the middle levels of the bureaucracy. These traditionally have often been trained in law, but recent decades have seen the rise of new professional groups: economists, scientists, and computer-based managers. Usually unknown and unsung (at least to the public generally), these professionals exercise much influence over policy; they are the experts or "technocrats" of a technologically oriented, bureaucratically managed society and government who control the dynamo of political power. In this development, the lawyer as lawyer is losing caste. Trained in the outmoded dialectic of a long-vanished world, the legal specialist is more and more being consigned to the role of a technician—not the "generalist," which was his historical

---

*Robert Michels, *Political Parties: A Sociological Study of the Oligarchical Tendencies of Modern Democracy* (paper ed.; New York: The Free Press, 1966) p. 15. (The book was first published in 1911.) See Seymour Martin Lipset's introduction to this book for a summary and evaluation of Michels' theory.

role in government.* In sum, it is suggested that elites ever increasingly control the exercise of political power in the United States and, secondly, that the economists, scientists, and computer-trained managers—the technocrats—are in the ascendency as elite groups. During the 1930s, the abortive movement known as "technocracy" was essentially a drive for government by expert; the suggestion here is that Americans are closer to that than they realize.†

Control of executive discretion: The necessary corollary to the first proposition about government by elite is that a high degree of discretion is exercised by officials in executive branch of the national government. Not only the President and the officers within the institutionalized Presidency, but also many subordinate officials are restrained not by those existing commands known as law, but by the operation of the political process. This is another way of saying, as has been outlined, that law is becoming politicized in the Positive State. Control is by power, not law, and power reposes in those with sufficient resources (votes, wealth, and so forth)—in short, in the pluralistic groups of the polity. The system may work tolerably well for some segments of activity—although no one has yet articulated an accepted set of criteria to evaluate whether it does or not—but for others (the disadvantaged, those who cannot call on group support) there can be and are many inequities.

Statutes do not administer themselves; it requires the active intervention of officials to put them into operative reality. Whether this is done or not rests, in the final analysis, on whether the administrator *wants* to do it. In other words, the power to do nothing is itself a major power, one that has significant consequences. This may be seen, for example, in a decision by a prosecuting attorney to prosecute or not, or by the Federal Trade Commission or some other

---

*See Arthur Selwyn Miller, "Public Law and the Obsolescence of the Lawyer," *University of Florida Law Review*, XIX (1967), 414. On the role of scientists in government, see Price, *The Scientific Estate*.
†See Harry Elsner, Jr., *The Technocrats: Prophets of Automation* (Syracuse, N.Y.: Syracuse University Press, 1967) for the history.

agency to investigate or not, or in many other ways. There is little that can be done about this by way of formal sanction. Vested with discretion, in such matters administrative officers are not often amenable to the judicial process. [It is only when an agency acts that review might be possible—and then not for most administrative decisions; to force administrative action, even if desired, may be impossible.*] The situation is otherwise when the administrative process or executive action is used as a forum for the adjudication of the rights of two or more private persons. But that is not the usual case, and the generalization about executive discretion remains valid.

Coordination of governmental policy: Given the immensely increased number of activities conducted by government, an obvious need arises for making the programs as consistent as possible. At present, there is no institutionalized means by which this can be done, although the enhanced activities of the Bureau of the Budget may portend a trend toward greater coordination.† Many programs are not congruent today, particularly as administered, a situation that at some time will become intolerable and will lead to greater control measures being instituted. One example of the present situation must suffice, an example that concerns the government-business relationship: the extent to which federal purchasing activities run counter to other programs and policies. For instance, the Pentagon and other agencies that annually spend billions of dollars tend, by and large, to favor big business over small business; for good and suffi-

---

*See Kenneth Culp Davis, *Administrative Law Treatise* (St. Paul, Minn.: West Publishing Co., 1958), chap. iv.

†See David Novick (ed.), *Program Budgeting: Program Analysis and the Federal Budget* (Cambridge, Mass.: Harvard University Press, 1965), for a collection of essays depicting the application of systems analysis to the executive branch. Although not its announced purpose, it seems evident that, to the extent that the planning-programming-budgeting system is introduced into the federal establishment, a necessary result will be enhanced power in the Bureau of the Budget; a serendipitous benefit from such a development would be greater congruency among federal programs. For further discussion, see Virginia Held, "PPBS Comes to Washington," *The Public Interest,* I, No. 4 (1966), 102.

cient military reasons, the government procurement officers thus pursue policies that have the effect of undercutting the antitrust laws. How this will be finally resolved cannot be forecast, although one would be safe in suggesting that nothing serious will be done by government to hamper or hinder the productive capacity of the large corporate enterprise.* The supercorporation is too important to be subjected to significant interference with their activities. (That this raises important questions for a constitutional order is discussed in Chapter Four.) But with consistency or congruency becoming a necessity, then what must give are the policies, such as antitrust, that hamper or hinder the production of the supercorporations (and their satellites). In all of this, including the very problem of bringing consistency to governmental policies, the Supreme Court will have little or nothing to say. Here as elsewhere the Court in the Positive State has little or no power.

The nature of human freedom: By no means is it a foregone conclusion that freedom is in fact high on the scale of values of most Americans. Despite the efforts by some Supreme Court Justices to give First Amendment freedoms a preferred position, it is far from certain that there is any deepseated and deeply felt commitment to that idea by the public at large. In some circumstances and in certain instances, perhaps, but the individual American probably neither wishes to accord a high degree of freedom to others nor does he desire it for himself. Freedom in the Positive State, dominated by corporate collectivities, must exist in a bureaucratized atmosphere; as such, it tends to become Hegelian, that is, the freedom to do what one should do— as determined by the elite. "All alone and afraid, in a world he never made," modern man tends ever more to "escape from freedom"—to use Erich Fromm's mordant label. The Positive State does not cause this condition; the flight from

---

*Cf. Arthur Selwyn Miller and W. Theodore Pierson, Jr., "Observations of the Consistency of Federal Procurement Policies with Other Government Policies," *Law and Contemporary Problems,* XXIX (1964), 277.

freedom merely characterizes that state. The cause lies elsewhere: in the organizational nature of American society, in
a proliferating government, in a population explosion, in a
recognition that the high ideals of the Age of Rationalism
have been invalidated. To whatever extent the Positive State
is an open society, it will probably be less so in the future.

CONCLUSION

In this chapter, we have traced the contours of the Positive State, which is by any criterion the most significant and
important constitutional alteration since 1787. That it came
without amendment, by Supreme Court decisions validating
legislative and executive action, is at once a tribute to the
flexibility of the Constitution and a reflection that the locus
of power is swinging ever more toward the executive-administrative branch of government. In this development, it should
be emphasized that the Court has been the *instrument* of
change, not its *cause*—something quite different. By updating
the fundamental law, the Court has enabled it to remain relevant and current in a nation far different from that which
existed in the late eighteenth century. Had the Court not
so acted, it is quite possible that the hydraulic pressures that
built up and found an outlet in the programs of the Positive
State would have swept the Court aside. In so doing, the
Court has lost power in economic-policy matters, probably
permanently, but, at the same time, it has asserted power
in other areas of societal concern. In other words, by legitimizing the Positive State, the Supreme Court was enabled
to remain viable and to operate in such important areas as
civil rights and civil liberties.

The scientific, technological revolution that has been
the primary cause of so much social change—its early origins
made up the Industrial Revolution—has at once made the
world in fact smaller, by way of communication and transportation, than the original thirteen states and has permitted
(perhaps, made necessary) the growth of private collectivi-

ties called corporations. These centers of private power are closely allied with public government. At the same time, a drive for equality in this country (and worldwide)* has produced demands for economic well-being that can be fulfilled only by mass production. The ineluctable tendency is toward the creation and maintenance of a system of corporate collectivism;† the danger is that the growing merger will lead to some sort of corporate state. At the very least, the politico-economic theory of American constitutionalism and the American economy has been shattered. The need, accordingly, exists for the development of a theory that will accord legitimacy to the corporation and also will place it into its position in a basically new constitutional order. It is to this question that we now turn.

---

*See Barbara Ward, *The Rich Nations and the Poor Nations* (New York: W. W. Norton & Company, Inc., 1962).

†Compare Price, *The Scientific Estate,* with Robert L. Heilbroner, *The Limits of American Capitalism* (New York: Harper & Row, 1966).

4

The Need for
New Constitutional Theory

We are seeing the gradual transition (in historical time of course not
gradual at all) of our vast country from a system of individual possessory
property (the norm a century ago) to a system of non-individual, non-statist,
non-possessory economic and social power (a system of corporations,
corporate insurance companies, and pension trusts, of labor unions,
professional guilds, and voluntary associations) which has concentrated
economic power to a degree unknown in recorded history.*

INTRODUCTION

Enough has perhaps been said in the foregoing chapters to
indicate a new socioeconomic order in the United States, one
dominated by huge collective combines called corporations
and one ever increasingly influenced by the activities of government. These developments, although so common today
that they seem to be the natural scheme of things, have come
about since the Civil War; for that matter, they are in the
main the product of the past few decades. The growth of
corporations has produced a new feudalism or a new federalism, all in the space of a few years—a change that, seen
against the backdrop of history, is as great or as basic as had
occurred in several thousand years previous. Very possibly
a product of the scientific-technological revolution, this alteration in man's patterns of behavior is as fundamental as the
agricultural revolution many millenia ago. The change thus

---

*Adolf A. Berle, Jr., "Coherency and the Social Sciences," in Lyman Jay
Gould and E. William Steele (eds.), *People, Power, and Politics* (New York:
Random House, 1961) p. 10. The passage is quoted in Richard Eells, *The
Government of Corporations* (New York: The Free Press, 1962), p. 283.

far is breathtaking and has not yet ended: here, as elsewhere, change is the law of life. Further alterations may be forecast. What they may be seems, at least in part, to be fairly clear, as will be shown in Chapter Five.

In this chapter, attention will be directed toward the most pressing intellectual need arising from the growth and dominance of the huge corporate collectivities and in the increasing role of government in the economy: the requirement for theory. For a nation of avowed pragmatists, Americans, particularly businessmen, have long espoused theoretical positions or ideologies.* The new political economy has so radically altered the social milieu in which the constitutional order exists that it requires, at the very least, a re-examination of ancient principles and beliefs and the substitution, when necessary, of new beliefs more in consonance with the facts of the modern era. The Constitution of 1787, still largely intact, makes no provision for either the corporation or affirmative government. That basic charter is still viable only because it has been progressively updated over the years —by Supreme Court decisions, in the main, but also at times by legislative or executive act. In so doing, some of the necessary theory has been created or is in process of creation, but much remains to be done. The need, in short, is for modernizing constitutional theory to fit the facts of onrushing social and legal change. The greatest stupidity is to forget what one is doing or trying to do—and that is precisely the danger unless and until theory is updated.

Involved in this quest is the application of such nebulous concepts as *responsibility, legitimacy,* and *accountability* to the corporate enterprise and to the Positive State. Each would require extensive treatment in any full-length exposition of the present problem. What follows of necessity is but an adumbration. It will be predicated on the assumption that the overarching concept is that of responsibility, and that legitimacy and accountability may be subsumed there-

---

*For a perceptive discussion, see Perry Miller, *The Life of the Mind in America* (New York: Harcourt, Brace & World, Inc., 1965), Part II.

under.* Attention is directed toward these concepts in the following discussion. As to responsibility, the definition of Professor William C. Mitchell is accepted:

> A persistent theme in the literature of political science and political discourse, generally, has been that of *responsibility*. In the case of Americans, the quest has been for political responsibility, that is, for governmental actions that are defensible in terms of our other political values. This has meant that we demand, and perhaps expect, that government decisions or policies be made with an objective of furthering our values of liberty and equality. . . .
>
> But there is one other element in the ideal of responsible political behavior: that concerns the consistency of the actions with the norms of our society and political system. In this case, the chief norm or set of norms is that of the Constitution and the laws of long-standing regarding the powers and duties of public officials. Every action is expected to be defensible in light of the basic norms of the Constitution, which, then, is the major normative reference point. Indeed, much energy and intellectual skill have gone into interpreting the document and applying it to the daily actions of citizens and officials. The Supreme Court, of course, has become a specialized agency in this task.†

In the ensuing discussion, the themes that Mitchell suggests will be developed in a series of propositions concerning the corporation and government. To anticipate a bit, the suggestion will be made that the corporation—particularly the supercorporation—is a species of private government and thus subject to the same evaluations that are and should be made about public government. Initially, however, brief attention must be accorded the question of power.

THE PROBLEM OF POWER

However defined, and surely it is one of the most difficult terms in the political lexicon, power in a social order is never left in abeyance. For present purposes, we accept

---

*See the several essays in Carl J. Friedrich (ed.), *Responsibility* (New York: The Liberal Arts Press, Inc., 1960).
†Mitchell, pp. 151-2.

the definition of Lasswell and Kaplan: "Power is participation in the making of decisions: *G* has power over *H* with respect to the values *K* if *G* participates in the making of decisions affecting the *K*-policies of *H*."* Power finds its source in the control of that which is valued by people; it is the ability to influence decisions and behavior of individuals and groups. The major point of departure for the following discussion is that power in the American polity, contrary to both the classical and neoclassical orientation of economics, tends to be concentrated, not diffused.† The antitrust laws, although no doubt partially successful, have not been able to stem the tide toward bigness. Those laws are ineffective and obsolescent in the present American economy—and will become even more so in the future. Bigness, it is interesting to note, is not invalid under the antitrust laws;‡ only when it tends toward monopoly or to lessen competition does it run afoul of the statutes.

Power *always* exists; it is an inevitable and indispensable attribute of any political community. The question is *who* exercises power, not *whether* it is being exercised. In classical economic theory the myriad decisions of the market—which supposedly consisted of entities roughly equal in power—was at once an attempt to explain away power in economic life and an utter failure to describe accurately the actual situation as it then (or thereafter) existed. The analogue of political liberalism (in the old, not the modern, sense of the term), economic theory could no more dispense with power than it could produce conditions of well-being for all.

Power, both political and economic, was in main part based historically on property; those who possessed property —tangible property, whether real or personal—also possessed

*Harold D. Lasswell and Abraham Kaplan, *Power and Society* (New Haven, Conn.: Yale University Press, 1950), p. 75.
†See Kalman Goldberg and Robin Linstromberg, "A Revision of Some Theories of Economic Power," *Quarterly Review of Economics and Business*, VI (Spring, 1966), 7.
‡So held in *United States* v. *United States Steel Corp.*, 251 U.S. 417 (1920).

power.* Those without or with little or no property had relatively little power—neither in an economic nor a political sense. They could command nothing. Without the right to vote, their access to or control over political institutions was nonexistent. In other words, the classical theory of economics never had a factual predicate; it stated an ideal, not a description of reality. The point is that, whatever reality classical theory may have had historically, it has been further vitiated by the rise of the supercorporations as decentralized centers of economic power.

How has the Supreme Court, which according to Dean Louis H. Pollak of the Yale Law School is the "ultimate arbitrator of values in the public arena,"† dealt with the problem of economic power as it exists today? Several propositions will be advanced, admittedly tentatively, propositions that illustrate the main lines of Supreme Court decision-making and the handling of power. The net conclusion from these propositions is that the Court has not evolved a viable theory of the corporation or of modern capitalism as the former exists in the American social order and as the latter possibly describes the American economic system.

Both legitimacy and accountability relate, as we have said, to the process of government. Legitimacy, according to Carl Joachim Friedrich, is the "right or title to rule, [which] has been founded upon a variety of beliefs, grounded in religious and metaphysical notions of a great range."‡ These include a magical belief in descent from the gods, blood descent that equates rule with the right of property, the divine right, custom and tradition, and—of present-day importance—by those who are being ruled expressing a preference for the ruler by voting for him. Thus, the ruler in the American system achieves legitimacy because he has been voted into office. Adolf A. Berle appears to accept custom or

---

*See the discussion in Adolf A. Berle, *Power Without Property* (New York: Harcourt, Brace & World, Inc., 1959).

†*New York Times,* May 13, 1966, p. 31.

‡Friedrich, *Man and His Government: An Empirical Theory of Politics,* p. 233.

tradition or consensus as his test of legitimacy. To him, the
term means "merely that the holders of power are considered
by the community to be justified in their tenure of it. . . ."*

"Accountability" is not nearly as pervasive a term in the
literature as is "legitimacy." In government, it is fairly easy
to discern so far as formal authority is concerned; far less
easy is accountability of those who have effective control
over governmental decisions. As businessman Paul O. Gaddis has put it, "The framers of the Constitution established
an American tradition when they declared that a holder of
power within a sphere of influence must answer for that
power in 'another place.' "† Under the tripartite division
of power within the federal government, holders of power are
ostensibly made accountable by the system of checks and
balances to offiicials in other branches; and, of course, they
are ultimately responsible to the electorate. Ultimate power
in the political order, according to the prevailing orthodoxy,
lies in the people—in popular sovereignty—and public officials, not excluding judges, know the weight of public opinion. A serious problem arises when notions of accountability
in the public sector are transferred to the holders of power
in the private sphere—the corporate managers, the trade
union leaders, the leaders of other social groups—or, as will
be shown, when the power wielders bridge both the public
and private sectors.

Accountability in business activities was built historically
on the doctrines of classical economics. The actions of "owners and proprietors in business found a clear responsibility.
Their own actions were guided unerringly, or so they believed, toward the public good and their own gain."‡ But
those doctrines have now been exploded by the rise of the
supercorporation and the consequent divorce of ownership
and control. The result is that the historic basis for accountability of the power of corporate managers has now vanished.

*Berle, *The American Economic Republic*, p. 42.
†Paul O. Gaddis, *Corporate Accountability: For What and To Whom Must
the Manager Answer?* (New York: Harper & Row, 1964), p. 5.
‡Gaddis, p. 3.

The crucial question is how to limit or control the power of the large corporate enterprise. This, according to economist Carl Kaysen, can be done in one of three ways (or a combination of all three): "The first is limitation of business power through promoting more competitive markets; the second is broader control of business power by agencies external to business; the third, institutionalization within the firm of responsibility for the exercise of power."*

The propositions set forth below relate to how the Supreme Court has contributed to, and what it might be able to contribute to, the twin concepts of legitimacy and accountability. The problem is both large and amorphous; what is said must perforce be more suggestive than exhaustive. A conclusion that will be reached is that the corporation has achieved legitimacy but that serious problems of accountability exist. The same may be said about government. A further conclusion is that, with the merger of political and economic power, something akin to an American version of the corporative state may be in process of creation.

A word of caution is in order. Terms such as "legitimacy" and "accountability" and "responsibility" are, of course, high-level abstractions. As such, they are not susceptible to precise definition; they may be discussed but not defined. They are analogous to such constitutional terms as "due process of law" and "equal protection of the laws," which have never been given definitive content by the Supreme Court. In all probability, they never will. Lawyers and others who follow the Court are able to forecast whether a given factual situation will accord with due process or equal protection only by viewing what the Court has done in the past and picking out an imprecise line. So it is with all of the constitutional terms that are litigable: they do not define themselves. The precise clauses of the basic charter never get into litigation. And it is to be remembered, as we have said, constitutional decisions are not brought by judicial

---

*Carl Kaysen, "The Corporation: How Much Power? What Scope?" in Edward S. Mason (ed.), *The Corporation in Modern Society*, pp. 85, 103.

storks; they do not necessarily follow by dint of rigid logic from the delphic phrases of the Constitution; they call for statesmanship on the part of the Court, statesmanship that is as much forward looking as backward looking, statesmanship that must in each generation apply the ancient words to new and emergent social problems and situations.*

PRIVATE ECONOMIC POWER

1. The Constitution, it is often said, runs against governments only. In legal terms, this means that, as far as constitutional limitations are concerned, a concept of "governmental action" was created by the Supreme Court. With respect to the Fourteenth Amendment's due process and equal protection clauses, a finding of "state action" is necessary to trigger the amendment. That amendment, which is now about one hundred years old, says in part that no state shall deprive any person within its jurisdiction of life, liberty, or property without due process of law or deny him equal protection of the laws. First announced in the Civil Rights Cases of 1883,† the state-action concept has never been repudiated, although it has been so watered down by subsequent Court decisions that a new concept seems to be in process of becoming. We have now reached the point where a private group that performs a public function or has some sort of tie to the state beyond that of the charter it has received from the state may at times fall within the expanding concept of state action.

The first proposition advanced concerning the Supreme Court's treatment of private economic power may be simply stated: *The governmental character of the private corporation is being recognized.* That recognition is only faint at this time with respect to judicial decisions, but, when legislative and executive actions are added to the Court's, it is becoming

---

*See, for discussion, Miller, "Some Pervasive Myths About the United States Supreme Court," p. 153.
†109 U.S. 3 (1883).

obvious that corporations are in some degree "private governments." The wheel has almost come full circle, for it seems that the corporation began as a device through which certain governmental goals were achieved. We have now reached the point where the corporation is seen as essential to national well-being. If the supercorporation did not exist, it would have to be invented. In fact, in some respects it is being invented, as the formation of Comsat—the Communications Satellite Corporation—attests and as the manner in which government financing is used to aid certain weapons producers further evidences.

In speaking of *the* corporation, particular reference is made to the supercorporations that, according to Robert L. Heilbroner, constitute "a bastion of formidable economic strength within the sprawling expanse of the American economy—indeed, . . . [almost an] economic system within an economic system."* We focus on these giants, the removal of which would effectively destroy the American economy, because they at once provide a more efficient means of perceiving the need for theory and do in fact dominate the remainder of the economy. They are, as Heilbroner remarks, the center of gravity within the American business world. Some have larger annual budgets than many states and even nations; one, the American Telephone and Telegraph Company, which is the largest single enterprise in this country, has assets that total on the order of *one million* smaller enterprises.

The supercorporations, or whatever other name they may be called, have so warped constitutional theory that the time is long past for scholars to put their minds to the task of producing an adequate and viable statement of their place in the politico-economic system. The task, as suggested, ultimately becomes twofold: establishing the *legitimacy* of the corporation, principally the supercorporation, and making it *accountable*. As to the former, as has been seen in Chapter Two, before the Civil War and for decades thereafter, a

---

*Heilbroner, p. 14.

serious controversy existed as to the place of the corporation and even whether it had any proper place at all. Possibly that battle may have been won. Heilbroner puts the matter well:

> . . . The position of business within society was never more solidly entrenched. By this I mean that its legitimacy is now virtually complete, its acceptance without question. For perhaps the first time in American history there is no longer any substantial intellectual opposition to the system of business nor any serious questioning of its economic privileges and benefits. In the past a few small but articulate groups, mainly comprising intellectuals and fringes of the labor movement, have imagined a New Order that would sweep away the Old, and have often placed the business system on the defensive. Today even these erstwhile dissenters have largely given up all thought of passage to a New Society, and exert their energies toward the improvement of things within the given economic structure. As a result, capitalism has become the virtually unchallenged order to which the ambitions of future American society must accommodate themselves.*

Even if that be so, it is a capitalism far different from that envisaged by its patron saints, such as Adam Smith. It is a hierarchically structured, bureaucratically managed capitalism of the supercorporations—conglomerates of economic power—that sets the tone for and makes American capitalism what it is today. Accordingly, the need for theory encompasses both the corporation as a center of economic power and capitalism—in short, the two facets of what may be called "corporate" or "collective" capitalism.

If the legitimacy of the corporation is accepted and thus settled, it is only because of long continued usage and familiarity and, of more importance, because the productive capacities of these collective organizations are necessary to provide the economic benefits now so manifest in "the affluent society." There is at least a tacit, and often an express, recognition that the material welfare of Americans is dependent on economic enterprise collectively organized and

---

*Heilbroner, pp. 55-6.

managed. Mass production, in short, means welfare for the masses; without it, any idea of a welfare state or other means of substantially elevating the well-being of all of the people becomes an impossibility.

At the same time, although it has come later and is still subject to controversy, legitimacy apparently has also been accorded to two other centers of power that contest with business: the labor union and affirmative government. The Supreme Court, in a sense, accorded constitutional legitimacy to the corporation in 1886 when it was recognized as a person within the meaning of the Fourteenth Amendment. A half-century later, by upholding the National Labor Relations Act in the famous Jones and Laughlin Case (1937), the Court may be said to have legitimated at one and the same time the union and the new power of government. This new governmental power has been given the label in the previous chapter of the Positive State. A consequence is a growing partnership, between business, labor, and government, in the management of the economy. And that partnership means, among other things, that the line between what is public and what is private is blurring increasingly.

But if the corporation has been given legitimacy, the problem of accountability has yet to be satisfactorily resolved. It is at least twofold: (1) the relationship of the individual person to the corporation, and (2) the manner in which the common good—the national or public interest—may be attained in the new social order. Corporations are centers of economic power; what they do touches and concerns many persons directly and, often, all persons indirectly. What they do is of great interest to government officials in the Positive State. They are, in brief, private governments, and will be treated as such in the balance of the exposition of this chapter.

Supercorporations are of such recent vintage, however, that the relationships between the units of the "American economic republic"—Adolf A. Berle's label—and their segments, as defined in Chapter One, are still in a state of becoming. The law is as yet inchoate. And the law here consists of far more than the judge-made constitutional law of the Supreme Court; there is also considerable legislation, as we have seen, and what is quantitatively the largest body of law: administrative law. Much, although not all, of administrative law—both the procedure by which the public administration acts and the substance of the decisions made there —is concerned with business affairs and thus with the corporation. Accordingly, what is said here about the judicial treatment of the emerging concepts of the accountability of business enterprises gives only a partial picture, probably not even its largest part. Even so, it is important; the Supreme Court to some extent has been concerned in recent decades with establishing the nexus between business and government, on the one hand, and business and the individual, on the other.

In speaking of the governmental character of the corporation, it is necessary to see these economic entities as but one of several decentralized power centers that exist within the American social structure. Others include farmers' organizations, veterans' legions, trade unions (if not considered part of the corporate community; see Chapter One), religious organizations, and other associations.* Of these, it seems clear that the corporation—at least, the supercorporation—is the most important. "There are three ways," Professor Emmette S. Redford has said, that "business reflects functions and operations, characteristic of government."† These include: (1) the manner in which business organizations have been employed as agencies of administration for government, largely through the system of contracts and grants; (2) business, the corporation, is itself a system of power—says Redford: "Imperfect competition, oligopoly, market power, adminis-

---

*For description, compare Grant McConnell, *Private Power and American Democracy* (New York: Alfred A. Knopf, Inc., 1966), with Corinne Lathrop Gilb, *Hidden Hierarchies* (New York: Harper & Row, 1966).
†Emmette S. Redford, "Business as Government," in Roscoe C. Martin (ed.), *Public Administration and Democracy: Essays in Honor of Paul H. Appleby* (Syracuse. N.Y.: Syracuse University Press, 1965), pp. 63-4.

tered prices, cost-plus inflation are concepts which register the breakdown of the assumptions of automatic control by market forces and the parallel recognition that business is a system of power"; * and (3) the corporation is procedurally political, that is, the decision-making process within the corporate community is not only a calculation of response to market factors, but also an adjustment of the conflicting interests of the several groups that make up the corporation. In these ways, and perhaps more, the corporation has a private governmental character. A recognition of that attribute may be seen, so far as law is concerned, in the complex interaction of statutes (federal and state), administrative decisions (from any one or several of the congeries of agencies and bureaus that constitute the public administration), and court decisions.

In another way, also mentioned by Professor Redford, the corporation may be said to have a governmental character: this is the way in which economic power (the corporation) and political power (government) interact in the formation of public policies. Accommodation rather than dominance is the rule, to be seen with particular clarity in the independent regulatory commission—an organ of government that is, as discussed in Chapter Two, essentially a compromise, a regulatory instrument acceptable to the regulated. Furthermore, corporate officials and corporate power is felt throughout the decision-making processes of the legislature and the public administration. The partnership of government and business inevitably means that business has a governmental facet. When to that political truism† is added the types of decisions, important to all Americans, left to be made by corporation officers, then the governmental character of the private corporation is indeed a fact. It is a political fact *and* a legal fact, and, as will be shown shortly, it may well be on the way toward becoming a constitutional fact.

2. The first steps toward development of a judicial

---

*Redford pp. 67-8.
†See Truman, *The Governmental Process.*

theory of the constitutional position of social groups may be found scattered throughout Supreme Court decisions going back several decades. As noted, the Court in 1886 accepted without question that the corporation was a person within the meaning of the Fourteenth Amendment. That decision was the culmination of a *constitutional* interest in the activities of corporations. Until recently, to be sure, that interest found an outlet almost exclusively in according the corporation the protections of the Constitution (due process of law, equal protection of the laws, and so forth). However, that emphasis, which shifted in the constitutional revolution of the 1930s to permit greatly increased governmental regulatory programs, now has another aspect. This may be stated in the form of a second proposition: *To some extent, limited thus far but capable of expansion, corporations are required to adhere to national constitutional norms.* The development is threefold—legislative and executive as well as judicial—and exemplifies the complex interaction of official organizations in the formulation of public policy.

The constitutional right of association, which, although not expressly set forth in the fundamental law, has nonetheless been made a part of American constitutional law by Supreme Court decisions,* has only recently received the express imprimatur of the Supreme Court. It is now a right guaranteed by the First Amendment (but should not be confused with the right of peaceable assembly, which is specifically stated in that amendment). The right of association, for corporations and, in recent years, for other social groups, has largely been employed by the High Bench to protect those groups against certain interventions by government. The other side of the medal—of limitations on groups—is much more inchoate. In fact, even the suggestion that social groups should be limited constitutionally is still such a novel proposition that it meets almost automatic resistance. The

---

*For example, *National Association for the Advancement of Colored People* v. *Button,* 371 U.S. 415 (1963); *National Association for the Advancement of Colored People* v. *Alabama,* 357 U.S. 449 (1958). Compare *Shelton* v. *Tucker,* 364 U.S. 479 (1960).

Constitution still runs against governments only—and it takes a deliberate mental leap to analogize or equate private associational activity with government. Our history and our tradition, our ethos and our ideology, is (at least, has been) against such a construction. But the time has come, as Alexander H. Pekelis asserted twenty years ago, for constitutional lawyers to discover the dimension of private governments.* That discovery is now in the process of becoming. This can be seen in one express constitutional holding and a number of other recent judicial decisions that, when read in terms of their effects as well as the doctrines they promulgate, may be said to place constitutional restrictions on the corporation. In addition, other cases have put restrictions on political parties (another form of private association), and there are even some scattered judicial statements that indicate that labor unions may at times fall within the concept. Furthermore, the manner in which the avowedly political branches of the federal government—both Congress and the executive—have accepted prior judicial pronouncements in the area of race relations and translated them into law is further testimony to the validity of the proposition that at times corporations must adhere to constitutional norms. In many respects, this is a logical corollary to the first proposition about corporations being private governments: If they are governments or are like governments, then they are subject to the time-honored limitations on government.

However, it must be repeated for purposes of emphasis that the development is far from widely recognized. The leading, and thus far only, case in which the Supreme Court applied the Constitution directly to a corporation is Marsh v. Alabama.† There the Court upheld the right of members of the Jehovah's Witnesses sect to proseletize their religion on the streets of Chickasaw, Alabama, even though the town

---

*See Alexander H. Pekelis, "Private Governments and the Federal Constitution," in Milton R. Konvitz (ed.), *Law and Social Action: Selected Essays of Alexander H. Pekelis* (Ithaca, N.Y.: Cornell University Press, 1950). (The essay was originally published in 1946.)
†326 U.S. 501 (1946).

was wholly owned by the Gulf Shipbuilding Corporation.
Conviction for trespass was reversed by the Court as a depri-
vation of liberty (freedom of religion) without due process
of law. Discussing the decision, Adolf A. Berle has said:

> The emerging principle appears to be that the corporation
> . . . is as subject to constitutional limitations which limit
> action as is the state itself. . . . The preconditions of appli-
> cation are two: the undeniable fact that the corporation
> was created by the state and the existence of sufficient eco-
> nomic power concentrated in this vehicle to invade the
> constitutional right of an individual to a material degree.
> This is new as a rule of law, but it is typically American in
> tradition. . . . The principle is logical because . . . the
> modern state has set up, and come to rely on, the corporate
> system to carry out functions for which in modern life by
> community demand the government is held ultimately
> responsible. It is unlimited because it follows corporate
> power whenever that power actually exists. . . . Instead of
> nationalizing the enterprise, this doctrine "constitution-
> alizes" the operation.*

Whether the Marsh decision is a sport cannot be determined
at this juncture. Certainly it has not been repudiated, and it
exists as a direct and square holding available at any time
that the Supreme Court should decide to use it. Whether the
Court will go that far—that is, extend the Marsh rule beyond
its particular facts—may depend on what other organs of
government do. For, as Robert A. Horn has said, "American
law governing the rights and duties of voluntary associations
is made by legislatures, administrative agencies, and courts,
both state and national. The law of association laid down by
the Supreme Court of the United States is only a small part
of the whole legal effort to define the place of groups in our
society, although a crucially important one."† The Court

*Adolf A. Berle, "Constitutional Limitations on Corporate Activity—Protec-
tion of Personal Rights From Invasion Through Economic Power," *University of Pennsylvania Law Review*, C (1952), 933, 942-3.
†Robert A. Horn, *Groups and the Constitution* (Stanford, Calif.: Stanford
University Press, 1956), p. vii.

will have an opportunity to operate in this area only if legislators and administrators fail to act.

The other decisions are of quite recent vintage; they revolve around attempts by Negro plaintiffs in the Sit-in Cases to have the Court declare a private business that holds itself out to serve the public (often, but not necessarily always, a corporation), "governmental" insofar as the Fourteenth Amendment is concerned. Although only Justice William O. Douglas has been willing to go that far, the Court found other means to uphold the claims of the Negroes. In so doing, the concept of state action was all but eliminated—if one looks at the *effects* of such decisions as well as the doctrine enunciated. Burton *v.* Wilmington Parking Authority provides apt illustration. There the Court found state action in a privately owned restaurant that had leased its facilities from Delaware's publicly owned parking facility. Said the Court: ". . . What we hold today is that when a state leases public property in the manner and for the purposes shown to have been the case here, the proscriptions of the Fourteenth Amendment must be complied with by the lessee as certainly as though they were binding covenants written into the agreement itself."* When to that is added the congressional commands enunciated in the Civil Rights Act of 1964, a part of which requires places of public accommodation within the concept of interstate commerce not to discriminate, then it may readily be seen that the corporation has been "public-ized" and, in some instances, required to observe national constitutional norms.† Further evidence in the same area may be found in executive action; since 1942, all federal contracts must contain a nondiscrimination in employment clause. Originally ordered by President Franklin D.

*365 U.S. 715 (1961). See Thomas P. Lewis, "*Burton* v. *Wilmington Parking Authority*—A Case Without Precedent," *Columbia Law Review* (1961), 1458. See also Jerre Williams, "The Twilight of State Action," *Texas Law Review,* LXI (1963), 347.

†That part of the Civil Rights Act was upheld by the Supreme Court in *Heart of Atlanta Motel* v. *United States,* 379 U.S. 241 (1964) and *Katzenbach* v. *McClung,* 379 U.S. 294 (1964).

Roosevelt and subsequently renewed by his successors, this provision, too, is found in the Civil Rights Act of 1964 (for all business firms in interstate commerce). The combination of all three branches of government may, accordingly, be seen to have created a duty on the part of corporate officials to adhere to the Fourteenth Amendment.

Little further judicial action in this area should be anticipated. The entry of the Congress and the President into the field has pre-empted it as a judicially cognizable *constitutional* matter. Nondiscrimination has now become a matter of avowed public policy, and there will be little further need for victims of racial discrimination to use the judiciary. What may well be of greater importance is one of those unanticipated side effects that often occur following changes or discoveries.* In this case, what the Court did in racial matters could well be the impetus to a greater recognition of the governmental character of the private corporation. It might even be suggested that, by such means, the essential privateness of enterprise can be retained while simultaneously the ideals and goals of the Constitution are realized. But whether this happens depends, in the first instance, on whether any group of disgruntled Americans is available to act as plaintiff in actions against corporations. Quite possibly, this will not come about. As has been suggested in Chapter Three, ever increasingly law has become politicized. The necessary conclusion is that energies will be directed toward controlling the decisional processes in the public administration and Congress, rather than the judiciary.†

To the extent that the first two propositions are valid, then it may be said that a measure—perhaps very small—of accountability has come to the corporation. Certain external standards are being erected through official action to which

---

*For a discussion of this phenomenon in scientific matters, see Barry Commoner, *Science and Survival* (New York: The Viking Press, Inc., 1966).

†A neglected but very useful discussion of the entire area covered by the second proposition advanced above may be found in Robert L. Hale, *Freedom Through Law: Public Control of Private Governing Power* (New York: Columbia University Press, 1952).

corporate management must pay attention; managers cannot be solely profit-motivated in modern corporate capitalism. Slowly, perhaps surely, its social role is evolving—by court decisions, by legislative pronouncements, by administrative actions.* This means that the state takes an interest in the internal governance of corporations, as well as their impact on the community at large.

However much the corporation may now be accountable, the requirement for theory is far from satisfied. It is by no means certain, as Professor Daniel R. Fusfeld has said, that the challenges of large-scale organization and modern technology to human rights and freedom will be adequately met. Says Fusfeld:

> This [will be] no mean task, for it will require structuring the organization of business, labor, government and education to provide a maximum of freedom while retaining the ability of large organizations to operate effectively. It may be that individualism and bureaucracy are ultimately incompatible, but an effort to reconcile the two has not been made on anything like the scale required.†

3. Whatever conclusions may be drawn from the first two propositions, it does seem clear, as Robert L. Heilbroner has said, that the corporation—even the supercorporation—has achieved legitimacy, legitimacy in the sense of well nigh universal acceptance of the corporate device for doing business (and, of course, for other purposes, including the nonprofit corporation‡). It performs tasks vitally necessary for fulfillment of the goals of the Positive State. Peter F. Drucker has put the matter well:

> The privately owned and privately managed business has been the carrier of economic recovery and of economic growth throughout the entire non-Communist world to an

---

*See Gaddis, *Corporate Accountability: For What and To Whom Must the Manager Answer?*

†Daniel R. Fusfeld, *The Age of the Economist* (Glenview, Ill.: Scott, Foresman and Company, 1966), p. 137.

‡See Bruce L. R. Smith, *The RAND Corporation: Case Study of a Nonprofit Advisory Corporation* (Cambridge, Mass.: Harvard University Press, 1966) for a discussion of one of the most well-known of such corporations.

extent to which no one in the sixteen years between 1929 and the end of World War II would have thought possible. . . .

One of the main reasons for this development is the "concept of the corporation"—that is, the concepts of order and structure and the principles of management which this book discusses. They have made it possible everywhere to create managements that can shoulder the tremendous tasks of a rapidly changing industrial economy in a Cold War world. Above all, they have created a new outlook by means of which the privately owned and privately managed enterprise is made capable of taking leadership in a world that differs so fundamentally from that in which the free-enterprise theory was first developed almost two hundred years ago. Whether there are more people in the industrial countries who are "for" big business now than there were a generation ago, or whether more are "against" it, I do not know. What matters is that most people, in developed as well as in underdeveloped countries, today accept that the corporation is a fact, and that it is the specific organ through which a modern society discharges its basic economic functions. . . .

. . . [There is increasing recognition] that managers have become a major leadership group in industrial society and as such have great responsibilities to their own profession, to the enterprise and the people they manage, and to their economy and society.

This may well be the most important—as it is also the most radical—of the new developments. The large-scale organization of the business enterprise is very new. It is therefore highly probable that we are not very good as yet in organizing and managing this social institution. That it has great potential has already been proved. The realization of this potential demands hard work on problems of order and structure, individual self-improvement, and community values and beliefs. It demands above all that our large corporations and their managers take the largest view of their functions and make the greatest demands upon themselves.*

The passage is quoted at length, for it states both a concept

*Peter F. Drucker, *The Concept of the Corporation* (New York: New American Library of World Literature, Inc., 1964), pp. 246-7.

of legitimacy, which Drucker affirms, and of accountability or responsibility—which is still inchoate. The third proposition, then, in this discussion of the need for a theory of the large corporate enterprise may be simply stated: *Although the corporation has been legitimated—in law and in custom— still unsolved are the equally important problems of accountability.*

We leave the latter to the next in this listing. So far as legitimacy is concerned, the corporation, having been accepted even by the intellectual community—grudgingly, perhaps, but nonetheless to the extent it is true still a remarkable achievement*—may be said to have a solid basis in the mores of the people. Although very new—a creature of this century —it is one of the most important social changes in the history of the nation (perhaps in man's social history). Even though the Founding Fathers did not envisage it, certainly not in the form of the supercorporation of today, by judicial decision it has become a part of the constitutional order; it is so enmeshed with government and societal goals that economic well-being cannot be achieved without it. However much modern-day followers of Jefferson may pine for yesteryear, reversion to an agricultural, small-shop economy is not even remotely foreseeable. (It may be, as Harrison Brown has said, that nuclear war would make it impossible to recreate the type of industrial society we have today,† but any discussion of industrialism and the corporation must be be based on an assumption that such a war will not take place.)

In law, legitimation came early, as we have seen above, both indirectly in the series of decisions of the Marshall and Taney eras and directly in the 1886 recognition of the corporation as a person. Of perhaps greater significance is the further concession by the Supreme Court that size alone is not invalid under the antitrust laws. As the Court said in

---

*See Clarence C. Walton, "Critics of Business: Stonethrowers and Gravediggers," *Columbia Journal of World Business,* I, No. 4. (1966), 25.
†Harrison Brown, *The Challenge of Man's Future* (New York: The Viking Press, Inc., 1954).

1932, "mere size . . . is not an offense against the Sherman Act unless magnified to the point at which it amounts to a monopoly. . . ."* Twenty years after that decision, David E. Lilienthal published *Big Business: A New Era,* a carefully reasoned argument for the acceptance of big business as necessary and desirable.† Others of like mind include J. A. Schumpeter, J. K. Galbraith, and A. D. H. Kaplan. These economists, it has been said, believe that, in the long run, "the activities of the giant business firm tend to bring about a more nearly optimum allocation of resources, raise the level and reduce inequality in the distribution of income, and promote the secular rise in total output."‡ However, if economists and lawyers are in essential agreement about the legitimacy of the corporation, just what form it will take is not so clear. Will its privateness be retained, or will there be a movement toward syndicalism or corporativism? This will be discussed.

As has been said, the essential question is one of power— and that is a political, not an economic, question. Hence, economic analysis alone cannot solve the problem of responsibility. Although the theoretical question of the position of the corporation in the American constitutional system has not been finally written (although some beginnings have been made), how to contain and control its power, both economic *and* political, is the most fundamental problem. This deserves separate treatment.

4. The fourth proposition is this: *The theoretical problem of the accountability of the corporation, or of corporate managers, has not yet been resolved.* In fact, far from having adequate answers, the correct questions have not yet been asked. Neither, for that matter, are sufficient facts available so that theorists may test their hypotheses and propositions against what corporations and managers actually do; the

---

United States v. *Swift & Co.,* 286 U.S. 106, 116 (1932).

†David E. Lilienthal, *Big Business: A New Era* (New York: Harper & Row, 1953).

‡Morton S. Baratz, "Corporate Giants and the Power Structure," *Western Political Quarterly,* IX (1956), 406-7.

business world is noteworthy for its reluctance to reveal the details of its activities. Until, then, the facts are produced and the correct questions posed, the need for theory is more than likely to remain unfulfilled.

The problem of accountability in final analysis is two-fold. First, it is concerned with the relationships of corporate managers to the other segments of the corporate community, and second, it involves the extent to which those managers need take the common good or the public interest into account when making decisions. Corporate managers, that is to say, are accountable—they are called to answer "in another place"—if they are responsive in their decision-making to more than profit maximization. In other words, the managers of our supercorporations, to be accountable, must take more into consideration than profits (by way of dividends, and so forth) to the shareholders (the owners). What that "more" may be is itself the subject of intense debate.

Such a view, of course, presupposes that a divorce of ownership and control of the corporation is a fact. And so it is—and has been so recognized since the seminal study by Berle and Means.* We live in a managerial society, dominated by organizations that are in turn led by self-perpetuating oligarchies. Of these organizations, the corporation is perhaps the most important. And of the segments of the corporate community, the managers are by far the most influential. The shareholders, who are the ostensible owners and, under traditional theories, the controllers of the corporation, in fact own a piece of transferrable paper—a promise by *the* corporation to pay dividends at such times as they are voted. The view also assumes that the other units of the corporate community can be identified with sufficient precision that the manager can feed their situations into his decision-making process and that the common good or public interest is or may be something other than profit maximization. Whether the first can be done and the second is valid are debatable propositions. Equally debatable is the thesis that the manager

*Berle and Means, *The Modern Corporation and Private Property*.

should have a responsibility to take these interests into account.

The question of accountability ultimately is a moral problem. It has been recognized in judicial decisions to the extent that corporations are subject to constitutional norms, in legislative actions by the application of external standards of behavior on corporate activity, and in executive decisions. Recognition by some corporate leaders—for example, Kappel of American Telephone and Telegraph—of the need for accountability does not solve the problem; it merely poses the question. How it will be solved is as yet unanswered. Two suggestions may be made:

The internal order of the corporate community: Discussed above is the notion that at times the corporation should adhere to national constitutional norms. That point involved the impact of the corporate community on persons outside of the community—for example, those who may wish to become a part of it by way of employment. It was suggested that as a species of private government, entrusted with the performance of major societal tasks, the corporation should be accessible to all without regard to invidious discriminations; and it was noted that some governmental decisions, judicial and legislative and executive, were tending in that direction.

We now turn to the other side of that coin. How may *the* corporation—that is, corporate managers—treat those who are already a part of the corporate community? The question is complex. Again, one may see the interplay of several types of official action, as well as the force of long-continued custom and usage. For example, a series of federal labor laws, the principal one being the National Labor Relations Act of 1935, may be said to constitute an attempt by Congress (and the executive) both to legitimize collective labor activity and to protect individual workers from arbitrary management decisions.* Judicial activity in this area becomes, as has been

---

*For discussion, see Charles O. Gregory, *Labor and the Law* (2nd rev. ed.; New York: W. W. Norton & Company, Inc., 1961).

noted, that of statutory interpretation and the review of administrative decisions.

Another area may be in process of establishment: that of the extension of procedural due process concepts to the internal activities of the corporate community. Professor Abram Chayes agrees that the "internal structure of the corporation can . . . be fruitfully seen as a federation of associational groupings."* How, if at all, may the ancient concept of due process be applied to this internal federation? The question can be no more than posed here. Sociologist William M. Evan has had this to say about it:

> There is a growing awareness of the need for restricting the powers of the corporation. In particular, it is being argued that the courts and the legislatures should extend constitutional guarantees of procedural due process to the corporation or that corporations should develop their own "supplementary constitutional systems." The venerable doctrine of due process, which dates back at least to the Magna Carta, includes a complex of procedural safeguards against the exercise of arbitrary and unlimited power. These norms seek to insure that disputes are resolved impartially and fairly. This complex of norms includes the right of all parties to a conflict to be heard, the right to confront witnesses, to cross-examine them, and to introduce evidence in one's behalf. Incorporated in the Bill of Rights in 1791, the Due Process Clause protects the citizen against the arbitrary exercise of power by the federal government. These rights were extended, about 75 years later, via the Fourteenth Amendment, to citizens vis-à-vis their state governments. Since then, this doctrine has diffused or is in process of being diffused to other spheres of government; and according to Berle and others it is likely to diffuse to the realm of private organizations. Thus, it is possible that pressures, internal and external to the corporation, may develop to institutionalize norms of procedural due process for all employees who come under its jurisdiction.†

*Abram Chayes, "The Modern Corporation and the Rule of Law," in Mason, (ed.), pp. 25, 45.
†William M. Evan, "Organization Man and Due Process of Law," *American Sociological Review*, XXVI (1961), 545.

Evan spoke of employees, but the need—if it exists at all—is for extension of the principle to the other units of the corporate community, the members of that "federation of associational groupings."

ᐟ Little has been done *in the courts* to constitutionalize the corporation internally. By and large, the judiciary has been content to leave the management of private associations to their own norms except where Congress has stepped in, as in labor legislation, to alter the situation.* But one may say, with little fear of error, that the problem will increasingly occupy the attention of constitutional scholars in the future, as the dimension of private governments comes to be seen in its fullest extent.

Social responsibility and the corporation: One aspect, then, of accountability yet to be worked out in the legal system is the set of limitations on corporate managers in their handling of relationships with the other units of the national community. In the same way, still in process of becoming is the manner in which those managers have a responsibility— are accountable—outside of the corporate community. The reference here is not to the way in which corporations touch and concern individuals as individuals, but to the question of the extent to which, if at all, corporate decisions must mesh with national policies enunciated by government. We have seen in Chapter Three the beginnings of a system of facilitative economic planning in the United States—noncoercive and largely an attempt by the executive branch of government to fulfill the goals of the Employment Act of 1946. External accountability in this sense is involved with the means by which that attempt can be furthered in the decisions made by corporate managers.

If the managers† have a social responsibility, and there

---

*See Note, "Judicial Control of Actions of Private Associations," *Harvard Law Review*, LXXVI (1963), 983.

†Cf. Michael Young, "Preface to the 1961 Impression," in James Burnham, *The Managerial Revolution* (Harmondsworth, Middlesex, England: Penguin Books, Ltd., 1962), pp. 7, 11: "Every industrial society is governed by a series of managerial bureaucracies, and it is surely right to speak of them

is growing recognition that they do, it is because the decisions they make have important consequences for identifiable people. Heretofore, the discussion concerned the individuals who are directly affected by the corporation; here, the problem revolves around the decisions the corporation makes and the public at large. These might be price decisions, wage bargains, investment decisions, and similar matters of public import. The problem of accountability—of social responsibility—is how to institutionalize a system so that these decisions may be taken in the public interest. Again, the question asks much that cannot be more than suggested. The system of facilitative economic planning outlined in Chapter Three points up the problem, which is more emergent than solved.

5. We have already noted the trend toward governmental intervention in the economy. This, with the growth of collective capitalism, has created a new social milieu and further points up the need for theory. Edward S. Mason said in 1958 that the attack on "the capitalistic apologetic of the nineteenth century has been successful, but a satisfactory contemporary apologetic is still to be created." According to Mason, economists likely will have little to offer in the creation of the new ideology. He thought the psychologists, sociologists, and political scientists would have more to contribute: "It is high time they are called to their job."* The last in this listing of propositions relating to the new theory of corporate capitalism is this: *The theory must encompass the twin facts of corporate collectivism and of governmental participation in the economy.* As a corollary, it may be said— it is far from certain as yet—that a form of corporativism is

as conforming to a common type. Managerial organizations are strikingly similar, in industry along with government, in education and research along with the armed services. Almost all institutions in almost all advanced societies are run by graded hierarchies of managers, officials, or officers who do not 'own' but control; the posts filled by appointment nominally on grounds of merit instead of by election or inheritance; the officials salaried, permanent, and pensionable; the whole structure governed by written rules and regulations."

*Edward S. Mason, "The Apologetics of 'Managerialism,'" *The Journal of Business*, XXXI (1958), 1, 11.

being created in the United States. A few brief reminders may
be suggested at the outset of the discussion: (1) Corporations
to a significant extent are becoming administrative arms of
the government; (2) corporations and government are locked
together in a public-law partnership; (3) theory will follow
the facts of economic life, rather than determine them; (4)
who controls the public-law partnership of government and
business is as yet uncertain; (5) the Supreme Court will have
little to say about the nature of the new system.

These do not merit extensive discussion, for they have
been covered previously. What requires present emphasis
is the outline of what may well turn out to be the corporate
state, American style. There seems to be developing in the
United States, in the symbiotic relationship between government and the supercorporations, an institution *sui generis*,
an indigenous organ of governance that has little parallel
elsewhere in the world or in history. The late Joseph A.
Schumpeter forecast a "march into socialism," and no doubt
it is true that the corporate conglomerates, simply by accumulating enormous assets within one legal framework,
make it easy for the state to socialize them. But that prediction seems faulty, for Schumpeter defined centralist socialism
as "that organization of society in which the means of production are controlled, and the decisions on how and what
to produce and on who is to get what, are made by public
authority instead of privately-owned and privately-managed
firms."* "Public-izing" the corporation, or even the advent
of some sort of economic planning, does not *in and of itself*
mean that public authority will actually control or make the
decisions. What Schumpeter neglected, and what is crucial,
is the political dimension; as Edward S. Mason has said, in
the passage quoted above, it requires more than the tools of
economic analysis to develop a new theory of corporate
capitalism. Furthermore, as another economist, Calvin B.
Hoover, has remarked, "Economic and political systems do

---

*Joseph A. Schumpeter, *Capitalism, Socialism and Democracy* (paper ed.;
New York: Harper Torchbook, 1962), p. 415.

not conform to precise and logical models. The capitalistic system was never adopted in any country as a social contract in some sort of constitutional convention. It gradually evolved in somewhat different forms in the various countries."*

So it is and so it probably will be in what Daniel Bell calls the "post-industrial age." The politico-economic structure of the present and emergent eras will not necessarily follow any preconceived ideology or theory. Robert L. Heilbroner, in his perceptive essay *The Limits of American Capitalism,* has said that "an economic transformation of such magnitude that its big businesses become, in effect, public agencies is not a serious possibility for the foreseeable American future, barring a military or other calamity that would wreck the existing order." But he does admit that, within twenty years (from 1966), there may be "a much more elaborate system of controls over the level of its total output and its grand division among various social purposes than exists at present."† Quite possibly, the essentially private character of the corporate community will be preserved, but whether this means that they will not become, in effect, public agencies may be said to be doubtful. Already, owing to the huge expenditures necessitated by the Cold War, a number of the largest corporations are almost wholly dependent for their viability on government contracts. Private industry, according to Professor H. L. Nieburg, "on an enormous scale has become the agent of a fundamentally new economic system which at once resembles traditional private enterprise and the corporate state. . . ."‡ On the other hand, it is by no means clear that public officials will in fact control; they may make the formal decisions, but that hardly means that they will be free from influence, even control. The possible emergence of the state as group-person,

---

*Calvin B. Hoover, *The Economy, Liberty and the State* (New York: The Twentieth Century Fund, 1959), p. 13.

†Heilbroner, pp. 90, 94.

‡H. L. Nieburg, *In the Name of Science* (Chicago: Quadrangle Books, Inc., 1966), p. 190.

postulated in Chapter Three, does not alter that conclusion. Nieburg's book, called by the publisher "a chilling account of the growth of the scientific-military-industrial complex in America," points up a dimension neglected by Heilbroner and suggests the need for viewing the corporate system against the imperatives of the social context of the day.

What those imperatives are may be briefly stated. They include (1) rapid, even cataclysmic social change, with the result that the world has changed more during the past one hundred years than it did in the previous two thousand; (2) the scientific-technological revolution, at once the cause of social change and the creator of new institutions; (3) the movement toward equality, foreseen long ago by Alexis de Tocqueville and brought to the fore during the present century; (4) the population explosion, with concomitant food shortages; (5) a shrinking planet and an interdependent world; (6) the emergence of the United States as the most powerful nation in the world's history; (7) the tendency toward multinationalism in American business (of which more in Chapter Five); (8) the "revolution of rising expectations" among the economically poor nations of the world; (9) a deepset, profound realization that the ideals of the Age of the Enlightenment have been shattered forever and that, consequently, man is far from the rational being that he once was considered to be; and (10) what may be a corollary of the last statement, the realization—at least, the possibility—that man is basically aggressive and a destroyer. All these, and more, are involved in the milieu in which government and business must operate. What these pressures—and they are just that—will produce by way of demands that will have to be met by the economic system of the nation can only be foreseen dimly. In general, they suggest increased governmental activity, often in concert with business, with the result that business will more and more become "public-ized."

What is emerging is a fusion of political and economic power. The supercorporation is coming to be seen as a political system as well as an economic device, with increasingly close ties to government, particularly but not solely through federal contracts. Robin Marris has said that, "the significant difference between managerial capitalism and managerial socialism lies less in the character of the rules of the game than in who sets them. In socialism, the rules are set by political government. In capitalism, they emerge indirectly from a body of law and custom, founded on the concepts of private property and slowly developed."* The suggestion here is that, in the emergent system of corporate capitalism, the rules are set by a combination of the elites of political government and of the supercorporations. The rules of the game are determined and the economic system has its tone set by the coalescing activities of the political managers and the corporate managers.

The dim outlines of corporativism may thus be seen. Corporations are the recipients of delegated power from the state. They act as administrative organs for the state: "The 'modern state,' or 'political power' . . . is increasingly focused upon the delegation of power to administrative commissions whose members are officials of government, while the 'new economic state,' or 'economic power,' is the corresponding delegation of power to private corporations whose officials are the boards of directors."† What this means in part is that a system of "functional" federalism has been created, superimposed on the system of "formal" federalism created by the Constitution.

Both delegation of power and federalism are constitutional doctrines with a time-honored history and a well-defined content insofar as official government is concerned. Some of the changes in federalism have been noted in Chapter Two; here, our attention is directed toward economic or functional federalism, created by the rise of the supercorporations, which perform governmental functions. Delegation

---

*Marris, p. 2.
†John R. Commons, *The Economics of Collective Action* (New York: The Macmillan Co., 1950), p. 302.

is another matter; it requires a considerable mental leap to accept the idea that corporations are the recipients of delegated power from the state. But, as Commons asserted, this is precisely what seems to be the situation. Justice Louis D. Brandeis hinted at this when he said in 1933: "Whether the corporate privilege shall be granted or withheld is always a matter of state policy. If granted, the privilege is conferred in order to achieve an end which the State deems desirable."* In some instances, of course, as has been shown, corporations act in fact as administrative agents of the state, and thus are clearly recipients of delegated power.

What may be said about the supercorporation that does not have such contractual ties to the state or that, if it does, has ones relatively insignificant as compared with the total amount of business done by the firm? Here is where it may be said that, if such entities did not exist, they would have to be invented, for they perform those tasks that government would otherwise have to do. What is crucial is the relationship of the corporations to government (and to society at large). We are just now beginning to learn to ask the correct questions in this area of government and business working together to achieve societal objectives. The suggestion, to repeat, is that the concurrent rise of the supercorporation and of big government makes for a modern form of the corporate state, American style. The companies and government are in some sort of symbiotic relationship, a partnership, and it is as yet unknown which of the duo is the senior or dominant partner.

Whatever the answer may be to that question, the modern American corporate state seems to be a reality. In saying this, it is emphasized that no allegation is made (or should be inferred) that American corporativism takes the totalitarian form that it did in, say, Mussolini's Italy. There the state deliberately established corporative enterprises as a means of control;† in the United States, corporate giants

---

Louis K. Liggett Co. v. *Lee,* 288 U.S. 517, 545 (1933).
†See, for a brief discussion, Carl J. Friedrich and Zbigniew K. Brzezinski,

have been created through extremely lax and seldom enforced chartering authorities in state governments, nurtured by a constitutional law that favored their growth, and have entered into close and continuing relationships with government.

There is little or no indigenous American corporatist theory, but a great deal exists in Europe.* The lack of theory, however, did not prevent an attempt to create a native system of corporativism in 1933 and 1934 under the National Recovery Administration. In effect, the National Industrial Recovery Act, one of the main items in President Roosevelt's New Deal, established self-governing units within the American business structure. It sought to legitimize cooperative activity among businessmen, activity that otherwise would have run afoul of the antitrust laws. The Act was declared unconstitutional in 1935 by the Supreme Court in two famous cases: Panama Refining Co. *v.* Ryan and Schechter Poultry Co. *v.* United States—often known as the Hot Oil and Sick Chicken cases.† Of the two, the latter is the more significant; in it, the Court invalidated the NRA both because of an improper delegation of legislative power to the President and because the activities at issue were not a part of commerce within the meaning of the commerce clause. Those rulings are of little present-day interest. Although the former has never been expressly overruled, it has been so chipped away that it is no longer viable; as for the latter, as has been seen in Chapters Two and Three, the commerce clause is read expansively so as to permit a wide latitude of regulation by Congress.

What is important, however, is what the NRA attempted

Totalitarian Dictatorship (Cambridge, Mass.: Harvard University Press, 1956), pp. 222-4.

*See, for example, Ralph H. Bowen, *German Theories of the Corporative State* (New York: McGraw-Hill Book Co., Inc., 1947); Matthew H. Elbow, *French Corporative Theory, 1789-1948* (New York: Columbia University Press, 1953).

†293 U.S. 388 (1935); 295 U.S. 495 (1935). For discussion of these and other New Deal cases, see Robert L. Stern, "The Commerce Clause and the National Economy, 1933-46," *Harvard Law Review*, LIX (1946), 645.

to do. In brief, "It provided for trade or industry associations to adopt, with approval of the President, 'codes of fair competition' that would proscribe unfair or wasteful competitive trade practices, establish minimum wages, maximum hours and free collective bargaining. Violation of an approved code would constitute a misdemeanor."* In other words, what was established was a system of government in which business organizations, acting in concert, set the rules of the game, subject to governmental approval—a grant of self-government to business to organize itself, in designated manufacturing categories, with the aim of reviving production and increasing employment and economic prosperity. In addition, price-fixing rights were granted as well as a concept of controlled competition. In exchange for this, business was to recognize the rights of labor to organize and bargain collectively and to comply with wage and hour standards set by the President. In short, the effort was to institutionalize a working partnership between business, labor, and government.

In this sense, the NRA was the corporate state, American style. This does not mean—and, emphatically, it should not be taken to mean—that it was an attempt to introduce into the government-business symbiosis something akin to the fascist corporate state as exemplified in Italy and other totalitarian nations. Professor Mario Eunaudi has stated the difference in these terms:

> On the grounds of principle, no difference can be found [between fascist Italy and the NRA]. The corporate state [of Italy] was a system in which the power of the totalitarian state was dominant. Both trade unions and employers were brought under the control of the fascist dictator and deprived of all freedom. The workers were compelled to join the one official trade union recognized by the State. The corporate system itself made no effort to fix minimum

---

*William B. Lockhart, Yale Kamisar, and Jesse H. Choper, *Constitutional Law: Cases—Comments—Questions* (St. Paul, Minn.: West Publishing Co., 1964), p. 210.

wages and standards of work. The whole mechanism was contrived purely for the purpose of mobilizing the national economy so that the fascist dictatorship could make adequate preparations for war.

The NRA was, on the other hand, an attempt to strike a bargain between government and business, whereby business acting under the fairly remote control of government would try to increase production, while at the same time it would give better working conditions to the worker and the utmost freedom of organization to trade unions.

The NRA shows, that is, the extent to which the New Deal remained within the framework of what has been loosely called the capitalistic system. Free enterprise was to acquire as much freedom as possible, provided it recognized its social responsibilities.*

What Congress sought to do directly by statute in 1933 may have become, less than forty years later, close to an operational reality—but through indirect means. With major segments of the economy dominated by the supercorporations, existing in a state of oligopoly and with administered prices and "fair" competition, accompanied by indifferent or nonexistent antitrust regulation of the giants, the only aspect missing from the picture today is the direct, expressly stated legal link between industry and government. Richard J. Barber, counsel for the Senate Subcommittee on Antitrust and Monopoly, has termed the development a "new partnership" between big government and big business.† And so it appears to be. What this suggests, at the very least, is the need for analyzing the government-business relationship both as to the formal—statutory and administrative—connections between them and as to the informal (and doubtless more significant) relationships that have sprung up. If Heilbroner's (and others', of course) analysis of the supercorporation is accepted, then something that might well be called "the

---

*Mario Eunaudi, *The Roosevelt Revolution* (New York: Harcourt, Brace and World, Inc., 1959), p. 83.
†Richard J. Barber, "The New Partnership: Big Government and Big Business," *The New Republic* (August 13, 1966), 17.

modern corporate state" has appeared and is still in process of formulation. We will have to know much more about the details of how government and business, including labor, interact before any solid conclusions may be drawn.

If, however, something that looks suspiciously like corporativism is being created, one should not leap immediately to the view that it will perforce be totalitarian in nature. In fact, by not being imposed by statutory decree, but by being worked out by trial and error, the values of freedom *could* be maximized, provided—and this is a big proviso—that some institutional means is available to take steps to insure the preservation of those values. Viewed in this perspective, the problem poses immense challenges to the American system and particularly to the Supreme Court of the United States. What in effect is being asked of the Court is for it to create the climate of freedom while the nexus between government and business is being developed. As has been shown in this chapter, the task will not be an easy one, and it is far from a foregone conclusion that the Court will attempt it and, if it does, that it will be successful. The Justices have not yet been asked to take on the job, and perhaps they will not. But if the Court does not, then no existing institution is available to accomplish that necessary task.

In any event, the very absence of a formal legal link between government and the corporation—save in the area of companies whose viability depends on federal contracts— means that the dangers of corporativism will be much harder to impose. Even if an effort was made to make the corporations arms of the state and instruments of repression, furthermore, the social milieu of the era does not augur for that development. There is more to be feared from the other direction—from government becoming the captive of industry, or, as President Eisenhower put it in his farewell address, from public policy being captured by a "military-industrial complex" and the "scientific-technological elite." The political consequences of the supercorporation, as yet unknown, may well tend in the direction of government by private elites who use the formal structures of government to enunciate public policies favorable to their entities.*

CONCLUSIONS

Responsibility, legitimacy, accountability, corporativism —these are large words and large concepts, tricky to analyze and difficult to explicate. Even to raise questions such as have been set out above will, for many, seem idle and futile speculation. But the questions must be posed and discussed not only by economists, but also by lawyers and sociologists, by political scientists and students of public administration. Not to do so would be to abdicate a prime responsibility of members of these scholarly disciplines. The United States Supreme Court, Professor Paul A. Freund once said, is a theme that forces lawyers to become philosophers. In like manner, the rise of the supercorporation and of the Positive State are themes, at once separate and entwined, that force themselves on the attention of students of diverse callings. The nature of economic endeavor and the type of government together have much, perhaps most, to do with the tone and style of life at any given time. That is particularly true for a business-oriented society such as the United States. Sustained and systematic attention to the new social order is overdue. Professor Richard B. Wilson has suggested in a recent paper that ultimately the corporation will be "constitutionalized":

> Both the "fact" of corporate revolution and the theoretical response which knows not what to make of that fact have had an obvious impact on American constitutional development. So, too, have they both obscured and made difficult attempts to measure the course of that development. The instruments of constitutional design—legislators, administrators, and judges—have found it imperative to recognize

---

*See Kariel, *The Decline of American Pluralism.*

(at least *sub silentio*) the "fact," but in seeking ways to legitimate and control it, they have been bounded and frustrated by the perplexities and uncertainties of current social theory. If, then, proliferating organizational power may properly be viewed as the dominant economic fact of our time, and if the economic arrangements of society can be said to be the paramount concern of an industrialized nation, then failure to develop a reasonably coherent theory of public affairs both to describe and to prescribe for that fact points to a constitutional crisis of considerable magnitude.*

The twin developments of organized business and mammoth government may thus be meaningfully seen as a problem in American constitutionalism. Some of the dimensions of that problem have been set out in this chapter.

The problem ultimately becomes one of power. How would the Founding Fathers have dealt with the twin facts of organized business and big government? Clearly, they fragmented political power in order to avoid despotism, and, equally clearly, they did not foresee the expansive reading that could be and has been given to some of the delphic phrases of the Constitution. The supercorporation was unknown at the time. It would have been odd indeed for the drafters of the fundamental law not to recognize power when it existed and to make proper provisions for its amelioration and control.† Had the corporation (and the labor union) been present in 1787 in anything like their position today, surely some effort would have been made to deal with them. What the Founding Fathers did not face because they did not have to has now become, in Professor Wilson's term, a "constitutional crisis." The need for theory has never been more pressing.‡ The late Senator Estes Kefauver was of the opinion that basic economic policy was in the hands of a few corporate managers. If this be true, then his conclusion that

---

*Richard B. Wilson, "Antitrust Policy and Constitutional Theory," *Cornell Law Quarterly*, XLVI (1961), 505.
†See *The Federalist* No. 10.
‡See Adolf A. Berle, *Economic Power and the Free Society* (New York: Fund for the Republic, 1957).

"it is difficult to believe that this country will for long tolerate" such power may well be warranted.* In any event, the most portentous constitutional question is presented, one that surely will occupy much of the attention of constitutional lawyers in the future.

Changes in both the economy and government have indeed been great since 1787. But one should not think that a plateau has been reached and that present-day institutions will continue in their present form. Nothing could be further from what is likely to take place. With change being a constant in the social order, the present is but prologue to the future, and what that future will bring cannot be forecast with any certainty. In this process, science and technology as harnessed by business and government will have a major if not dominant part. As Dean Don K. Price has said, "the main lines of our [public] policy, over the long run, are likely to be determined by scientific developments that we cannot foresee, rather more than by political [and legal] doctrines that we can now state."† Nevertheless, enough is known today for one to be able to project some of what will occur in the future. One of these possibilities deserves special attention: the multinational corporation and its relationship to government, including the Supreme Court. It will be the focus of attention in Chapter Five.

---

*Estes Kefauver, *In a Few Hands: Monopoly Power in America* (New York: Pantheon Books, Inc., 1965), p. 238.
†Price, p. 186.

5

An Industrial America
in an Industrial World

The world is entering a new age—the age of total industrialization. Some countries are far along the road; many more are just beginning the journey. But everywhere, at a faster or slower pace, the peoples of the world are on the march toward industrialism. They are launched on a long course that is certain to change their communities into new and vastly different societies whose forms cannot yet be clearly foreseen. The twentieth century is a century of enormous and profound and worldwide transformation.*

INTRODUCTION

As should be obvious by now, the Supreme Court has not produced a comprehensive or consistent theory of economic behavior in the United States. Neither, for that matter, has anyone else, not even economists—although there may be a higher degree of agreement among specialists in economics about certain basic tenets of their profession than is true in other disciplines. The failure to produce a viable theory is traceable to an intellectual lag that exists between social fact and politico-economic doctrine (and also to the fact that the system of corporate collectivism now dominant in the American economy simply cannot be understood if viewed solely through the eyes of a specialist in one discipline). That lag is endemic in this nation—a country peopled by avowed prag-

---

*Clark Kerr, John T. Dunlop, Frederick H. Harbison, and Charles A. Myers, *Industrialism and Industrial Man* (New York: Oxford University Press, 1964), p. 3.

matists who presumably worry not about ideology, but who in fact are intellectual prisoners of defunct academicians, as John Maynard Keynes said.* The gap between fact and theory is particularly evident in the manner in which the Supreme Court handles economic-policy questions.

We have seen how the Court has abdicated its once-assumed role of making ultimate economic-policy decisions. The nexus between government and business is now being worked out, both in detail and in basic decisions, by the political branches of government—and, of those, mainly the public administration branch (including, of course, the President). Politics necessarily prevails, even in the so-called independent regulatory commissions. And that means that concepts of balance and of accommodation, rather than pre-existing doctrine or ideology, will control. It also means that the short-range view—meeting the problems of the moment in an *ad hoc* manner—will dominate (as in the past) over long-term perspectives. Of all the organs of government, only the Supreme Court can take longer views into consideration. But it is not at all clear that the High Bench has the institutionalized means to make effective judgments in this area. We will inquire into that question and also pose the problem of substantive areas with which the Court might deal in Chapter Six.

This chapter, necessarily short, thus defers discussion of the institutional adequacy of the Court, even though it is

---

*John Maynard Keynes, *The General Theory of Employment, Interest, and Money* (New York: Harcourt, Brace & World, Inc., 1936), pp. 383-4: ". . . The ideas of economists and political philosophers, both when they are right and when they are wrong, are more powerful than is commonly understood. Indeed the world is ruled by little else. Practical men, who believe themselves to be quite exempt from any intellectual influences, are usually the slaves of some defunct economist. . . . I am sure that the power of vested interests is vastly exaggerated compared with the gradual encroachment of ideas. Not, indeed, immediately, but after a certain interval; for in the field of economic and political philosophy there are not many who are influenced by new ideas after they are twenty-five or thirty years of age, so that the ideas which civil servants and politicians and even agitators apply to current events are not likely to be the newest. But, soon or late, it is ideas, not vested interests, which are dangerous for good or evil."

basic to much of what is said here. In main theme, the implications of an essentially new phenomenon will be explored:
the rise of the multinational corporation.* At the outset,
the American corporation will be described as it has spilled
out over national borders and now operates throughout the
world. Then will come a delineation of certain problems and
consequences of that development. Finally, the role of the
Supreme Court will be assayed.

AMERICAN BUSINESS GOES MULTINATIONAL

Speaking in 1963, Mr. Michael G. Duerr, European
Economic Specialist of the Chase Manhattan Bank, made the
following observation:

> Many U.S. companies today are looking at European opera-
> tions not as an isolated arm of their domestic business, but
> as a part of an integrated world-wide business. It is easy to
> exaggerate this, but the president of a U.S. company with
> its headquarters in Chicago is now more likely to look on
> his plant in Amsterdam and his plant in Atlanta as inter-
> related parts of the company's global operation than he
> might have a few years ago. I think this is a trend which
> will continue—as markets overseas continue to grow and
> as American companies become better and better educated
> in the ways of serving them.
>   I had a conversation two years ago with a New Eng-
> land manufacturer that has stayed in my mind ever since.
> I had commented on his ambitious plans for overseas ex-
> pansion, and he said:
>   "About 40 years ago I remember the big topic of
> conversation among New England manufacturers was
> whether to confine themselves to the territory they knew
> well—the Northeast—or to 'go national.'
>   "Our company did decide to 'go national,' and—al-
> though we had some anxious moments—we did very well.
>   "Now," he went on, "I look back to that period and,
> do you know? It's hard to remember the names of the firms

---

*So labeled in David E. Lilienthal, "The Multinational Corporation," in
Melvin Anshen and George Leland Bach (eds.), *Management and Corporations 1985* (New York: McGraw-Hill Book Co., Inc., 1960).

that decided not to venture outside of New England. Most of them have disappeared.

"Today," he went on, "I have the feeling I've lived through this before. Maybe I'm exaggerating a little," he concluded, "but if you ask me today you 'go international' or you're dead.*

Going national by American business has been one of the principal reasons for the changes in the nature of the federal system that have taken place since 1787. Once the economy became national, this meant that a continental economic system was superimposed on a decentralized political order. Inevitably, changes had to and did take place in federalism once nationalization had occurred; states rights became an anachronism, resurrected periodically in political campaigns, but more as a hortatory slogan than a description of reality. The simple—and hard—fact is that no one state can hope to control the corporate giants, even if some state wanted to. (Furthermore, should a state seriously attempt really effective regulation of the supercorporations, the Supreme Court would probably strike the attempt down because of interference with interstate commerce.)

Something roughly analogous is taking place with American firms going international—which they have been doing ever increasingly since the end of the Second World War. The American corporation—American capitalism—is in process of becoming multinationalized. Corporations are transcending *national* boundaries, just as, during the nineteenth century, they found *state* lines no barrier. Asserts Professor M. Y. Yoshino:

One of the most significant business trends today is the emergence of many American firms in the world market. The United States Department of Commerce reports that direct private investments overseas have almost tripled in the last decade, reaching $44 billion in 1964. . . . Over 3,300 American firms have some interest in overseas

---

*Michael G. Duerr, "Alternative Methods of Operation Within the EEC; Factors to Weigh in Doing Business in Europe," in *Doing Business in the Common Market* (Chicago: Commerce Clearing House, Inc., 1963) pp. 3, 13.

production either through licensing agreements or direct investments. For a substantial number of these, international business represents over 50 percent of earnings.*

The physiognomy of American business is changing dramatically; no longer is the continental United States the limit of the interest or thinking of the corporate executive. National boundaries are being dropped from business thinking. This does not apply to all corporations, of course, for the bulk of American enterprises are still relatively small; but, for those we have called the supercorporations, it has become by and large a necessity.

The development is a consequence of the fantastic technological advances of the past few decades—those that have so telescoped time and space that the planet is now indivisible, and interdependence among nations may meaningfully be contemplated. It finds a counterpart in the vastly increased political arrangements, now so prevalent, of a larger than national scope. The primary force may well be technology, in that it leads both to the increase in size of corporate collectivities and also makes it far easier and quicker to trade across national boundaries. But, whatever the cause, there seems to be little question that great changes are taking place in the form and nature of American capitalism. Of these changes, the tendency toward multinationalism coalesces with—perhaps influences—analogous developments in politics and military strategy. In net result, this has considerable importance for American public policy.

The development in its entirety may be put in the form of a trend (or a hypothesis): *The tendency is toward the obsolescence of the nation-state as a form of social order.* We may digress briefly from our main inquiry in order to set a larger pattern. In a time of rampant nationalism, when more nations exist than at any time in world history—the membership in the United Nations has almost *tripled* in twenty years—it may seem odd to suggest the desuetude of

---

*M. Y. Yoshino, "Toward A Concept of Managerial Control for a World Enterprise," *Michigan Business Review*, XVIII, No. 2 (March, 1966), 25.

the nation-state. But precisely this is advanced, and, moreover, the activities of the business community are helping to provide a social basis for a larger-than-national resolution of the problems of the human condition.

Nations are relative latecomers to human organization. Only within the last two to three hundred years have they become the characteristic form of social order. The modern state system emerged during that time out of a contest between the Church, feudal entities, and kings. Commercial and economic interests had great influence. The Peace of Westphalia in 1625 may be considered to be the great divide between partly medieval structures and the modern era of clear-cut territorial units with sovereignty. From the time of the French Revolution, nationalism increasingly has been the focal point of the loyalties of men. Paradoxically, the movement has now reached its peak—at precisely the time that the nation can no longer perform the functions for which it was originally created. At a time, then, of frenetic nationalism, the nation-state seems to be in the beginnings of a process of fundamental change. Compare these statements:

> Like all political arrangements, the nation-state system is a means for the realization of human goals; it is not a consummatory value—an end in itself. . . . [In this century, that system] has been conspicuously failing . . . [and] is increasingly unable to satisfy [the] minimum requirements for self-defense, self-support and economic growth.

* * *

> Nationalism has had its day. It was the political principle appropriate to the post-feudal and pre-atomic age. For the technology of the steam engine, it was indeed in good measure a force for progress. In the atomic age, it must make way for a political principle of larger dimensions, in tune with the world-wide configurations of interests and power of the age.*

---

*The first quotation is from William Y. Elliott, *The Political Economy of American Foreign Policy* (New York: Henry Holt & Co., Inc., 1955), p. 396; the second is from Hans Morgenthau, "The Paradoxes of Nationalism," *Yale Review*, XLVIII (1957), 481.

What seems to be emerging from the welter of nationalistic politico-economic policies is a clear tendency toward a *multi*national, although not a true *inter*national, resolution of policy making. The movement, glacial and massive, may be in the direction of the formation of what have been called "civilizational" or "ideological" groups. However loosely knit they may at present be, it is possible to discern three great transnational groups: the North Atlantic community and its satellites; the Sino-Soviet bloc and its satellites (however, that group may now have split); and the developing countries—those in the southern part of the planet, in Asia, Africa, and South America. "The reality of global society at the present time shows the ideological group, consisting of a superstate and its allies or satellites, as the basic social group. [And this may be projected as a working hypothesis, even though] we continue to act 'as if' the nation-state were the basis of international society and 'as if' its rules have to be created by the nation-state of the nineteenth century."* For the United States, the development can be seen in a congeries of policies and programs enunciated since the end of the Second World War.† It may also be seen in the growth of multinational corporations, which exercise *economic* sovereignty side by side with the nation-states, which exercise *political* sovereignty. Often the economic power of the corporation is contradictory to political loyalties and allegiances embedded in the concepts of nationality and citizenship. Those concepts have become meaningless insofar as the corporation is concerned. Washington lawyer Sigmund Timberg, writing in 1952, put the matter into effective focus:

> England, Holland, and the other great trading powers of the seventeenth and eighteenth centuries were delegating

---

*The notion of civilizational or ideological groups is taken from B. Landheer, "Contemporary Sociological Theories and International Law," *Recueil des Cours,* XCII (1957), 519.

†See Miller, "Foreign Trade and the 'Security State': A Study in Conflicting National Policies, p. 37.

political power to their foreign merchants, when they permitted those merchants to engage—collectively and under the corporate aegis—in foreign trade. In Maitland's classic phrase, these were "the companies that became colonies, the companies that make war." The same proposition holds for the modern large corporation. The modern state undeniably delegates *political* power to large private corporations, as it does to large labor unions with which the corporate behemoths deal. The authorization of collective activity has, at least since the time of the early Christian and Jewish communities had their difficulties with the Roman emperors, always been a state prerogative. Furthermore, the activities authorized for a large corporation involve such functions as price-fixing, the division of markets, the setting of wages, and the general development of local communities, functions which in a pre-Industrial Revolution era had been the primary responsibility of the State. It has been said of international cartels that some of the more powerful of them "are little empires in themselves, and their decisions are often more important than those of 'sovereign, political' entities like Holland, Denmark, or Portugal."*

Sovereignty-sharing with private collectivities is, as Timberg indicates, not a new phenomenon. Put another way, the present political framework is nationalist, almost frenetically so, while simultaneously, the economic base is transnational. What Adolf A. Berle has termed "the twentieth-century capitalist revolution" is coalescing with other forces to break up the familiar pattern of international relations. National frontiers are becoming increasingly irrelevant; the nation-state is becoming obsolescent.† What does the corporate development mean? What role will the Supreme Court have in resolving the inevitable disputes that will arise? It is to these questions that we now turn.

---

*Sigmund Timberg, "The Corporation as a Technique of International Administration," *University of Chicago Law Review*, XIX (1952), 739, 742.

†See Adolf A. Berle, *The Twentieth Century Capitalist Revolution* (New York: Harcourt, Brace & World, Inc., 1954). See also Arthur Selwyn Miller, "Toward A Concept of National Responsibility," *Yale Review*, LI (1961), 185.

CONSEQUENCES AND PROBLEMS OF CORPORATE MULTINATIONALISM

It is a condition, President Cleveland was wont to say, that confronts us, not a theory. That condition (multinationalization of American capitalism) presents problems of a new and critical nature to the constitutional order, problems that will increasingly occupy the attention of policy makers in the years to come. It meshes with "the age of total industrialization." On a collision course are the national policies of individual nation-states throughout the world. But the extension of American business abroad also creates opportunities, which when taken in their entirety at least give the promise of improved economic well-being for the peoples of the world. Multinationalism, in other words, is neither an unalloyed affliction nor is it an unmitigated blessing. Like any other institutional development in human history, it has two sides. For present purposes, we single out one aspect of each side for brief discussion. An entire volume could be written on the multinational corporation; some, in fact, have been, but none of a thoroughly systematic nature.* The "problem" and the "benefit" are really two sides of one coin: the inability of political sovereignty to control corporations.

A representative problem of multinational business is *control.* "Multinational firms," Professor Howe Martyn has said, "are a far cry from the traditional form of international trade that was based on the physical movement of goods. In addition, they generate a powerful international force that not only transcends the usual economic barriers, but political barriers, as well."† Conflict exists, as a consequence, between

---

*Compare Howe Martyn, *International Business* (New York: The Free Press, 1964) with Richard D. Robinson, *International Business Policy* (New York: Holt, Rinehart & Winston, Inc., 1964) and John Fayerweather, *Facts and Fallacies of International Business* (New York: Holt, Rinehart & Winston, Inc., 1962).

†Howe Martyn, "Multinational Corporations in a Nationalistic World," *Challenge: The Magazine of Economic Affairs* (November-December 1965), 13.

the multinational corporation and the sovereignty of the nation-states. Corporate power operates with little regard to national frontiers, although it acknowledges one political jurisdiction here and another there; a powerful social force, it influences "tax revenue, foreign exchange earnings, the balance of payments, the rate of new capital formation, and the earnings of local lawyers and newspaper publishers, as well as salesmen and engineers."*

How, then, can American multinational corporations be controlled? Law, such as it is, follows national boundaries; it has little extraterritorial application. Furthermore, there is no international law (or legal system) through which the activities of such corporations may be controlled. They are responsible to no one. As economist Kenneth E. Boulding has said,

> The international corporation faces a peculiarly difficult problem in establishing its universal legitimacy. Within a nation, the corporation achieves a certain legitimacy simply from the fact that it is incorporated by some public body. . . . The international corporations do not have even this shred of legitimacy, simply because there is no international body that can charter them. The international corporation, that is, operates in a kind of governmental vacuum, and it has to depend for its survival on legitimacies which are derived from special skill, from bargaining power, or from the prestige of the national government with which it is most closely associated.†

This is a philosophical problem—a constitutional problem, if you will—but one of concern to academics, not to businessmen. The latter, most of them at any rate, do not seem to be particularly perturbed that they may lack legitimacy.

The problem may be seen with particular clarity in the administration of the antitrust laws. Early in the history of the Sherman Antitrust Law, Mr. Justice Holmes said that "it is surprising to hear it argued" that the law should apply to acts "outside the jurisdiction of the United States, and

---

*Martyn, "Multinational Corporations in a Nationalistic World," p. 13.
†Quoted in *ibid.*, p. 15.

within that of other states."* In this case, it was alleged that
the defendant (a New Jersey corporation) had monopolized
and restrained trade in violation of the Sherman Law. The
case was a private suit between two corporations, not an
action brought by the United States government. Plaintiff,
another American corporation, maintained that he had been
damaged by defendant's alleged illegal activities in Costa
Rica. Justice Holmes pointed out that the damage was done
outside of the territorial limits of the United States and that
"general and almost universal rule is that the character of
an act as lawful or unlawful must be determined wholly by
the law of the country where the act is done."† In other words,
from this decision it would seem that the Sherman Law has
no application to acts done abroad. But that "is not the law,"
as the Supreme Court made clear in 1911 in United States
v. American Tobacco Company;‡ there, American Tobacco
and the Imperial Tobacco Company of Great Britain had
entered into contracts in England that allocated world markets and assigned the foreign export business of both companies to a third. These contracts were held unlawful. In net,
then, as a recent study concluded: "The fundamental principles of antitrust applied to foreign trade are the same as
those applied to interstate commerce."§

But the problem is less the positive law than the willing-
ness and the ability of government administrators to ascertain
the facts of foreign commerce—of the multinational corporations—and to prosecute the law in appropriate circumstances.
Little zeal is apparent within the Department of Justice's
Antitrust Division, whose Foreign Commerce Section is
sparsely manned and has few resources to deal effectively with
the burgeoning situation. As a consequence, almost nothing

American Banana Co. v. *United Fruit Co.*, 213 U.S. 347, 355 (1909).
†213 U.S. 347, 355 (1909).
‡221 U.S. 106 (1911).
§W. Wallace Kirkpatrick, "U.S. Antitrust Law and Its Relations to American
Firms Doing Business Within the EEC," in *Doing Business in the Common
Market* (Chicago: Commerce Clearing House, Inc., 1963), pp. 152, 168.
Professor Kirkpatrick went on to say, however, that the courts do take into
consideration special circumstances of foreign trade.

is done to enforce the antitrust laws in this expanding field.

The fault is even broader than a lack of zeal on the part of the United States government. Many American businesses operate through foreign subsidiaries and other arrangements. As Professor Howe Martyn has pointed out, "many businessmen argue that operations of foreign subsidiaries are properly private and no business of the United States government. This view is even stronger in [such countries as] the Netherlands and Switzerland. . . ." Merely getting the facts—as, for example, trying to learn how much profits are made in foreign operations by multinational companies—raises "thorny questions of sovereignty"; there is, in addition, "a certain reticence among businessmen themselves, which is attributable to an understandable [*sic!*] doubt about the capacity of public and government to understand the complexities of modern business."* In net result, then, the American multinational corporation operates in a region beyond the confines of the political nation-state and territorial ideas of law. The consequence, as Professor Boulding has said, is that the corporation lacks legitimacy—and that seems to be true even though, according to A. A. Berle, it may be doing a better job of governing its part of the world community than has the territorial nation-state.† The corporation seeks the protection of political government when desirable or necessary, but, otherwise, it tends to have as little as possible to do with it. In other words, as said above, the corporation exercises economic sovereignty in the world community and seeks the benefits but not the burdens or responsibilities, even though, in net effect, it is a species of private governing power‡—accountable to no one or no public government.

Essentially, thus, the rise of the multinational corporation poses acute problems of constitutionalism, revolving

---

*Martyn, *International Business,* pp. 260-1.

†Adolf A. Berle, *The Twentieth Century Capitalist Revolution.*

‡The point is developed in Arthur Selwyn Miller, "The Corporation as a Private Government in the World Community," *Virginia Law Review,* XLVI (1960), 1539.

around the concepts of legitimacy and accountability. One of the important questions for the future—it is already evident— is how and in what circumstances these entities may be brought within the ambit of public control. The nation-state is apparently unable either to learn the facts or effect the necessary controls over multinational business. But the problem, if that it be, is not without benefits. At work is a subtle process by which the activities of transnational business enterprises contribute substantially to the progressive erasure of the line between foreign and domestic, external and internal—or, put another way, the multinational corporation is one of the main forces leading to the obsolescence of the nation-state. Through its activities, as a by-product and not as a result of conscious design, may be seen the development of the social conditions that lead to what may validly be termed the "living law of multinational constitutionalism." Nationalism and its concomitant legal principle, sovereignty, are being eroded in the myriad transactions that transcend national boundaries, transactions of an economic character that sooner or later will have political repercussions.

The development is particularly to be seen within the North Atlantic community—those nations, of varying degrees of industrialization, existing along the North Atlantic littoral. One would have to be naïve or a glandular optimist to believe that the development has proceeded very far; but more than faint signs are evident. The "constitution" for the North Atlantic community is to be found in the twin organizations of NATO (the North Atlantic Treaty Organization) and OECD (the Organization for Economic Cooperation and Development). Both are products of the Cold War, emanating from American aid to Europe after World War II. They are multilateral treaties, one for military and the other for economic cooperation, couched in vague language and not outwardly supranational. But in their administration, in the day-to-day routine activities of those charged with carrying out the details of their missions, may be found one example of a living law of multinational cooperation. This is accomplished without fanfare or publicity. As President Kennedy put it in his State of the Union message in 1962: "The emergence of the new Europe is being matched by the emergence of new ties across the Atlantic. It is a matter of undramatic daily cooperation in hundreds of workaday tasks: of currencies kept in effective relation, of development loans meshed together, of standardized weapons and concerted diplomatic positions. The Atlantic community grows, not like a volcanic mountain, by one mighty explosion, but like a coral reef, from the accumulating activity of all."* What is being built up is a body of practice—of living law—that transcends national boundaries and that, to a very minor degree, constitutes an example of supranationalism in practice.

Such political actions are finding a counterpart in the commercial activities of American multinational corporations. The two aspects mesh together to form an ever increasing basis for the desuetude of the nation-state. As has been said, the paradox is that this is coming at the very time when nationalism is at its height and seemingly triumphant. It is not—and will not be. Replacing it, slowly but inexorably, is that system of multinational cooperation that is blurring the line between foreign and domestic in much the same manner as the line between public and private is being erased within the United States.

Where does the Supreme Court fit into this development? Little, if at all, although it will be suggested in Chapter Six that one of the new areas for judicial concern in the future will be the adaptation of a national Constitution to an interdependent world. The problems of cooperation between nations are political; they constitute a large area of what the Court has wisely called "political questions" and thereby avoided ruling on problems that have erupted therein. Those problems are not susceptible to judicial treatment, save in the

---

*For recent discussion, see Harold van B. Cleveland, *The Atlantic Idea and Its European Rivals* (New York: McGraw-Hill Book Co. Inc., 1966). On OECD, consult Arthur Selwyn Miller, "The Organization of Economic Cooperation and Development," *Yearbook of World Affairs,* XVII (1963), 80.

exceptional instance when a proper case can be brought before the Court, as when a treaty or other international agreement has internal consequences of direct impact on persons
within the United States. The cases are rare and handled by
and large by the Court so as to accord a high degree of deference to the President in his conduct of foreign relations.*

Much the same may be said for the business corporation
—but in a different way. It is odd but true that very few of the
disputes that arise in international trade are ever brought to
a national court—in this nation or any other—for settlement.
Rather, the businessman has established a broad network of
private judiciaries—of arbitration tribunals—that operate
either on an *ad hoc* or a continuing basis to resolve within
the framework of each industry or commodity the inevitable
disagreements that crop up. Little known and seldom studied,
that network is an important segment of the private economic governments in the world community. "The very
apprehension of the dangers inherent in litigation, the de-
spair of ever achieving a speedy and satisfactory settlement
of differences, may inhibit certain transactions from taking
place at all. International commercial arbitration, by providing an alternative method for the resolution of controversies,
may remove this impediment. . . ."† Accordingly, the role of
national judiciaries, including the Supreme Court of the
United States, is attenuated indeed. The businessman needs
a quick solution to his controversies; the politician looks
with disfavor on the judiciary; even the Court itself feels
uneasy in the area.

The situation is nowhere better seen than in the recent
important decision involving the seizure by Cuba of Ameri-

---

*See, for example, *United States* v. *Belmont*, 301 U.S. 324 (1937) and *United
States* v. *Pink*, 315 U.S. 203 (1942). These decisions involved U.S. recogni-
tion of Soviet Russia and the disposition within the United States of
Czarist Russian assets.

†Richard N. Gardner, "Economic and Political Implications of International
Commercial Arbitration," in Martin Domke (ed.), *International Trade
Arbitration* (New York: American Arbitration Association, 1958), pp. 15, 17.

can assets, part of which assets (sugar) got to the United States and became the subject of litigation. This is Banco Nacional de Cuba *v.* Sabbatino,* one of the most significant cases in Supreme Court history. Involved was the ownership of sugar, nationalized by the Castro government in Cuba and levied on in New York. Banco Nacional de Cuba, the state-owned bank in Cuba, was permitted to bring an action in the federal courts in which it asserted ownership of the sugar. The Supreme Court, in a case that raised issues important to American foreign relations and "more particularly to the proper role of the judicial branch in this sensitive area,"† reversed the lower federal courts and held that the "act of state" doctrine applied. That doctrine relates to the "capacity to reflect the proper distribution of functions between the judicial and political branches of the Government on matters bearing upon foreign affairs." In net effect, the Court said it was without competence to rule on the question, since it involved an act of state of another government, albeit an unfriendly power. This effectively removed the Court from that sensitive area—as of the time of the decision.

However, that was not the end of the matter, and at this writing the case is still pending final resolution in the federal courts. American business interests, incensed and alarmed at the Sabbatino decision, prevailed on Congress to hurry through an amendment to the Foreign Assistance Act whereby Congress sought to reverse the Supreme Court's holding and to require that courts take jurisdiction and decide such cases unless the President specifically determines that the foreign-policy interests of the United States made it inappropriate.‡ What the amendment, to cut away the legal technicalities, requires is that courts are not to apply the act-of-state

---

*376 U.S. 398 (1964). The case engendered voluminous comment in legal and other periodicals.
†376 U.S. 398 (1964), p. 407.
‡For discussion and criticism of this legislation see Stanley D. Metzger, "Act-of-State Doctrine Refined: The Sabbatino Case," in Philip B. Kurland (ed.), *Supreme Court Review* (1965), 223.

doctrine unless the President so requests; what Sabbatino decided was that the Supreme Court would determine in each instance whether the doctrine was to be applied.

The case, and its still-pending aftermath, is important for several reasons. First, it illustrates in classic style the reluctance of the Supreme Court to intervene in the foreign-policy process. In this respect, it is by no means certain that the Court will agree that Congress can order the judiciary to take jurisdiction over such disputes.* Second, Sabbatino is another example of the manner in which Congress reverses or overrules the Court in economic matters. Although this may ultimately be stricken down, the post-Sabbatino legislation fits into the pattern of Congress as a super court of appeals, discussed in Chapter Three. Third, what happened after the case was decided illustrates again the power of business interests to get government—in this instance, Congress—to do its will, even in the face of judicial (and executive) unwillingness. Seen in operation in the post-Sabbatino amendment are private power interests working together to force the act through Congress.† American business and American lawyers, not excluding some academics, made an effective team. Finally, the case is noteworthy for the absence of clear law—in the sense of precise normative, ordering principles to be applied—and for the need for the Supreme Court to create new law to fit the situation. In this respect, it was even more a case of judicial law-making than is often the situation—although it is not invalid to posit that every case decided on the merits by the Supreme Court involves judicial creativity in some degree.

Sabbatino may be a sport, or it may be typical of an increasing number of cases that will wend their ways toward the United States Supreme Court. Although it is perilous to

---

*The federal district court has upheld the legislation. *F. Palicio y Compania, S.A.* v. *Brush,* 256 *Federal Supplement* 481 (U.S. District Court, Southern District, New York, 1966). The decision has been appealed and is pending ultimate resolution.

†See McConnell, *Private Power and American Democracy,* for a thorough discussion of this phenomenon.

forecast any development in such an uncertain world, none-theless one may, with some confidence, say that the attitude of the Court in Sabbatino is likely to prevail, whatever Congress does. The Justices seem to feel uneasy when faced with the abrasive problems of foreign policy; they do not consider them amenable to the adversary process. Likely they are correct. One would be hard put to find a more unwieldy way of making policy—which, after all, is the result of judi-cial decisions—than through litigation. The nation is past the time when judges will seek out new areas of concern, unless in some way some person, natural or corporate, is directly and adversely affected. The problems of multinationalism in corporate affairs, in other words, likely will continue to be settled politically, if by public government, or through arbitration, if by the private economic governments.

That conclusion is nowhere better illustrated than in the well-known Chicago & Southern Case, decided in 1948. Under the terms of the Federal Aviation Act, applications to operate within the United States from abroad are passed on by the Civil Aeronautics Board, subject to the approval of the President. In that case, the Court held that "approval" meant not "a mere right of veto . . . but a positive and de-tailed control over the Board's decisions. . . ." The CAB's conclusions in the Chicago & Southern Case had been altered by the President "because of certain factors relating to our broad national welfare and other matters for which the Chief Executive has special responsibility."* That was all the President said in explanation of the changes made in the Board's order. In reviewing the case, the Supreme Court was wholly clear in its opinion that such a presidential decision

> is political, not judicial. Such decisions are wholly confided by our Constitution to the political departments of the government, Executive and Legislative. They are delicate, complex, and involve large elements of prophecy. They are and should be undertaken only by those directly re-

---

Chicago & Southern Airlines, Inc. v. Waterman Steamship Corp., 333 U.S. 103 (1948).

sponsible to the people whose welfare they advance or imperil. They are decisions of a kind for which the Judiciary has neither aptitude, facilities nor responsibility and which has long been held to belong to the domain of political power not subject to judicial intrusion or inquiry*

—as classic an example of judicial abdication as has ever been seen. The point to be emphasized is the reluctance of the Supreme Court to intrude into matters for which they have "neither aptitude, facilities nor responsibility. . . ." As will be discussed in Chapter Six, it is this attitude that seems to be contributing to the desuetude of the Supreme Court.

IN SUMMATION

A basic problem confronting the American nation is how to fit a *national* Constitution, one designed for the resolution of internal problems, to the exigencies of life on an interdependent planet, one in which the public-policy problems more and more are becoming *larger than national*. One aspect of the development is the tendency for American business to go international. This produces fundamental problems of legitimacy and accountability, problems that may have been solved for the domestic corporation but that are not even approached for the transnational or multinational corporation. Businessmen in these companies think of themselves, "not as . . . American [companies] with overseas interests, but as . . . international [companies] whose headquarters happen to be in the United States."† The Supreme Court's demonstrated reluctance to intrude into the area means that control, if effected (which is doubtful), will be by the political branches of government, and also that the Court is further diminishing in power. It is to that latter basic question that we now turn.

---

*333 U.S. 103 (1948).
†An officer of a large chemical company, quoted in Geoffrey Owen, *Industry in the U.S.A.* (Harmondsworth, Middlesex, England: Penguin Books, Ltd., 1966), p. 129.

6

The Desuetude of the Supreme Court?

I believe that for by far the greater part of their work it is a condition upon the success of our system that the judges should be independent; and I do not believe that their independence should be impaired because of their constitutional function. But the price of this immunity, I insist, is that they should not have the last word in those basic conflicts of "right and wrong—between whose endless jar justice resides." You may ask what then will become of the fundamental principles of equity and fair play which our constitutions enshrine; and whether I seriously believe that unsupported they will serve merely as counsels of moderation. I do not think that anyone can say what will be left of those principles; but this much I do think I do know—that a society so riven that the spirit of moderation is gone, no court *can* save; that a society where that spirit flourishes, no court *need* save; that in a society which evades its responsibility by thrusting upon the courts the nurture of that spirit, that spirit in the end will perish.*

INTRODUCTION

We return now to a question raised but deferred in Chapter One: the relationship between Supreme Court decisions and the economic order. Put more concretely, what difference has it made for the nature of American capitalism that the Court has exercised its powers of judicial review of other governmental acts? As was noted before, little is known about the causal connection between law and social change, or, in present context, about such a connection between judicial decisions and the manner in which the economy is conducted.

---

*Learned Hand, "The Contribution of an Independent Judiciary to Civilization," in Irving Dilliard (ed.), *The Spirit of Liberty: Papers and Addresses of Learned Hand* (New York: Vintage Books, Inc., 1959), pp. 118, 125. The quotation is from an address made in 1942.

To be sure, there has been much discussion and many confident assertions to the effect that the Court has made a difference; but these views, without any noteworthy exception, are advanced without benefit of factual studies that would tend to indicate the absence or presence of such a causal connection. Here, as in so much of constitutional law, the *a priori* pronouncement, plus exegesis of established texts, substitutes for carefully delineated hypotheses tested by factual evidence. Even such a thoughtful modern student of the Court as Professor Walter F. Murphy of Princeton University has stated flatly: "No serious student of public law has ever doubted the immense power of the justices. . . ."* Murphy implies that the Court has played a key role in American history. But is "government by judiciary"—historically or contemporaneously—really possible? Would the nation be different today if the cases reviewed in the foregoing chapters had been decided differently or had not been decided by the Supreme Court at all? Suppose that the social problems inherent in those judicial decisions had been decided politically, as in other democratic nations; would the net result be fundamentally different?

In many respects, the question is idle and impossible to answer. The Court did exist and did make decisions; the nation has changed from situation *A* in 1787 to situation *B* in 1967. Many commentators and scholars have acted "as if" the Court has made a difference. Presidents of bar associations and Supreme Court Justices, among others, have maintained that fundamental changes could be and have been wrought in the fabric of government by the Court. Even the cool-minded Holmes, who saw things whole and who was not likely to be deluded by images of judicial grandeur, could say that the Court had made a great difference in the nature of federalism—even though he asserted that little difference would result if the Court lost its power to declare acts of Congress and the executive unconstitutional.

*Walter F. Murphy, "Deeds Under A Doctrine: Civil Liberties in the 1963 Term," *American Political Science Review*, LIX (1965), 64, 75.

Against that array of talent, one might be thought rash indeed to suggest a contrary view. However, as Alfred North Whitehead once said, "the doctrines which best repay critical examination are those which for the longest period have remained unquestioned."* The essential question involves the relationship between legal and social change; here, the most that can be said is that we simply do not know the impact the Supreme Court has had on the structure and nature of American society. Rather than factual studies, what is available are the *ipse dixits* of a number of observers. The Court, accordingly, *may* have made a difference, but no one can tell —precisely or broadly—what the difference is. Picking up a theme outlined in Chapter Two, what is required are studies that would validate (or invalidate) such grand pronouncements as that of Professor (later Justice) Felix Frankfurter, who said in 1938:

> We speak of the Court as though it were an abstraction. To be sure the Court is an institution, but individuals, with all their diversities of endowment, experience, and outlook, determine its actions. The history of the Supreme Court is not the history of an abstraction, but the analysis of individuals acting as a court who make decisions and lay down doctrines, and of other individuals, their successors, who refine, modify, and sometimes even overrule the decisions of their predecessors, reinterpreting and transmuting their doctrines. In law also men make a difference. It would deny all meaning to history to believe that the course of events would have been the same if Thomas Jefferson had had the naming of Spencer Roane to the place to which John Adams called John Marshall, or if Roscoe Conkling rather than Morrison R. Waite had headed the Court before which came the Granger legislation. The evolution of finance capital in the United States, and therefore of American history after the Reconstruction period, would hardly have been the same if the views of men like Mr. Justice Miller and Mr. Justice Harlan had dominated the decisions of the Court from the Civil War to Theodore

---

*Alfred North Whitehead, *Adventures of Ideas* (paper ed.; New York: New American Library, 1959), p. 179.

Roosevelt's administration. There is no inevitability in history except as men make it.*

The difficulties with this statement are several. First, it reveals a philosophy of history that itself is the subject of deep dispute among historians. Men make a difference, says Frankfurter, but how does he know? How much of a difference? And, of much more importance, *which* men? How can it possibly be said that a group of middle-aged or elderly men, even though they sit on the highest bench, can have that much power? By what possible means can such propositions be validated? "How can one discover in history a coherent sequence of cause and effect, how can we find meaning in history, when our sequence is liable to be broken or deflected at any moment by some other, and from our point of view irrelevant, sequence?"† Frankfurter proves both too much and too little. A lifetime student of the Court, soon to wear the robes of the high office himself, might be pardoned such a belief. After all, one would not willingly wish to believe that his time had largely been spent in studying history through Supreme Court opinions when that history in the sense of causality between decision and society might not actually be ascertainable. As Arthur Koestler has said, "The inertia of the human mind and its resistance to innovation are most clearly demonstrated not, as one might expect, by the ignorant mass—which is easily swayed once its imagination is caught—but by professions with a vested interest in tradition and in the monopoly of learning."‡

Whatever conclusion one draws on the question of inevitability in history "as men make it," historical interpretation, it seems clear, is bound up with value judgments. "The search for causalities in history is impossible without reference to values. . . . Behind the search for causalities there

*Felix Frankfurter, "Justice Holmes Defines the Constitution," in *Law and Politics,* pp. 61, 62.

†Edward Hallett Carr, *What is History?* (London: Macmillan & Co., Ltd., 1961), p. 93.

‡Arthur Koestler, *The Sleepwalkers: A History of Man's Changing Vision of the Universe* (New York: The Macmillan Co., 1959), p. 427.

always lies, directly or indirectly, the search for values."*
When one views the past and attempts to achieve understanding, furthermore, it can only be done through the eyes
of the present. The historian is the product of the age in
which he lives, unavoidably so, and is bound to it by the
conditions of human existence. Even the words he uses—
such words as "democracy" or "capitalism" or "property"
—have present-day connotations from which he cannot divorce them.

Finally, causation itself as a legal concept, whether it is in
the context of the present inquiry of the relationship between
judicial decision and social change or in such matters as a
primary factor in the determination of tort liability, is complex and difficult—far different from causation in the labora-
tory, where, within rigidly limited circumstances, a natural
scientist can "cause" certain results through the operation of
known, invariable natural laws. Put water in a pot on a stove
and it will boil at a certain temperature. But causation in law
and in human affairs is quite another matter, not subject to
such uniformities and badly in need of reliable data that will
reveal some of the connections and relationships.

That, however, is a most difficult task, perhaps impossible. "The craving for an interpretation of history is so
deep-rooted that, unless we have a constructive outlook over
the past, we are drawn either to mysticism or to cynicism."†
In the present context, the Frankfurter position tends toward
mysticism; to be able to avoid cynicism, it seems to be necessary to have available—at the very least—deep and continuing
studies into the manner in which the American people
"obey" Supreme Court edicts. Without such studies, one can
give meaning to history if he so chooses, but his conclusions
tend to be merely a reflection of his personal valuations. One
sees meaning—or historical causation—where one wants to
see it.

But there should be no optimism that such studies will

---

*Carr, p. 93.
†Carr, p. 93.

soon be made. Legal scholars, whether lawyers or political scientists or others who have singled out the Supreme Court for scrutiny, have been anything but quick to produce the necessary data. One searches the literature in vain for anything more than sporadic forays into the uncharted sea of "impact analysis." In the main, such studies have been in the area of the influence Court decisions have had on the church-state relationship. So far as economic matters are concerned, the Court neither knows nor have scholars studied just what difference judicial decisions have made—or might make. Felix Frankfurter as Justice, as compared with Frankfurter as professor, again provides apt quotation:

> Take a problem that has been confronting the Supreme Court, Sherman Law regulation of the movie industry. A number of decisions have been rendered finding violations under the Sherman Law. Does anybody know, when we have a case, as we had one the other day, where we can go to find light on what the practical consequences of these decisions have been? . . . I don't know to what extent these things can be ascertained. I do know that, to the extent that they may be relevant in deciding cases, they ought not to be left to the blind guessing of myself and others only a little less uninformed than I am.*

At best, then, the impact of the Supreme Court on the nature of the American economy is unknown. Frankfurter's off-bench statement, to which we will revert below in discussing the expertise of the judiciary in economic-policy matters, reveals that a person who was one of the better constitutional scholars of this century could not forecast what a given decision might do. Nor could he say what impact decisions had had in the past. In other words, the confident assertion, in 1938, by Professor Frankfurter that "men make a difference" seems to become, in 1954, a position of bafflement.†

Even the elementary jurisprudential question of the

---

*Felix Frankfurter, *Some Observations on Supreme Court Litigation and Legal Education* (Chicago: University of Chicago Press, 1954), p. 17.
†The point is discussed at greater length in Miller, "On the Need for 'Impact Analysis' of Supreme Court Decisions," p. 365.

meaning to be given to Supreme Court decisions is not settled. Does a decision merely settle the matter as between the parties then before the Court? If so, then the Court is stating the *law of the case*. Or does it have a broader implication? Is the Court stating the *law of the land* in constitutional adjudications? This question has never been satisfactorily answered. Certainly, the Court has no general amendatory power to update the Constitution. Certainly no one not before the bar of the Court—unless it is a "class action"—can be said to be personally bound by the judicial decree; this means that one not party to litigation cannot be held in contempt of court for failing to adhere to the decree. From this, it would seem that the Court's pronouncement is in fact the law of the case, not of the land. On the other hand, there can be little question that the general judicial practice is to follow precedent and that, accordingly, once a rule governing a particular factual situation has been announced, a lawyer may predict what will happen in identical or similar factual situations. Furthermore, some decisions are widely reported and are thought to state a general, not a particular, norm. Laymen as well as lawyers may look upon Supreme Court rulings as binding on them personally— although the absence of empirical data makes this uncertain.

On the whole, moreover, it should be noted that constitutional rules and principles tend to travel in pairs of opposites. Cases accepted by the Supreme Court for ruling on the merits tend to be the "trouble" or "hospital" disputes— those that cannot be resolved without resort to the High Bench—which means that the law is not settled and that the Justices have choices to make from a multiplicity of rules or principles. Whatever the lay view may be, then, a Court constitutional adjudication, as a matter of legal technicality, merely settles the law of the case; it determines the rights and duties of only the parties before the Court.

This has considerable importance, elementary though it may be, for businessmen who must fit their practices into the framework of law. Is corporation X bound or constrained by a decision affecting corporation *Y?* Does an administrative agency adhere to the commands rendered by courts with respect to other agencies? The short answer to these questions is "no"; neither the enterprise nor the government is necessarily bound by decisions to which they are not a party. Certainly, in neither instance do they appear to be bound. Rather, they continue on their practices until a specific judicial decree is aimed at them. The binding effect of law announced by the judiciary may well be minimal.*

Moreover, even if one still maintains that the Court in the past has wielded immense power in economic matters, that power surely is attenuated at the present time. As we have already seen (in Chapter Three), the Court's economic pronouncements are in the field of statutory rather than constitutional interpretation and are thus always subject to eventual reversal by Congress. Furthermore, much of the basically important economic matters never get to Court— and indeed cannot; for example, monetary and fiscal policies and most contractual matters. When the Positive State came into fruition and public law proliferated, lawyers and others attempted to employ the institutions of a private-law system in making some public-law decisions. As Lon L. Fuller has said, we are faced with new problems of institutional design unprecedented in scope and importance. "As lawyers we have a natural inclination to 'judicialize' every function of government. Adjudication is a process with which we are familiar and which enables us to show to advantage our special talents. Yet we must face the plain truth that adjudication is an ineffective instrument for economic management and for governmental participation in the allocation of economic resources."† When, in other words, government and law changed from umpire of the private decisions of the market to that of active manager of the economy, adjudication became inadequate as a decision-making institution. And that

---

*See Arthur Selwyn Miller and Alan W. Scheflin, "The Power of the Supreme Court in the Age of the Positive State," *Duke Law Journal* (1967), 273.

†Lon L. Fuller, *The Morality of Law* (New Haven, Conn.: Yale University Press, 1964), p. 176.

is valid even though, because of an inability to escape the heritage of the past, many of the regulatory functions of government—for example, the Federal Communications Commission—operate at least outwardly in a judicial manner. Courts, whether truly so or in the form of administrative tribunals, are, to use Aristotle's classification, adequate and indeed indispensable for problems of *corrective* justice but are wholly inadequate when it comes to problems of *distributive* justice. The Positive State is more and more concerned with the latter.

THE NEED TO ADAPT

The desuetude of the Supreme Court *in economic matters* is already a hard fact of life. Its importance is minimal at best, nonexistent at worst. An occasional antitrust decision, of course, is made, but John Kenneth Galbraith's assertion in his Reith Lectures in 1966, that "the anti-trust laws are a charade"* may be close to the mark. Seldom do these decisions affect, directly or indirectly, the supercorporations. Their administration, in the main, is directed toward the small enterprise. And on occasion, review is made of the economic decisions of the regulatory commissions, but these, too, are rareties and do not invalidate the conclusion that the Court has abdicated whatever role it may once have had in the setting of basic economic policy.

Since that shift in judicial function took place, the High Bench ever increasingly has taken on the role of protector of civil liberties and civil rights. In other words, it found itself a new role. The change has been so abrupt that, when reviewed retrospectively, it is difficult to think of any important civil-rights or civil-liberties case older than forty years; those that are, moreover, have often been overruled by more recent decisions. These cases mean that the Court has become immersed in the travail of society to a degree never before

---

*John Kenneth Galbraith, "The New Industrial State: Control of Prices and People," *The Listener* (December 1, 1966), 793, 794.

known in American history. Had this role not been undertaken by the Court, likely it would by now have largely sunk into oblivion. But, by tackling the situation of the Negro, the position of the urban voter, and the shortcomings of the administration of the criminal law—these are some but not all of the recent important categories of cases—the Justices not only kept their status but enhanced it. By becoming "activist" in new areas, by being willing to confront some of the abrasive problems of the human condition that had been ignored by the avowedly political branches of government, the members of the High Bench have helped create breakthroughs that are enabling resolution of those problems.

One should not read too much into these decisions, however. In the future, they may be viewed as an isolated burst of judicial energy that permitted pent-up forces to have an outlet. Moreover, the very success of the Court in recent years—and, outwardly at least, it has been highly successful, perhaps more so than at any other comparable period in history—raises at least two critical questions: (1) Has the Court about worked itself out of critical social problems with which to deal? and (2) Why has the Court had this success? The second question relates to the power of the Court; as noted above, so little is known about the impact of judicial decisions that posing the question is about all that can be done. We limit ourselves here, accordingly, to the first question, itself complex enough to merit extended discussion, but which can get only summary attention.

The basic proposition advanced is that the Court must, if it is to remain a viable and significant organ of government, adapt itself to changing reality. The need, in short, is twofold: for the identification of new areas of constitutional concern and for enhancement of the institutional capacity of the Court to handle those problems. Each will be separately discussed. First, however, a few words on the need for adaptation. The court, in the past, has been able to meet new constitutional exigencies when needs arose. More may be expected in the future, since the nation (and the world) is in the midst of a period of extremely rapid social change. What these new areas of constitutional concern may be cannot be forecast with any degree of certainty. It is, furthermore, outside the scope of this volume to develop the question in detail. Nevertheless, it is possible to reiterate and thus re-emphasize some suggestions made in previous chapters, particularly those that have some relevance to the nature of American capitalism. Unless the Court is able to find new constitutional issues to grapple with, one may without excessive temerity raise the question as to whether much more remains to be done in the area of civil rights and civil liberties. The main guidelines have been set—in ethnic relations, in legislative apportionment, in criminal law administration, and in like matters—and what remains is to fill in the details. Of course, this could—and will—keep the Court busy for a number of years; any change will not be as abrupt as was the coming of the Positive State. Looking ahead, say, twenty years and trying to forecast what will be the areas of concern then, leads to the conclusion that few of the burning issues of the past two decades will still be foremost in the eyes of the Court and its followers.

We are on the verge, in short, of a decline of the Supreme Court—unless and until it can find new issues of constitutional importance to decide. If change is the law of life, as President John F. Kennedy was fond of saying, then the analogue is adaptation; *adapt or die* would seem to be a terse, not invalid, way of putting it. Government institutions, if they are to survive, must be Darwinian, not Newtonian;* they must accept the changing needs of each generation and mold their practices to those exigencies. We have become accustomed, in recent years, to a Court that avidly

---

*"Government is not a machine, but a living thing. It falls, not under the theory of the universe, but under the theory of organic life. It is accountable to Darwin, not to Newton. It is modified by its environment, necessitated by its tasks, shaped to its functions by the sheer pressure of life. . . . Living political constitutions must be Darwinian in structure and practice."— Woodrow Wilson [*Constitutional Government in the United States* (New York: Columbia University Press, 1908), pp. 56-7.]

pursues the values of human dignity embedded in the Bill of Rights and the Fourteenth Amendment.* It is, at the very least, highly unlikely that such judicial activism can be long continued, simply because there are few basic constitutional issues remaining subject to the Court's determination. What can be foreseen are some areas that arguably are amenable to at least partial judicial exposition; these may well occupy an increasing part of the Supreme Court's annual agenda.

NEW AREAS OF CONCERN

To be able to predict with any accuracy what might be the main issues before the Court in the future depends on whether one is able, in the first instance, to forecast what social problems and drives will obtrude. For it is these problems and drives that, in the past, have so often been sent to the High Bench for resolution. We have sketched, in the foregoing chapters, how the Court met the challenge of an industrializing America; and we have indicated that, in the past few decades, it has met in like manner the drive toward equality of disadvantaged Americans. As for the future, at least three main problem areas seem possibly suited for judicial action. (All have been previously mentioned; they are drawn together here to summarize and to attempt to indicate the flow of future decision.)

Oversight of the public administration: In discussing the rise of the Positive State in Chapter Three, it was suggested that the position of the Court vis-à-vis the public administration had changed, at least with respect to economic-policy decisions. No longer does the High Bench make what appears to be the final decision; that is in the hands of the avowedly political branches of government. (Many of the decisions were never really "final.") The sug-

---

*See Alpheus Thomas Mason, "The Warren Court and the Bill of Rights," *Yale Review,* LVI (1967), 197.

gestion now is that, in the future, the Court possibly may find increased opportunities for oversight of the public adminis- tration in two principal areas: (1) in the myriad instances where the public administration touches and concerns the individual as an individual, and (2) in the field of economic regulation. This suggestion is based on the assumption that the bureaucratization of American society will proceed apace, exemplified both in the growth of huge private col- lectivities and in the increasing proliferation of government. The further assumption is made that one area of concern for thoughtful Americans will be the manner in which pub- lic administrators operate, both as they affect individuals directly and as they deal with private collectivities. The pen- dulum may well be swinging toward an attempt to counter- act the excessive deference to the public administration here- tofore shown.

Some portents of greater judicial activity may already be seen. In Greene *v.* McElroy and Kent *v.* Dulles,* for example, the Supreme Court invalidated administrative actions adverse to individuals. Greene dealt with the industrial security pro- gram of the Department of Defense; the Court held that, since that program had not been authorized by Congress or presidential order, it was invalid insofar as it applied to an employee of a Navy contractor. (But the defect was soon cured through the issuance of an Executive Order, so that the *status quo ante* was restored—another example of where judicial decisions get overruled by the political branches of government.) In Kent, the Court held certain State Depart- ment passport procedures improper. On the other hand, in the Phillips Petroleum Company Case of 1954,† the Federal Power Commission was ordered to take jurisdiction for rate- making purposes over sales at the "wellhead." The Commis- sion had said that it did not have the power to do this. (In this case, the FPC in effect ignored for years the judicial decree—a classic example of how Court orders do not enforce

---

*360 U.S. 474 (1959) and 357 U.S. 116 (1958).
†347 U.S. 672 (1954).

themselves.) And in the more recent United Church of Christ Case, the Court of Appeals for the District of Columbia significantly enlarged the category of persons who can challenge orders—in this case, the granting of licenses—of the Federal Communications Commission.* A group of consumers was permitted to sue and to get a license renewal reversed. In like manner, a conservation group in New York was permitted to sue—in technical language, they were accorded "standing to sue"—the Federal Power Commission when the FPC granted Consolidated Edison Company a permit to build a facility at Storm King on the Hudson River.†

In net effect, such cases as these may be seen as attempts by the judiciary to attain a greater scope of control over the flow of administrative decisions. What their long-range impact will be is difficult to foresee. Likely it will not be great. Surveillance over the myriad of such decisions is simply not possible for such an outmoded institution as courts. Some other techniques must be developed if ever the discretion administrators admittedly have is to be made more accountable. In this connection, increasing attention will probably be paid to such devices as the ombudsman (the name is derived from the Scandinavian officer who acts as a focal point for complaints to be channeled and investigated). The system has spread to other countries, including some with legal systems not unlike the United States—England and New Zealand, for example.‡ Whether similar offices will be created is uncertain. But, if they are, it may be said that many of the questions of interest to the officers of America's capitalism will *not* be within their jurisdiction. Those questions will continue to be resolved through the operation of

---

Office of Communication of the United Church of Christ v. *FCC,* 359 Federal Second 994 (1966).

†*Scenic Hudson Preservation Conference* v. *FPC,* 354 Federal Second 608 (1965).

‡For comprehensive discussion, see Walter Gellhorn, *When Americans Complain* (Cambridge, Mass.: Harvard University Press, 1966) and the companion volume by the same author, *Ombudsmen and Others: Citizens' Protectors in Nine Countries* (Cambridge, Mass.: Harvard University Press, 1966).

the political process.* At the present time, approximately
40 percent of the cases decided each year by the Supreme
Court involve some aspect of administrative law. That number may well increase. If it does, it still will not touch the
bulk of the public administration, either directly or indirectly. The time-honored system of checks and balances,
assuming it was once valid, simply no longer operates in the
age of the administrative state. Simplistic notions of constitutionalism have to give way to the realities of the modern
era.

*Adaptation of a national constitution to multination-
alism:* Writing in 1956, Professor Paul A. Freund maintained
that any thorough-going American commitment to supranationalism would have to come by constitutional amendment.†
That might well be valid, provided that the commitment
were to come in one swoop. But it might be questioned if the
process of adapting a Constitution designed largely for the
resolution of *national* problems to multinationalism or supranationalism were to be one of slow accretion. This seems to
be the greater likelihood. The faint, though unmistakable,
signs may already be seen (see Chapter Five). But the well-
known reluctance of the Supreme Court to intervene into
foreign policy matters is likely to keep it out of the fray. The
decisions of adaptation, in other words, are being and will
continue to be taken by the Congress and, more importantly,
by the executive. Speaking sententiously, no serious constitutional obstacle exists to an ever increasing commitment
of American policy to multinationalism or even supranationalism. We are in fact already doing just that, to a much
greater extent than many realize. The process, of course is
far from complete; it has barely been started. But the imperatives of the age—technological, economic, military, political
—all are working in that direction.‡ Much of the disquietude

*As seen in Chapter Three.
†Paul A. Freund, "Law and the Future: Constitutional Law," *Northwestern
University Law Review*, LI (1956), 187.
‡See, for example, Louis H. Mayo, "The New Technology and Multinational
Cooperation," *Minnesota Law Review*, XLVI (1962), 869.

displayed by American officials in the mid-1960s over the activities of President Charles de Gaulle of France seems to be attributable to the fact that he is trying to reinstate nationalism at a time when Americans look upon it as an anachronism.

One can overestimate the extent of larger-than-national resolutions of public-policy questions, but it is difficult to gainsay the idea that those resolutions, when and if taken, will be by Congress and the executive, not the Supreme Court. The unhappy history of the International Court of Justice is ample testimony that national leaders will not permit judicial determinations in the important issues of policy. The Supreme Court does not demur from that attitude.

The individual and the group: A final area of possible increased concern for the Supreme Court is in developing the position of the individual vis-à-vis the pluralistic social groups of American society. To some extent, the tendency has already begun. We have seen in Chapter Four, for example, a few scattered decisions that may be read as applying constitutional norms to corporations. Labor unions, too, may well come within the ambit of the Court's decrees.* Yet to be worked out in constitutional theory is the constitutional position of the decentralized power centers of the American polity. It is possible that the Court will find increased opportunity to make decisions that will have the effect at once of protecting individuals against group activity and of producing a theory of the group in the social structure. The extent to which this will take place cannot be predicted. Suffice it for present purposes to say that the dimension of private governments may well be recognized and that, as with public government, the Supreme Court will make decisions when individuals are adversely affected by either form of government.†

---

*For discussion, see Arthur Selwyn Miller, "The Constitutional Law of the 'Security State,'" *Stanford Law Review*, X (1958), 620.
†See Arthur Selwyn Miller, *Private Governments and the Constitution* (New York: Fund for the Republic Occasional Paper, 1959).

EVALUATION AND PROGNOSIS

More than three decades ago, in a book prophetically entitled *The Twilight of the Supreme Court,* Professor Edward S. Corwin reached this conclusion:

> The success of the spending power [of the national government] in eluding all constitutional snares, goes far to envelop the entire institution of judicial review, as well as its product, constitutional law, in an atmosphere of unreality, even of futility. With the national government today in possession of the power to expend the social product for any purposes that may seem good to it; the power to make itself the universal and exclusive creditor of private business, with all that this would imply of control; the power to inflate the currency to any extent; the power to go into any business whatsoever, what becomes of judicial review conceived as a system for throwing about the property right a special protection "against the mere power of numbers" and for perpetuating a certain type of industrial organization?
>
> Nor can the reflection be avoided . . . that if government had been able to regulate private business without having its efforts constantly frustrated by the courts in the name of "due process," the "federal equilibrium," or what not, it might not today be under the compulsion to supersede private enterprise directly. In short, having gone in for political democracy, it might have been as well if we had courageously faced the logical consequences of our choice from the outset, instead of trying "to cover the bet" by resigning the ultimate voice as to matters of vital social import to the consciences of nine estimable elderly gentlemen. Today, willy-nilly, we have to face these consequences, and we are ill-equipped in important respects to do so.*

Professor Corwin meant that the Court would decline in importance and governmental significance because it no longer would be pre-eminent in economic-policy matters. He did not foresee the burst of activity of the Court over which Chief Justice Earl Warren presides. There is a lesson here. One is well advised not to be overly confident in

---

*Edward S. Corwin, *The Twilight of the Supreme Court* (New Haven, Conn.: Yale University Press, 1934), p. 179.

his predictions about the court or official decisions or which institutions will make them. Corwin was as astute a constitutional scholar as this nation has produced, but his crystal ball was cloudy a bare three decades ago. Why he erred is itself a fascinating question; that he did err is sobering and chastening. He did not make a mistake, of course, about the economic powers of government; as seen in Chapter Three, these are now sufficient to the need and the "nine elderly gentlemen" no longer have the "ultimate voice."

In any event, it seems possible to venture a few suggestions about the future of the Supreme Court. What follows is built around the following proposition: *The Court will diminish in power and importance unless certain improvements are made in its method of operation.* These include: (1) the flow of information to the Court; (2) the expertise or competence of the Justices, including institutional aids that may be given them; and (3) alterations in the adversary system of constitutional adjudication. Each will be briefly discussed. The proposition about the diminution of Court power is based on two factual assumptions: that the complexity of human problems will increase, rather than decrease, and that the center of gravity for government will continue to be in the executive-administrative branch. These have been discussed above (Chapter Three) and will not be further mentioned here. One conclusion that will be drawn is this: No one should be sanguine about the likelihood of the High Bench making necessary and desirable changes to improve its methodology; if a prediction had to be made, it would be that the Court will continue in its time-honored manner, making some incremental alterations, and that it will dwindle into an essentially impotent organ of government. The effectiveness of the Court as a power in government—and it should be again iterated for emphasis that no one knows just how powerful the Court is or has been—may well depend on such institutional changes as the following; these of course overlap—the first and second are really preliminary to the third—but they are listed separately.

Improvement in the flow of information to the Court: One of the more persistent of the myths that eddy about the Court is that it is to be equated with any other court of law. Two students of the Court, for example, have asserted that the judicial process in constitutional litigation "is but a specific instance of the judicial process," and that the Supreme Court is not different from other courts.* This at best is a dubious proposition. Although it is true that the Justices of the Supreme Court have been raised in the common-law and case-law system, it is also true that the cases they decide concern far more than the routine disputes of *meum* and *tuum* as are handled by, say, the Supreme Court of Missouri. In discussing the Supreme Court, we should never forget that it is a Constitution the Justices are expounding, a Constitution designed to endure for the ages to come, a Constitution that, in Woodrow Wilson's language, is not "a mere lawyers' document" but the "vehicle of the nation's life."†

Parallel to the idea that the Supreme Court is no different from any other court is what may be called the "declaratory" theory of law, often attributed to Blackstone. Under this theory, it is the function of the judge to find the law and then to apply it impartially and without any evaluation of the consequences of alternative decisions. Such a view has long been exploded; the task of the judge is not to be a human automaton rigidly applying the one rule or principle to the facts of a given case. Rather, he must be aware of the consequences of his decisions, however much he may try to avoid such an inquiry and however much it may go against the conventional wisdom. In other words, he must look forward—to the possible effects of alternative decisions as well as backward—to antecedent principle. Oliver Wendell Holmes, soon to be appointed to a seat on the Supreme Court, put the matter in this manner in 1897: "I think that the judges themselves have failed adequately to

---

*Jacob D. Hyman and Wade D. Newhouse, "Standards for Preferred Freedoms: Beyond the First," *Northwestern University Law Review,* LX (1965), 1, 41-4.

†Wilson, *Constitutional Government in the United States,* p. 157.

recognize their duty of weighing considerations of social advantage. The duty is inevitable, and the result of the often proclaimed judicial aversion to deal with such considerations is simply to leave the very ground and foundation of judgments inarticulate, and often unconscious. . . ."*

If judges unavoidably must be forward-looking as much as they search for existing doctrine, then the way in which the judicial mind is informed becomes a matter of critical import. Under the prevailing orthodox theory, the flow of information to the Court is by briefs and argument of counsel, the record of the trial court, and the amorphous concept of "judicial notice," under which a judge, as the saying often goes, may take notice of things of common knowledge as well as certain other noncontroversial matters. But what orthodoxy proclaims seems to be far from the fact, for the Justices at times roam far afield to seize upon knowledge (facts or arguments) that will help them reach a conclusion. Thus, as Justice William O. Douglas has said, the problems with which the Court deals are "delicate and imponderable, complex and tangled. They require at times the economist's understanding, the poet's insight, the executive's experience, the political scientist's understanding, the historian's perspective."† Certain it is that more than the orthodox methods of getting information to the Justices must be employed if they are to perform their delicate and complex duties. This has a dual aspect. In the first place, the Justices themselves require more reliable data on which to base their decisions; secondly, some means must be provided for adversaries to know about and counter information from outside the record. Both facets must be analyzed in any comprehensive discussion.

Here, however, the question may merely be raised, not

---

*Oliver Wendell Holmes, "The Path of the Law," *Harvard Law Review*, X (1897), 457, 467-8. As Dr. Judith Shklar has pointed out, judges look upon such matters as "frightful occasions" and try as much as possible to avoid performing their inevitable norm-setting function. (Judith Shklar, *Legalism* [Cambridge, Mass.: Harvard University Press, 1964], pp. 101-2.)
†Douglas, pp. 401, 414.

analyzed and not answered. It is an unresolved problem, as
witness the following statements of contemporary Justices,
the former by the late Felix Frankfurter and the latter by
William Brennan:

> Can we not take judicial notice of writing by people who
> competently deal with these problems? Can I not take
> judicial notice of Myrdal's book without having him called
> as a witness? . . . How to inform the judicial mind, as you
> know, is one of the most complicated problems. It is better
> to have witnesses, but I did not know that we could not
> read the works of competent writers.

* * *

> The briefs of counsel are always helpful, but each of us is
> better satisfied when he not only checks but also supple-
> ments those materials with independent research.*

As the problems coming before the Court become, in many
respects, ever more complicated, it is vitally necessary that
improved means of informing the judicial mind be de-
vised. If the Court is ever to achieve—or regain—a meaningful role in economic-policy matters, whether by statutory
interpretation or constitutional adjudication, it must have
some institutional method by which it can become privy
to the esoterica of economics and politics. It must, in short,
improve the flow of information to the bench.†

One should not be optimistic that this will be done. The
Court has not been quick to reform its procedure to take
care of the impact of public law on the legal system. Rather,
it has been content to proceed on basically the same lines
that it always has, using the same institutions and methods,

---

*Felix Frankfurter, quoted from oral argument in Walter F. Murphy and
Herman Pritchett, *Courts, Judges, and Politics* (New York: Random House,
1961), p. 318; William Brennan, quoted in Alan Westin (ed.), *An Auto-
biography of the Supreme Court* (New York: The Macmillan Co., 1963), p.
303.

†See Mark S. Massel, "Economic Analysis in Judicial Antitrust Decisions,"
American Bar Association Section of Antitrust Law Bulletin, XX (1962), 46;
Dean Alfange, Jr., "The Relevance of Legislative Facts in Constitutional
Law," *University of Pennsylvania Law Review*, CXIV (1966), 637; Francis
Wormuth, "The Impact of Economic Legislation upon the Supreme Court,"
Journal of Public Law, VI (1957), 296.

with little or no change. This may have been satisfactory, for the nineteenth century, but it is hardly adequate for the needs of the modern era. The problems, particularly in the government-business relationship that is the subject of so much administrative law and that makes up about 40 per cent of the Court's annual workload, are simply too complicated to retain ancient methods. It is for this reason—the lack of information—as well as the lack of expertise, that has led the Court in recent years to defer so much to the political branches of government. The tendency is likely to continue, particularly in economic-policy matters. The decisions discussed in this chapter may well be an aberration or a last gasp of an organ of government vainly seeking to regain lost powers.

The competence of the Justices: The point about information becomes clearer when viewed from another perspective: the comparative competence of judge and administrator to deal with the continuing problems of the public administration. When Congress established the Positive State, it did so by way of delegations of power to the agencies, accompanied (often, but far from always) by a provision for judicial review of administrative decisions. This meant, among other things, that the Supreme Court had to face up to the question of how far it would substitute its judgment for that of the agency officials. One answer was given quite early. In a decision that dealt with review of state administrative proceedings but that had a larger significance, the Court in 1941 reached the conclusion that its inquiry by and large would look to the *procedure* by which agency decisions were reached and would not substitute judgment on the substantive issue. In Railroad Commission *v.* Rowan & Nichols Oil Co., the Court, speaking through Mr. Justice Frankfurter, had before it the question of whether a "proration" of oil permitted by the Texas Railroad Commission to be produced violated the Constitution; Frankfurter "rejected a judicial judgment for the expert process invented by the state in a field so peculiarly dependent upon specialized

judgment." All procedural requirements having been satisfied, "sounder foundations are only to be achieved through
the fruitful empiricism of a continuous administrative process." And further: "On the basis of intrinsic skills and equip-
ment, . . . the federal courts [are not] qualified to set their
independent judgment on such matters against that of the
chosen state authorities." The administrative agency "presumably" possessed "an insight and aptitude which can
hardly be matched by judges who are called upon to intervene at fitful intervals."*

The case, accordingly, presents as clear an answer as the
Court has ever given to the question of comparative competence. Were it an isolated instance, it would merit little
attention. But it exemplifies a judicial attitude that reached
a peak in the 1940s and that has continued since then, although some effort to counteract it may be discerned. Noted
have been some examples of decisions in which the judiciary,
through expanding ideas of "standing" to bring actions for
review of administrative determinations, appears to be trying to regain some of the ground lost in the wholesale abdication of power in the 1940s. Its success is to be doubted, if for
no other reason than that the Court itself has actively fos-
tered inconsistent tendencies in other areas.

Of interest here, since it is largely confined to antitrust
and other economic-policy matters, is the so-called "primary
jurisdiction doctrine." Although this is not a doctrine governing judicial review, it nonetheless involves the relative
positions of court and agency; it is concerned with priority
of decision-making. A creation of the Supreme Court, primary jurisdiction means that, if both a court and an administrative agency seem to have jurisdiction over a particular
controversy, the court will say that the agency should make
the initial determination.† However, the question of comparative competence or expertise transcends the primary

---

*311 U.S. 570 (1941).
†For a brief discussion, see Kenneth Culp Davis, *Administrative Law* (St.
Paul, Minn.: West Publishing Co., 1959), chap. xix.

jurisdiction doctrine; it runs through many cases involving judicial review of administrative action, either outwardly (as in the Rowan & Nichols Case) or implicitly. The author of the leading treatise on administrative law, Professor Kenneth Culp Davis, has concluded that, "the Supreme Court sometimes substitutes judgment and sometimes refuses substitution of judgment."* He has found the discretion exercised by a reviewing court to be influenced by many inarticulate factors and concludes that the most important in guiding that discretion is the comparative qualification of court and agency to decide the particular issue—as determined, of course, by the court. "Courts are experts in such areas as constitutional law, common law, ethics, overall philosophy of law and government, judge-made law developed through statutory interpretation, most analysis of legislative history, and problems transcending the agency's field."† Although Professor Davis does not have a functional breakdown of the types of issues in which administrators have the final word and those in which the courts will substitute judgment, it does seem fair to say that the more complicated or novel the question the more likely the Court is to defer to the purportedly greater expertise of the administrator. Here again, as Justice Frankfurter said in Rowan & Nichols, the "fruitful empiricism of a continuous administrative process" is apt to prevail over a judiciary institutionally able only "to intervene at fitful intervals."

Given the self-admitted declaration of lack of expertise to deal with many of the complex issues of the Positive State, the question that arises is whether by some means the capability of the judiciary could be enhanced. Are there techniques that would at once provide a more adequate flow of information to the Supreme Court and enable the Justices to be more confident in approaching the issues thrown before them for decision? Although some suggestions in this vein have been made, the short answer to that question

---

*Davis, sec. 30.14.
†Davis, sec. 30.14.

appears to be negative. Such suggestions include: (1) providing panels of experts in economics to assist the Justices in making economic decisions—antitrust, for example; and (2) replacing the present system of law clerks drawn from new graduates of the law schools with lawyers including law professors, who have had at least ten years of experience. Neither seems particularly promising. The former would merely add another group of experts to those allegedly already available in the public administration; the notorious differences of opinion among experts, including economists, would do little to enlighten and possibly much to confuse the Justices. As to the latter, it seems more useful, but could be risky. There has been considerable talk already about the influence law clerks are alleged to have on decisions. For a Justice to take a more mature lawyer as his assistant would give him the benefit of additional experience; on the other hand, it could be pointed to as a system by which each member of the Court had an *eminence grise* behind him—not a pleasant prospect. In any event, there seems to be no discernible movement toward changing the present system. The conclusion, in net, must be that the Court will continue to be manned by lawyers whose expertise outside (sometimes, inside) of law may be expected to be minimal—accidental at best.

The changing nature of the adversary system: If the flow of data to the Court and the very competence of the Justices may, thus, be questioned, this should not be taken to mean that slow changes are not taking place. Indeed they are and in the adversary system itself. That system, borrowed from a feudalistic, private-law oriented legal edifice, is a poor vehicle at best for permitting grave issues of public policy to be debated. Perhaps because of the burgeoning of the law schools, which now means that most lawyers are graduates from some law school, there is increased attention being paid to the methodology of the Justices. Political scientists, too, have pioneered in this inquiry. Furthermore, the use of recent law graduates as clerks means that the Justices are furnished with some of the best new talent the legal profession can boast. Most of the Supreme Court clerks come from law schools whose faculties are manned by people with brilliant legal minds. All of this adds up to new ways in which opinions are written. More and more, for example, articles in legal periodicals are cited in the footnotes of Court opinions. To some immeasurable extent, thus, one of the inputs of the constitutional adjudicatory system is what is written in professional journals.

Another input is an expanded use of briefs *amici curiae,* sometimes at the request of the Court, when special need for argument from other than one of the adversaries is desired, but more often on request from some party (usually a group) that wishes to have its interests heard by the Court. In either instance, it is discretionary with the Court to permit filing of such briefs. In recent years, the tendency has been to allow briefs much more often than formerly. This has not come by any announced policy shift by the Justices, but is a fair conclusion from the number of briefs now being accepted from parties other than the actual adversaries.* This at once increases the flow of information to the Court and is illustrative of what seems to be at least a partial breakdown of the adversary system. For acceptance of briefs from non-adversaries means, in effect, that it is recognized that the importance of Supreme Court cases often transcends the immediate litigants. The litigants, in constitutional cases, have a limited function to perform: to get a case to the Supreme Court. The Justices must await some proper case before issuing opinions; they cannot reach out and seize upon issues simply because there might be portentous public-policy questions involved. (And they may at times refuse to rule on certain matters, even though proper parties are before the Court, simply because the time is apparently not propitious. For example, there was a consistent failure for many years to rule on the validity of miscegenation laws,

---

*See Samuel Krislov, "The Amicus Curiae Brief: From Friendship to Advocacy," *Yale Law Journal,* LXXII (1963), 717.

even though ample opportunities have been afforded the Court to do so. The Court finally did so in 1967.)

The Supreme Court operates with pomp and ceremony. Prescribed ritual is all important. One strays outside of the ritual at his peril. Louis Dembitz Brandeis, as lawyer, was successful in making such a foray when he introduced the Brandeis Brief in Muller *v.* Oregon (1908).* But behind the facade are nine men who operate, as Justice Robert H. Jackson said, "less as one deliberative body than as nine. . . ." As a result, the Court's working methods "tend to cultivate a highly individualistic rather than a group viewpoint."† This may be seen in the tendency of the Justices in important cases to issue multiple opinions—the opinion for the Court, concurring opinions, and dissenting opinions. It may also be seen in the different ways that the Judges approach their high function. There is no prescribed methodology for them to follow, although institutional norms and habits do circumscribe their freedom of operation to some extent. As a result, the Court is splintered in important areas between activists and self-restrainers, to take one classification. But of more basic importance, the members of the High Bench view their tasks in differing ways. As recently as 1936, Justice Owen J. Roberts could state that the task of the Court, when a statute was challenged, was to lay the statute against the Constitution, to see if the former squared with the latter. (That was as simplistic a view of constitutional adjudication as has ever been taken.)

Whatever the individual idiosyncracies of the Justices may be, it does seem clear that the orthodox views of the adversary system are not adhered to. Information is garnered from wherever a Justice may find it—and according to his personal standards of relevance. The parties who bring the suit—the individual litigants—are important only because they trigger the judiciary into action. Once they have

---

*208 U.S. 412 (1908).

†Robert H. Jackson, *The Supreme Court in the American System of Government* (Cambridge, Mass.: Harvard University Press, 1955), p. 16.

done that, any constitutional case transcends the litigants in importance. (Cases are decided by the Court because of the importance of the issues, not of the litigants who bring them.)

IN SUMMATION

The Supreme Court assumed its role of constitutional lawmaker nearly two centuries ago. Since the time when Chief Justice John Marshall seized upon an otherwise unimportant case* to enunciate the principle of judicial review of the actions of other parts of the government, the Court has experienced many ups and downs. Until the Civil War, its economic decisions for the most part concerned what state governments could do. In the next period, from the end of the Civil War to the middle 1930s, it considered both federal and state actions. This was the heyday of economic due process and the time in which the country came closest to having judicial government. Ultimate policy was formally enunciated by the nine Justices, often by only five of them—for the Court was bitterly divided. The cases decided during that period were those that reflected the first responses of government to the industrialization of the nation. Although more active than in the early nineteenth century, government was relatively small and relatively weak. The situation, as we have seen, abruptly changed in the 1930s; and with the rise of a new posture of government—the Positive State —came the end of economic due process. The Court found a new role in the issues of civil rights and civil liberties that has plummeted it into the center of new controversy during the past score of years. The question that is now beginning to obtrude is this: Where does the Court go next? What role will it take on?

The answer given here, admittedly tentative and subject to all of the uncertainties of prediction in an age of rapid social change, is that the High Bench is diminishing

---

Marbury v. *Madison,* 1 Cranch 137 (1803).

in power and importance. If the process has not already
set in, it soon will. No longer will political problems be cast
before the Court for resolution; de Tocqueville's assertion
is even today at best a half-truth. Public policy issues of the
most profound and portentous import are increasingly by-
passing the Court and being dealt with by the avowedly political branches of government. Not only war and peace, which
have always been little litigated, but such important questions as monetary and fiscal policy—of economic planning—
do not come before the judiciary. The Supreme Court, in
short, is a nineteenth-century institution that, at the seeming
height of its powers, already is declining into desuetude.
Speaking colloquially, it is running out of (constitutional)
gas.

Of course, it will not disappear overnight. We will continue to witness judicial decision-making in constitutional
matters. But the sweep and tide of affairs is gradually—and
surely—sweeping it aside. The accident of litigation cannot
be depended on to set public policy. Needed is the continuing scrutiny of those who can both adjudicate present-day
disputes and plan for the exigencies of the future. Needed, in
other words, is a full realization that this is indeed the age
of administration, that the bureaucracy is firmly in command, and that command is shared with political leaders,
not with the judiciary. Lawyers probably will continue to
act as if the courts were central to the legal system, something that has not been true for decades. Courts will continue
to act—the Supreme Court may well continue to be the
most prestigious of governmental institutions—but the signs
are clear and unmistakable. Speaking again sententiously,
America's unique contribution to the art of government—
judicial review—is on the verge of becoming a historical od-
dity. Ironically, the development comes at the very time
when there is more recognition that courts can and do make
policy than at any time in history. By the year 2000, there
will be little policy of any importance still entrusted to the
judiciary. That is already true for the issues involving Ameri-

can capitalism; it will also be true for other areas of public importance.

In making such statements, it is recognized that they run counter to what most commentators and observers of the Supreme Court believe. Only time will prove which position is correct. However, past history seems to reveal at least this: that during the nearly two centuries of constitutional adjudication, it is difficult, even impossible, to locate one instance where the Court has been able to do more than postpone what a determined people or legislative majorities wanted. Sometimes the avenue taken was constitutional amendment (for example, the Eleventh and Sixteenth Amendments), but more often it was by the Court overruling or "distinguishing" prior decisions. In any event, neither the Constitution nor the Court has proved to be an insuperable barrier to what the American people wanted to do. Perhaps some of what they wanted to do has been pointed out by Court decisions, as when the judiciary has acted as a national conscience and erected standards for social improvement. In characteristically luminous prose, the late Professor Edmond Cahn put apt expression to the concept of judicial review in these terms:

> *Marbury* v. *Madison* has proved to be one of those very special occurrences that mark an epoch in the life of the republic. Culminating the great achievements of the Constitutional Period, it accomplished the transition from perpetuity to efficacy, from immutability to adaptation, and from heavenly to judicial sanctions. Finally, it introduced an unending colloquy between the Supreme Court and the people of the United States, in which the Court continually asserts, "You live under a Constitution but the Constitution is what *we* say it is," and the people incessantly reply, "As long as your version of the Constitution enables us to live with pride in what we consider a free and just society, you may continue exercising this august, awesome, and altogether revocable authority.*

---

*Edmond Cahn, "An American Contribution," in Edmond Cahn (ed.), *Supreme Court and Supreme Law* (Bloomington: Indiana University Press, 1954), p. 25.

It is not suggested that Professor Cahn would agree with the idea of the desuetude of the Supreme Court. (Nor does one have to agree entirely with him.) What he is saying is that the Court, to be able to operate, must articulate the deep-felt aspirations of the American people. We take that position one step further and maintain that the American, a political animal living in a scientific-technological age, will not much longer cast burning issues of public policy before the nine Delphic oracles in the Marble Palace. What is already true of the judiciary and American capitalism will, it is forecast, become true of other areas of social importance.

In saying all of this, it is recognized that the Court during Chief Justice Earl Warren's tenure (since 1953) has been running on all cylinders and not "running out of gas," as suggested above. The Warren Court has been the most activist in history; more constitutional law has been created during the past two decades than during any comparable period in American history. In ethnic relations, church and state, legislative apportionment, and criminal-law matters, the Court has made major doctrinal breakthroughs. The point, however, is not so much that of what it has done as what it can do in the future. Other than the areas suggested above, it is difficult to discern further doctrinal forays the Court might take—if it were of such a mind, which is by no means certain. For that matter, it is far from certain that the High Bench can do anything substantial in those three areas. Those who dispute the coming desuetude of the Supreme Court must suggest problems of constitutional concern that are both ready and appropriate for settlement by that institution.*

---

*See Miller and Scheflin, "The Power of the Supreme Court in the Age of the Positive State."

Epilogue

The imaginative creation of new institutions and relations between governments and private groups is a critical need of our time*

Some strands of thought set out in the foregoing chapters may now be drawn together. We take as our theme in this concluding chapter both Professor Blough's statement reproduced above and Eric Hoffer's recent aphorism: "The business of a society with an automated economy can no longer be business."† During the two centuries since the Declaration of Independence, there has been one principal constant in American economic life: change, of a nature and character that makes the nation of today fundamentally different from that of the late eighteenth century. Change is not only built into the social structure; it is accelerating. The impact of the scientific-technological revolution means that even more rapid social and legal change may be foreseen in the future.

One consequence of the development is what Dean Don K. Price has called "constitutional relativity":

> Science, by helping technology to increase prosperity, has weakened the kind of radicalism that comes from a lack of economic security. But science has helped to prdouce other kinds of insecurity: the fear of the new kind of war that science has made possible; the fear of rapid social and economic change; and the fear that we no longer have a fixed and stable constitutional system by which to cope with our political problems. And these fears are breeding a new type of radicalism.
>
> The new radicalism is ostensibly conservative. It springs in part from the resentment men feel when their

---

*Professor Roy Blough of Columbia University, quoted in Victor Obenhaus, *Ethics for an Industrial Age* (New York: Harper & Row, 1965), p. 184.

†Eric Hoffer, *The Temper of Our Time* (New York: Harper & Row, 1966), p. 32.

basic view of life is unsettled—as medieval man must have felt when he was asked to think of a universe that did not revolve around the earth, or as some physicists felt a generation or two ago when their colleagues began to talk about relativity and indeterminacy. The new conservative radicalism had a fundamentalist faith in the written Constitution, and the high priests of that faith seem to have desecrated it. The Supreme Court has applied relative policy standards in place of the fixed rules of precedent; and worse still it has admitted into its system of thinking not only the moral law as revealed in tradition, but arguments from the sciences, even the behavioral sciences.*

The Constitution does not embody absolutes. In any clause that is the subject of litigation, constitutional relativity is the rule, whether it be in personal liberties, such as freedom of speech, or whether it be in economic liberties, such as due process of law. Decisions on constitutional matters are made either by according a high degree of deference to the political branches of government (as in economics) or by balancing the interests between individual and society (as in personal freedoms).

Dean Price's observation about constitutional relativity is drawn from a book that develops the impact of the scientific-technological revolution on the constitutional order. One such impact is affirmation of a proposition advanced by others—for example, Adolf A. Berle and Paul P. Harbrecht— that traditional ideas of property are in need of redefinition. Price makes this acute statement:

> The most fundamental disagreement between the nations of the Western political tradition and those of the Communist world does not turn on their attitudes toward private property. The greatest mistake in Western political strategy consists in committing itself to the defense of property as the main basis for the preservation of freedom. Private property is indeed a useful and important means to that end, but it is not an absolute end in itself, and the effect of scientific advance on a technological civilization

*Price, p. 163.

has made property less and less important as a source of
power, and as a way of limiting political power. Far more
fundamental is the way men think about the desirability
of organizing truth in the service of power, and using
power to determine truth.*

New institutional forms are being created; property as the
basis of both political *and* economic power is being redefined.
Ownership of things is less important than ownership of
promises (such as shares of stock); and both are less important
than the ability to control the gigantic entities of the modern
American economy. Control lies with the corporate managers, who in many respects are self-perpetuating oligarchies
wielding immense economic (and political) power.†

Even more, power in a political sense may well be
passing to other centers: To take two noteworthy illustrations, the scientific-technological elite—what Dean Price labels
the "scientific estate"—and those who control the universities and other "nonprofits" in what Professor Daniel Bell
has called the "post-industrial society." Says Bell: "To
speak rashly: if the dominant figures of the past hundred
years [in American society] have been the entrepreneur, the
businessman, and the industrial executive, the 'new men'
are the scientists, the mathematicians, the economists, and
the engineers of the new computer technology."‡ The shorthand term for the new man of power is "technocrat" and
for the social system that of "technocracy." Both terms are
not new; according to Bell, they were coined in 1919. During the 1930s, technocracy had a brief flurry as a social
movement and as a panacea for the depression. With the
coming of the Second World War, it became moribund. Its
revival in the present era takes a different form and is not
tied in with a social or political movement, as was technocracy in the 1930s. Rather, it may be seen in the rise of possible new centers of decentralized power within the body

---

*Price, 161-2.

†See Berle, *Power Without Property*.

‡Daniel Bell, "Notes on the Post-Industrial Society," *The Public Interest*,
No. 6 (Winter, 1967), 24.

politic; Bell identifies these as the universities and other nonprofit institutions, such as research corporations, industrial laboratories, and experimental stations. If this description proves valid, then the post-industrial society—technocracy—will, in large part, be the resultant, as Dean Price avers, of the scientific-technological revolution. More, it will be closely allied with the government-business complex. We suggested above (Chapters Three and Four) that a form of economic planning was coming into existence, the institutions of which were given the shorthand label of "the corporate state." The direction in which American society may well be moving, then, is toward the corporate state, the governing elite of which is a corps of technocrats (as defined above) rather than businessmen or political officers. Time only will tell whether this tendency, already evident, will become a fact—whether, that is, the forces of science and technology and the pressures from living in an interdependent world will produce such a radically new social order.

To the extent that such a social order does come into being, then one with an eye to history can well cast back to the early 1930s in order to show that two notions then current are ideas "whose time has come." These are the governmental attempt in 1933 to establish a form of the corporate state in the National Industrial Recovery Act (discussed in Chapter Four) and the social movement called technocracy. As has been seen, the attempt to graft the corporate state on the American economy fell before the Supreme Court, which invalidated it in 1935;* and technocracy died out with the coming of the war. Both were premature in the 1930s, but they seem now to be flowering (without, however, the same labels). The result likely will be a fusion of corporativism and technocracy. If so, it may be said without fear of contradiction that the Supreme Court is emphatically not

---

*Not, be it said, because it was a form of corporativism, but on technical grounds. See *Schechter Poultry Corp.* v. *United States,* 295 U.S. 495 (1935) and *Panama Refining Co.* v. *Ryan,* 293 U.S. 388 (1935).

going to invalidate the new system. Rather, it will content
itself at most with hit-and-miss review of individual acts of
parts of the techno-corporate complex. This should occasion
no surprise, for certain it is that the Justices have neither the
desire nor—more importantly—the competence to deal with
the complex issues presented therein. The nature of the
American political economy of the future, in other words,
will be little dependent on what the nine middle-aged or
elderly men who sit on the highest tribunal might say
about it.

The other side of that coin is that the governmental decisions of basic significance for the economy will come from
the avowedly political branches of government, and from
them, mainly the executive-administrative agencies. During
the course of American history, a steady tendency may be
perceived in the growing intervention of government in
decisions previously thought to be private. The state has
become an important and pervasive participant in economic
matters. The American economy, as a consequence, is well on
its way toward becoming managed. Governmental decisions
to spend, to tax, to regulate currency, and to do a host of
other economic matters, will become far more important
than sporadic judicial decisions issued by a Court that must
depend on the *bona fides* of others to put its commands into
reality and that must depend on the accident of litigation to
act at all.

In saying this, however, it is not implied that government is autonomous—that the elites of the private corporations and the institutions of the post-industrial society do not
and will not have a great influence on the nature of official
decision-making. Quite the contrary. In all probability, decisions will be a product of a mixture of law and politics—of
pre-existing command or interdictory rule and of the accommodation of conflicting interests in the political arena.* This
means that the question to ask is not only, Who has *formal*

*For recent discussion of some of this, see William L. Cary, *Politics and the
Regulatory Agencies* (New York: McGraw-Hill Book Co., Inc., 1967).

authority to make economic decisions in government? but rather, Who exercises *effective control* over those decisions? When one probes beneath the surface, it is soon apparent that the decisions of governmental agencies—of the political branches generally—are the result of a parallelogram of conflicting political forces. Even in the ostensibly independent regulatory commissions, decision-making is a marriage of politics and law. Accordingly, the desuetude of the Supreme Court does not necessarily mean the pre-eminent power of the bureaucracy or of Congress; rather, it means a complex interaction of power wielders in the techno-corporate state.* The content of decisions, in other words, is influenced by the actions of private groups in the polity. The government official has the *authority* to make the decisions, that is, he is clothed with the formal capacity to decide, but what is decided is not necessarily, or even usually, within his control. Effective *power* over decisions, that is to say, often lies elsewhere.

Whatever may be the situation, then, with respect to other issues of public policy—and it is by no means clear that the pattern is essentially different in those other areas—within the field of economic decisions, the United States Supreme Court has little or no real *power*. It may be clothed with some *authority*, but what its impact might be is quite another matter. The suggestion made here is that the impact is minimal at most, and probably even less, as the United States ever increasingly becomes the techno-corporate state.

Another factor to be emphasized is that old lines of political and economic demarcation are breaking down. At one time, perhaps, it was possible for students of government and of society to make credible distinctions between what was in the public sector and what was consigned to private initiative and to say that policy problems could be divided between foreign and domestic. If so, that state of affairs no

---

*For insightful discussion, see Truman, *The Governmental Process;* and John Kenneth Galbraith, *The New Industrial State* (Boston: Houghton Mifflin Co., 1967).

longer is true: America has moved beyond that to a new order, one in which the public and private sectors are inextricably intertwined* and in which the line between external and internal is increasingly being blurred. The old order is gone, irretrievably; a new order is being created; the age is one of transition, beset, as never before in human history, with changes of the most far-reaching nature. In its most fundamental aspect, the problem facing policy makers is that of managing change—something rather new for Americans. As Daniel Bell has said, "Perhaps the most important social change of our time is the emergence of a process of direct and deliberate contrivance of change itself. Men now seek to anticipate change, measure the course of its direction and its impact, control it, and even shape it for predetermined ends."† Within the United States, this has produced the interlocking of public government and private corporation, aided and abetted by the universities and other segments of the third sector of the economy.‡ A continuum may be constructed, in this respect, running from the corporations (such as the major weapons producers) that are obviously closely allied to government to those (such as A.T. & T.) that have only a minor part of their overall income coming from government. At both ends of the continuum, and also in between, may be seen a growing partnership between government and business, a partnership widely recognized by corporate managers. Witness, for example, this statement by a prominent business executive: "Since the early part of this century we have been developing a new form of public-private society. . . . Call it what you will, the fact remains that this kind of government is here to stay, and those who would accomplish almost anything of public interest must work with the government. I say work 'with' it, not 'for' it."§ The

---

*See Nieburg, *In the Name of Science.*
†Bell, p. 25.
‡See Ginzberg, *et. al., The Pluralistic Economy.*
§Melvin H. Baker, Chairman of the Board of the National Gypsum Company and a Vice-President of the National Association of Manufacturers, quoted in *Christian Science Monitor,* July 2, 1959, p. 10.

essential point is that certain societal demands exist, which must and will be fulfilled, if not by business then by government. More likely, these demands—mainly those for higher material levels of well-being—will be realized, if at all, through a partnership of government and business. (What this means, among other things, is that individualism is dead; this will be discussed shortly.)

The same sort of blurring may be seen in the fact that public-policy problems tend to have both external and internal—foreign and domestic—characteristics. In a statement that encompasses both dimensions presently under discussion, Arnold Toynbee in 1959 asserted: "The businessman of the future . . . will be one of the key figures in a world civil service." By this, Dr. Toynbee apparently meant that business and government would grow closer together, while simultaneously transcending national boundaries. If this forecast be accurate, then some sort of corporativism seems to be in the offing.

In sum, then, the nation-state and the corporation—the twin institutions of the postfeudal and early industrial era—are in the process of profound alteration; they are breaking up and moving closer together. What the ultimate form will be cannot be predicted with certainty. What can be said, however, is that the sharp separation between government and business, once so evident in the United States, will be increasingly blurred. The demands of the American people, articulated through government in what has above been called the Positive State, finds a counterpart in the principle of the social responsibility of business. The two institutions are partners. More, the problems of economic, and political, order now are planetary, not national. The government-business partnership will more and more have to face up to that hard fact.

Finally, it must be said that the American ideal of individualism is dead. Although the autonomous man has long been the democratic hero, it is nevertheless true that the core of industrialization, and thus of modern capitalism, is not independence, but interdependence. The autonomous individual does not exist as such; the human being spends his life as a member of groups and gets his significance only as a member of a group. He is important in the economic sense only insofar as he can become part of a collectivity—a corporation, a trade union, a farm group, a consumers cooperative, and the like. As Professor John William Ward has said in a perceptive essay, "Our society, like all modern industrial societies, is characterized by economic and social interdependence, specialization of activity, and large-scale organizations—social phenomena that pose troublesome problems for traditional American attitudes toward the relation of the individual to society."* It is a paradoxical fact that, whereas the Supreme Court in recent decades has been busily engaged in seeking to maximize individual liberties—in effect, through a merger of the concepts of liberty and equality—the growth of economic enterprise has created a social milieu in which individual liberties or freedoms are not high on the list of preferred values. Uniformity cultivated through mass advertising and astute use of the mass media is a requirement of industrialism. In the final analysis, furthermore, Americans, according to Professor William Withers, are "more wedded to materialism than to individualism"; where they have had a choice, or could make conscious decisions, "they chose the solution that led to greater material satisfaction, even at the sacrifice of individual freedom."†

Thus it is that the recent Supreme Court decisions that appear to enhance the liberty and dignity of the individual came at precisely the time when on-rushing technology and industrial organization make the realization of those values unlikely at best, impossible in all probability. The technological imperatives demand social organization and social control; these organizations are both public and private, and

---

*John William Ward, "The Ideal of Individualism and the Reality of Organization," in Earl F. Cheit (ed.), *The Business Establishment* (New York: John Wiley & Sons, Inc., 1964), p. 37.
†Withers, p. 8.

the controls emanate from both sources. The Court is a weak reed indeed on which to rely to further a vanished individualism—even if it could be convincingly demonstrated that people generally wanted that sort of society, by no means a self-evident proposition. Erich Fromm's *Escape from Freedom,* although written about the Europe of the 1930s, seems particularly apposite. The clear lesson to be drawn is not that people want freedom or that the Supreme Court can force them to be free, but that they want material prosperity —and are quite willing to pay the price of organization and control to achieve it.*

In the final analysis, the impact of the Supreme Court on the nature and thrust of the American economy will be, in the immortal words of Senator Everett McKinley Dirksen, about like that of "a snowflake wafting down upon the bosom of the mighty Potomac." Even if one assumes (without hard evidence) that the decisions of the Court have had importance in the past, the economics of the future will be determined by other factors—by the actions of government generally, which in turn will reflect the exigencies of the times. It simply does not seem possible that the American people—or American business—will permit nine men, with no special economic competence, to set fundamental policies in economic affairs. However wise the nine may be, the very nature of present litigation techniques and the adversary system is not adequate to the need of either the routine day-to-day decisions nor to the setting of fundamental policy.† Doubtless, decisions will emanate from the High Bench, but their total impact will be small indeed; they will be of importance to that segment of the legal profession, academic and practicing bar, that earns its livelihood following what the Court does. For others—those who live in the rarified

---

*See Roderick Seidenberg, *Anatomy of the Future* (Chapel Hill: University of North Carolina Press, 1961) and his earlier *Post-Historic Man* (Chapel Hill: University of North Carolina Press, 1950).

†See Mark S. Massel, "Economic Analysis in Judicial Antitrust Decisions," *Report of the Section of Antitrust Law of the American Bar Association,* XX (April, 1962), 46.

heights of big business and big government—what the Court might say will have less and less significance as the years go by. At the most, the Justices will be in the position, and have the same approximate power, as someone writing editorials about some of the issues of economic policy. (As discussed in Chapter Six, that conclusion may also prove valid for other areas of public policy.)

If the Court reorganized itself so as to permit a more adequate flow of information to it and to enhance its institutional capacity to grapple with the complicated factual issues present in economic-policy cases, then it might be possible to project a greater role for the Court in the future. But there is little evidence that such a reorganization can or will take place. The High Bench remains essentially static in the age of what economist Kenneth E. Boulding has called "the second great transition in the history of mankind."* Litigation—courts, generally—are products of a feudalistic, preindustrial age; even legislatures may be said to be in the same category. Beyond feudalism, beyond industrialism, is the technologically oriented society, manned by technocrats, governed by "rational" processes, and highly organized and bureaucratized—a situation in which the Supreme Court seems oddly out of place.

One need not—indeed, should not—welcome such a development. For it means that the United States has entered an era dominated by administration and by the expert. Humanistic values are being lost in the quest for efficiency. The individual is being submerged in a melange of collectivities, public and private, that interlock in a system of the "new feudalism." American capitalism is far different today from what it was in 1787, when the Constiution was written. (It is the conceit of lawyers that the Supreme Court has had a major part in effectuating those changes.) Capitalism will be different "tomorrow"—in the next two or three decades. Possible preservation of the values of individualism and even

---

*Kenneth E. Boulding, *The Meaning of the 20th Century* (New York: Harper & Row, 1965), p. 1.

perhaps of the dignity of the individual will depend on whether new institutions can be created; as Professor Blough said in the headnote to this chapter, there is a critical need for the "imaginative creation of new institutions and relations between governments and private groups." The need is critical simply because the factor of change—epidemic in society—means that time-honored ways of doing things are in need of re-examination and restructuring. Law and lawyers tend to react to change, rather than guiding or managing it, and thus seem to be fated always to be bringing up the rear. The legal profession, including the august Supreme Court of the United States, appears at times to be trying to preserve values—of individualism, of humanism—that, because of advancing technology and the organizational revolution, seem forever to be gone.

Those values are gone even though, as Victor Obenhaus has recently put it, two polar forces seem now to be in tension. On the one hand, are those that are freeing man from burdensome physical labor and thus creating a leisure society; and, on the other hand, is "the closer integration of society and the mutual dependence of men, intra- and internationally."* In the final analysis, the question of American capitalism is a question of the nature of man. The efforts of courts and even of governments to alter that nature, whatever it might be, seem feeble indeed. What does not seem feeble is the possibility of control over the individual by the collectivities produced through the organizational revolution. *That* not only appears possible; it seems to be probable. For the nature of man is to some indeterminate extent a resultant of the environment in which he lives. Man's technical resources have become enormous, but his social and psychological conflicts are far from resolved; they may in fact have been exacerbated in recent decades. War, overpopulation, excessive use of scarce resources, environmental pollution, mass hunger in the developing nations, economic and intellectual

---

*Victor Obenhaus, *Ethics for an Industrial Age* (New York: Harper & Row, 1965), p. 220.

stagnation that may appear with the achievements of the Positive State—all these and more add up to the nightmarish possibility of an Orwellian world of *1984* looming ever closer.* The economic institutions of the future may well be a part of George Orwell's prescient forecast of things to come.

Should this dreary prospect in fact come about, then it will likely be without major amendment or other alteration to the basic Constitution. Americans have learned well what Henry George long ago called "an axiom of statesmanship . . .—that great changes can be brought about under old forms." The words of the Constitution will remain the same, but techniques of interpretation that already have embedded concepts of relativity deeply and probably irretrievably will mean that new institutions can be produced within the framework of the Constitution of 1787 as interpreted not only by the Supreme Court, but also by other governmental officials. The exigencies of the future can be accommodated within that document.

---

*See Boulding, *The Meaning of the 20th Century.*

A Note on Further Reading

The primary source for what the Supreme Court has said about American capitalism is, of course, the cases in the several hundred volumes of the *United States Reports* (U.S.). These volumes are printed and sold by the government; when sufficient decisions and other data have emanated from the Court, a volume is published. (During the early years of American independence, Court opinions were issued under the name of the reporter rather than by number; later, these cases were reissued with the same pagination under *United States Reports.* Thus, for example, the case of Marbury *v.* Madison, decided in 1803, is cited as 5 U.S. (1 Cranch) 137—Cranch being the reporter for the Court.) So-called "slip" opinions are distributed to the press and other interested parties on the days that decisions are rendered. In addition to the government publication, two commercial publishers collect and index Supreme Court decisions; these are the *Supreme Court Reporter* (S.Ct.) (St. Paul, Minnesota: West Publishing Co.) and the *Lawyers' Edition* (L.Ed.) (Rochester, New York: Lawyers' Cooperative Publishing Co.). The latter is particularly valuable for its analytical notes of the decisions in terms of preceding decisions. Since all of these publishers are several months in arrears, so-called "advance sheets" are issued; however, these are also issued several weeks after a given decision. To keep up to date, consult the commercially published *United States Law Week* (Washington, D.C.: Bureau of National Affairs, Inc.), which makes the full opinions of the Court available with minimal delay.

The Table of Cases lists references to the official set of reported cases (U.S.) cited in the main portion of this volume and, in addition, those for the two other series, the *Supreme Court Reporter* (S.Ct.—does not cover earlier cases cited by the reporter for the court) and *Lawyers' Edition* (L.Ed.).

(The reader should note that three cases decided by lower federal courts are also listed; the citations to these are in the *Federal Reporter, Second Series* (F.2d) and *Federal Supplement* (F. Supp.), both of which are available in any law library.) If the reader has a law library available to him, he will usually find all three series of Supreme Court decisions; most college and public libraries acquire only one set. The two nonofficial publications provide considerably more analytical data for the student, particularly for linking one decision with others on the same subject, but all three contain exactly the same text of the decisions. One should be aware that the *United States Reports* is the only official publication and that the additional matter in the two commercial series has not been approved by the Supreme Court. For those who do not have any of the three series available, it may be possible to find a casebook published for use in law school or college classes in constitutional law. Many of these are in print, those designed for law school use being the most comprehensive and useful. For reasons of space, the cases are usually substantially edited, so that the full opinion is not printed. Many of the cases discussed in the text of this volume may be found in such casebooks. In addition, the editors of these books often include commentary about specific cases. One of the better casebooks is William B. Lockhart, Yale Kamisar, and Jesse H. Choper, *Constitutional Law: Cases—Comments—Questions* (St. Paul, Minn.: West Publishing Co., 2nd ed., 1967).

SECONDARY SOURCES

Most of the works cited in the text of this volume contain extensive references and bibliographies. In this essay, only three repetitions are made of books or articles mentioned in the footnotes of the text. The reader is cautioned that *all* commentary about the Supreme Court is not official; the voluminous literature about the Court is to be considered a secondary source, the only primary source being the opinions of the Justices of the Supreme Court.

Discussions of the relationship of the Court to the American economic order may be found scattered through the literature of political science, economics, sociology, and law. The bulk of these relate to individual decisions; there is nothing of a comprehensive nature. For analyses of individual cases, the best single resource is the *Index to Legal Periodicals,* available in any law library. Everything published in the hundred-odd law journals is listed there. Other indexes may be consulted for publications in political science, economics, and sociology.

The best single volume discussing the full sweep of Supreme Court decisions throughout American history is Norman J. Small and Lester S. Jayson (eds.), *The Constitution of the United States of America, Analysis and Interpretation* (Washington, D.C.: Government Printing Office, 1964). Even though this book is published by the government, it is not an official commentary in the sense that it has been sanctioned by the Supreme Court; the High Bench does not comment on cases it has decided. Valuable histories are Carl Brent Swisher, *American Constitutional Development* (Boston: Houghton Mifflin Co., 2d ed., 1954); Alfred H. Kelly and Winfred A. Harbison, *The American Constitution: Its Origins and Development* (New York: W. W. Norton Co., 3d ed., 1963); Robert G. McCloskey, *The American Supreme Court* (Chicago: The University of Chicago Press, 1960). See also Alexander Bickel, *The Least Dangerous Branch: The Supreme Court at the Bar of Politics* (Indianapolis, Ind.: The Bobbs-Merrill Co., Inc., 1962); Charles Black, *The People and the Court* (New York: Macmillan Co., 1960); Bernard Schwartz, *A Commentary on the Constitution of the United States* (New York: Macmillan Co., 1963). In process of being written is a multivolume history of the Supreme Court, written under the terms of the will of Justice Oliver Wendell Holmes, which may prove to be the definitive historical treatment.

For an argument that business interests determined the outcome of the constitutional convention of 1787, see Charles Beard, *The Economic Basis of the Constitution* (New York, Macmillan Co., 1925). Beard's thesis has been disputed in Robert E. Brown, *Charles Beard and the Constitution* (Princeton, N.J.: Princeton University Press, 1956).

The literature on capitalism is enormous. The student

should find the following treatments of value. Werner Sombart, "Capitalism," *Encyclopedia of the Social Sciences,* Vol. III, p. 196; Miriam Beard, *A History of the Business Man* (New York: Macmillan Co., 1938); Henri Pirenne, *Economic and Social History of Medieval Europe* (New York: Harcourt, Brace & Co., 1937); R. H. Tawney, *Religion and the Rise of Capitalism* (New York: Harcourt, Brace & Co., 1926); Eli Hecksher, *Mercantilism* (London: Allen & Unwin, 1935); Robert L. Heilbroner, *The Worldly Philosophers: The Lives, Times, and Ideas of the Great Economic Thinkers* (New York: Simon & Schuster, 1953). The foregoing are mainly historical analyses. For contemporary statements, see Francis X. Sutton, Seymour Harris, Carl Kaysen, and James Tobin, *The American Business Creed* (Cambridge: Harvard University Press, 1956); Robert A. Dahl and Charles E. Lindblom, *Politics, Economics and Welfare* (New York: Harper & Bros., 1953); V. A. Demant, *Religion and the Decline of Capitalism* (New York: Charles Scribner's Sons, 1952).

The standard economics texts will give the economist's version or versions of the economic order. The split of "political economy" into at least two separate disciplines (political science and economics) has had the unhappy result that political scientists, with only rare exceptions, have not concerned themselves with economic policy matters. Such periodicals as *Fortune* and *Harvard Business Review* routinely publish articles discussing facets of contemporary politico-economic affairs. The *Wall Street Journal* often carries insightful discussions of current relations between government and business, and also about the economic decisions of the Supreme Court.

CHAPTER ONE

On corporate America, compare Peter Drucker, *The New Society* (New York: Harper & Bros., 1950) with John Kenneth Galbraith, *The New Industrial State* (Boston: Houghton Mifflin Co., 1967). See also Scott Buchanan, *The Corporation and the Republic* (New York: Fund for the Republic, Inc., 1958) (one of a series of pamphlets issued by the Fund for the

Republic on the corporation). Clarence C. Walton, *Corporate Social Responsibilities* (Belmont, Calif.: Wadsworth Publishing Co., Inc., 1967) is a valuable account of the changing role of the corporation. Richard Caves, *American Industry: Structure, Conduct, Performance* (Englewood Cliffs, N.J.: Prentice-Hall, Inc., 1964) is an excellent generalized account of the American economy. Fritz Machlup, "Theories of the Firm: Marginalist, Behavioral, Managerial," *American Economic Review,* Vol. LVII (1967) p. 1, surveys the field and lists the pertinent literature. Richard Eells, *The Meaning of Modern Business* (New York: Columbia University Press, 1960) is a provocative assessment of the modern "metrocorporation." See also George B. Hurff, *Social Aspects of Enterprise in the Large Corporation* (Philadelphia: University of Pennsylvania Press, 1950). A careful study is A. D. H. Kaplan, *Big Enterprise in a Competitive System* (Washington, D.C.: The Brookings Institution, 1954).

CHAPTER TWO

Valuable histories of American business may be found in Thomas C. Cochran, *The American Business System: A Historical Perspective* (Cambridge, Mass.: Harvard University Press, 1957); Edwin M. Dodd, *American Business Corporations Until 1860* (Cambridge, Mass.: Harvard University Press, 1954). A vast literature exists on the government-business interface, although nothing significant has been published on the impact of Supreme Court decisions on that relationship. See, for two useful and comprehensive accounts, M. Fainsod, L. Gordon, and J. C. Palamountain, *Government and the American Economy* (New York: W. W. Norton Co., 1959) and V. A. Mund, *Government and Business* (New York: Harper & Bros., 1950). Calvin Woodard, "Reality and Social Reform: The Transition from Laissez-faire to the Welfare State," *Yale Law Journal,* Vol. 72 (1962) p. 286, traces the growth of the welfare principle in American history; his footnotes are extensive and valuable. Jacques Ellul, *The Political Illusion* (New York: Alfred A. Knopf, 1967) is a dour essay on the impact of technology and the decline of individ-

240 A Note on Further Reading

ualism. Emmanuel G. Mesthene (ed.), *Technology and Social Change* (Indianapolis, Ind.: Bobbs-Merrill Co., Inc., 1967) reprints several essays on the technological imperatives of the age. In *The New Industrial State,* cited above, John Kenneth Galbraith links those imperatives with the growth of business enterprise and the interlocking relationship of government and business. An acerbic account of big business, written by a former high official of General Electric, is T. K. Quinn, *Giant Business: Threat to Democracy* (New York: The Exposition Press, Inc., 1952), to which should be compared Gardiner Means, *The Corporate Revolution in America* (New York: Crowell-Collier Publishing Co., 1962) and Wilbert E. Moore, *The Conduct of the Corporation* (New York, Random House, Inc., 1962).

For important studies from differing viewpoints of the early years of Supreme Court activity, compare Albert J. Beveridge, *The Life of John Marshall* (Boston: Houghton Mifflin Co., 1916) with Charles G. Haines, *The Role of the Supreme Court in American Government and Politics, 1789-1835* (Berkeley, Calif.: University of California Press, 1944). Robert L. Hale, "The Supreme Court and the Contract Clause," *Harvard Law Review,* Vol. 57 (April, May, June 1944) is a worthy discussion. For the development of substantive due process, particularly in the late nineteenth century, compare Walton Hamilton, "The Path of Due Process of Law," in Conyers Read (ed.), *The Constitution Reconsidered* (New York: Columbia University Press, 1938) (the book has a number of other useful essays on various aspects of the Constitution) with Carl B. Swisher, *Stephen J. Field: Craftsman of the Law* (Washington, D.C.: Brookings Institution, 1930). Also well worth consulting are R. L. Mott, *Due Process of Law* (Indianapolis, Ind.: Bobbs-Merrill Co., Inc., 1926) and Benjamin F. Wright, *The Growth of American Constitutional Law* (New York: Reynal & Hitchcock, 1942).

CHAPTER THREE

The changing relationships of governmental organs is well set out in Carl Brent Swisher, *The Growth of Constitu-*

tional Power in the United States (Chicago: University of Chicago Press, 1946). Charles A. Reich, "The Law of the Planned Society," *Yale Law Journal,* Vol. 75 (1966) p. 1227, is a provocative delineation of the legal problems of the Positive State. A symposium, "The Legal Basis for Managing the Economy: The Employment Act After Twenty Years," *George Washington Law Review,* Vol. 35 (1966) p. 170, is a valuable collection of articles dealing with various facets of action under the Employment Act of 1946. Publications of the Joint Economic Committee, U.S. Congress, delineate the full sweep of problems of managing the economy.

CHAPTER FOUR

John Kenneth Galbraith, *The New Industrial State,* cited above, is a trenchant call for a new way of thinking about the government-business symbiosis. A symposium, "Freedom in the Modern American Economy," *Northwestern University Law Review,* Vol. 55 (1960) p. 1, has a number of valuable essays about the rise of the supercorporations. William T. Gossett, *Corporate Citizenship* (Lexington, Va.: Washington and Lee University, 1957) is a businessman's discussion of the new economic order. Walton Hamilton, *The Politics of Industry* (New York: Alfred A. Knopf, Inc., 1957) should be consulted, as should Richard Eells, *The Government of Corporations* (New York: The Free Press, 1962) and Gardiner Means, *Pricing Power and the Public Interest* (New York: Harper & Bros., 1962). A volume of NOMOS, the publication of the American Society of Political and Legal Philosophy, entitled "Voluntary Associations," is scheduled for early publication by the Atherton Press, New York, edited by Roland Pennock and John Chapman. Firmin Oulès, *Economic Planning and Democracy* (Harmondsworth, Middlesex, England: Penguin Books Ltd., 1966) is a very useful discussion by an economist of many of the problems set forth in Chapters Three and Four of the text.

CHAPTER FIVE

The *Columbia Journal of World Business,* published by the Graduate School of Business, Columbia University, prints many excellent essays on the multinational corporation. A good brief essay is Donald Kircher, "Now the Transnational Enterprise," *Harvard Business Review* (March-April 1964) p. 7. The best introduction to the subject matter is George Steiner and Warren Cannon (eds.), *Essays on the Multinational Corporation* (New York: Macmillan Co., 1967). A useful delineation of the various roles of the three branches of government in foreign relations is Louis Henkin, "The Treaty Makers and the Law Makers: The Law of the Land and Foreign Relations," *University of Pennsylvania Law Review*, Vol. 107 (1959) p. 903. See also Michael Cardozo, "Judicial Deference to State Department Suggestions," *Cornell Law Quarterly*, Vol. 48 (1963) p. 461; Louis Henkin, "The Foreign Affairs Powers of Federal Courts: Sabbatino," *Columbia Law Review*, Vol. 64 (1964) p. 805.

CHAPTER SIX

The theme of this chapter runs against the tide of most commentary on the Supreme Court. The power—past, present, and future—of the Court is assumed by the great bulk of those who write about the High Bench. Many of the books cited in the first part of this bibliographical essay, accordingly, are written on the assumption that such power does exist and will continue to exist. See, however, Robert Dahl, "Decision-Making in a Democracy: The Supreme Court as National Policy-Maker," *Journal of Public Law*, Vol. 6 (1957) p. 279; this is an essay in a symposium dealing with the Supreme Court as a policy-maker. See also, Walter Murphy, "Lower Court Checks on Supreme Court Power," *American Political Science Review*, Vol. 53 (1959) p. 1017; Jack Peltason, *Federal Courts in the Political Process* (New York: Doubleday & Co., 1955). Dean Alfange, "The Relevance of Legislative Facts in Constitutional Law," *University of Pennsylvania Law Review*, Vol. 114 (1966) p. 637, is an excellent account of the difficulties of informing the judicial mind. William K. Muir, *Prayer in Public Schools: Law and Attitude Change* (Chicago: University of Chicago Press, 1967) presents a quite different viewpoint from that set forth in the text of this chapter.

Table of Cases

Index

Index

Reason and Law (Cohen, 30
Recueil des Cours, 178
Redford, Emmette S., 144-145
Regulating Business by Independent Commission (Bernstein), 66
Reich, Charles A., 73, 113, 123
Reincourt, Amaury de, 123-124
Report from the Secretary of the Treasury on the Removal of Public Deposits from the Bank of the United States, 45
Report of the Section of Antitrust Law of the American Bar Association, 231
Responsibility (ed. Friedrich), 135
Reubens, Beatrice G., 71
Rich Nations and the Poor Nations, The (Ward), 132
Richards, I. A., 31
Roberts, Owen J., 217
Robinson, Richard D., 180
Roche, John P., 8
Rockefeller, John D., 51
Roosevelt, Franklin D., 99, 149-150, 165
Court packing scheme of, 79
Roosevelt Revolution, The (Eunaudi), 166-167
Roots of American Economic Growth, 1607-1861: An Essay in Social Causation, The (Bruchey), 44
Rostow, Eugene V., 43, 64, 72, 75, 89
Rule of Reason, meaning of, 63

St. Louis University Law Journal, 4, 29
Satterfield, John C., 81, 82
Scheflin, Alan W., 198, 221
Schultz, George P., 100
Schumpeter, J. A., 154, 160
Science, 6
Science and Survival (Commoner), 150
Scientific Estate, The (Price), 8, 128, 132
Second United States Bank, 42

Seidenberg, Roderick, 231
Shapiro, Martin, 4
Sharp, Malcolm Pitman, 19-20
Sherman Antitrust Act of 1890, 62-67, 73, 181-182
enacted, 48
enforcement of, 65
Shklar, Judith, 210
Sleepwalkers: A History of Man's Changing Vision of the Universe, The (Koestler), 194
Smith, Adam, 7, 51, 118, 142
Smith, Bruce L. R., 151
Social change, 80, 191-199, 201
Social Darwinism, 51
Social Darwinism in American Thought (Hofstadter), 51
Social ethic, the, 14
Social Science Research on Business: Product and Potential (Dahl, Haire, and Lazarsfeld), 16
Socialism, 160, 163
Some Observations on Supreme Court Litigation and Legal Education (Frankfurter), 196
Spencer, Herbert, 51
Spirit of Liberty: Papers and Addresses of Learned Hand, The (ed. Dilliard), 191
Stanford Law Review, 113, 206
State legislatures, apportionment of, 120-121, 221
Steel mill strike of 1952, 80
Steele, E. William, 133
Stern, Robert L., 41
Stockpiling program, 117
Stone, Justice Harlan F., 79
Story, Joseph, 92
Struggle for Judicial Supremacy, The (Jackson), 32, 78
Sumner, William Graham, 49, 51
Supreme Court in the American System of Government, The (Jackson), 217
Supreme Court in the Political Process, The (Krislov), 4
Supreme Court Review, The, 54, 187